Feeding Iran

Feeding Iran

SHI'I FAMILIES AND THE MAKING
OF THE ISLAMIC REPUBLIC

Rose Wellman

UNIVERSITY OF CALIFORNIA PRESS

University of California Press
Oakland, California

© 2021 by Rose Edith Wellman

Library of Congress Cataloging-in-Publication Data

Names: Wellman, Rose, author.
Title: Feeding Iran : Shi'i families and the making of the Islamic Republic / Rose Wellman.
Description: Oakland, California : University of California Press, [2021] | Includes bibliographical references and index.
Identifiers: LCCN 2020049981 (print) | LCCN 2020049982 (ebook) | ISBN 9780520376861 (cloth) | ISBN 9780520376878 (paperback) | ISBN 9780520976313 (epub)
Subjects: LCSH: Kinship—Religious aspects—Islam. | Paramilitary forces—Social aspects—Iran—21st century. | Rites and ceremonies—Iran—21st century.
Classification: LCC BP190.5.K55 W45 2021 (print) | LCC BP190.5.K55 (ebook) | DDC 204/.41—dc23
LC record available at https://lccn.loc.gov/2020049981
LC ebook record available at https://lccn.loc.gov/2020049982

Manufactured in the United States of America

29 28 27 26 25 24 23 22 21
10 9 8 7 6 5 4 3 2 1

For Ayla

Contents

	List of Illustrations	ix
	Acknowledgments	xi
	Note on Translation and Transliteration	xv
	Introduction: Kinship, Islam, and the State	1
1.	Blood, Physio-Sacred Substance, and the Making of Moral Kin	38
2.	Feeding the Family: The "Spirit" of Food in Iran	76
3.	Regenerating the Islamic Republic: Commemorating Martyrs in Provincial Iran	124
4.	Creating an Islamic Nation through Food	153
	Epilogue	192
	Notes	201
	References	221
	Index	237

Illustrations

1. View of Fars-Abad, Iran, from the town park — 27
2. Alley, Fars-Abad, Iran — 28
3. Mr. Hosseini's diagram of the course of human existence — 46
4. Nushin praying at the tomb of a *sayyed* in Fars-Abad's graveyard — 55
5. Votive *sofreh* featuring *kāchi* — 82
6. Pomegranate statue in Fars Province, Iran — 96
7. Nushin and Ahmad making pomegranate sauce — 97
8. Women praying and stirring votive soup for teething children — 116
9. Women sharing votive soup — 117
10. Mothers of martyrs sitting behind the graves of two unknown martyrs from the Iran-Iraq War — 136
11. Event welcoming the martyrs to their final resting place in the town park — 137
12. Sign created for the martyrs' commemoration in Fars-Abad — 138
13. Women attending a commemoration for Fatemeh Al-Zahra — 145

14. Parvin, Mahmud, and their two sons in the parking lot
of the Mausoleum of Ruhollah Khomeini   154
15. Kiosk serving hot milk in Zahra's Paradise   157
16. Nushin praying at the shrine of Imam Reza's descendant 169
17. Hajji Hamed's Muharram vow   176

All photographs are by the author.

Acknowledgments

My late grandmother, Edith L. B. Turner, is the reason I became an anthropologist. She believed in people, in their stories, and in the reality of spirits. She thrived on human connection, friendship, and intellectual collaboration, and it is in this spirit that I now turn to thank all who have supported me in writing this book.

First and foremost, thank you to my hosts in Iran for your love, support, and endurance through life's difficulties. I will never forget your kindness and hospitality. Many thanks also to my research assistants, Mohammad and Hoda, in Fars-Abad and Tehran, who always encouraged me to finish this work and who trusted me with their stories. My deepest thanks to the person who is the heart of this book, "Nushin."

I am also immensely grateful to my dissertation committee at the Department of Anthropology at the University of Virginia. Susan McKinnon, Ira Bashkow, and Richard Handler provided invaluable advice, support, and constructive criticism over the course of this project. I have been especially honored to work with my committee chair, Susan McKinnon, who has taught me everything I know about kinship and the anthropological critique of domains. Without her stalwart support and encouragement, this project would not have been possible. Special thanks also to my other committee members, Ira Bashkow and Richard Handler, who have offered their perceptive feedback and backing. Finally, thank you to Farzaneh Milani, my esteemed outside reader at the University of Virginia, who supported my research and shared with me her love of Iranian poetry, prose, and film.

In the world of Iran studies, I am indebted to John Haldon, Kevan Harris, and Cyrus Schayegh, who helped hone my knowledge of Iranian history, politics, and sociology during my postdoctoral research position at Princeton University. I am also indebted to all of the attendees of Ethnography of Iran: Past and Present, a conference I organized at Princeton University in 2015. The participants pushed me to better understand and convey the complexities of Iran in the present moment. I'm especially indebted to Mary Hegland; William O. Beeman, who provided insightful comments on this manuscript; and Amina Tawasil, who encouraged me in this publication and provided feedback on earlier chapters.

During the life course of this project, I have received incredible support, insight, and education from my friends, anthropologists, and other scholars. I am thankful to Debbora Battaglia, who was one of my first guides through the terrain of anthropology. I am also thankful to Zjaleh Hajibashi (who taught me Persian), Eve Danziger, Wende Marshall, Daniel Lefkowitz, Abdul Aziz Sachedina, Roy Wagner, George Mentore, and Lise Dobrin. Emiko Ohnuki-Tierney has been an incredible voice of encouragement and support. I have also been continuously inspired by the brilliant Janet Carsten.

This book would not have been possible without my sisters in spirit, Todne Thomas and Asiya Malik, the coeditors of *New Direction in Spiritual Kinship*. I am grateful for the intellectual curiosity and friendship of Dionisios Kavadias. I am always thankful to my dear friend and writingmate Lydia Rodriguez. Arsalan Khan, Julie Starr, David Flood, Roberto Armengol, and Jack Stoetzel provided me with invaluable and incisive feedback in earlier drafts of this project. Daniel Birchok and Ana Vinea insightfully commented on chapters and book proposals in Michigan, as did my friends and colleagues Susan Ellison, Erin Raffety, and Bridget Purcell during my time at Princeton. Others have provided me with amazing friendship and support over the years. I am grateful to Alison Broach,

Irtefa Binte-Farid, Grace Reynolds, Claire Snell-Rood, Yu-chien Huang, Nathalie Nahas, Dannah Dennis, Carolyn Howarter, Jennie Doberne, Sue-Ann McCarty, Jason Hickel, and Jacqueline Cieslak, who have all been a part of this adventure in one way or another.

I presented various parts of this book's arguments at Princeton University, Yale University, the University of Edinburgh, NYU Abu Dhabi, Goucher College, the University of Michigan-Dearborn, the University of Virginia, the American Anthropological Association Annual Meetings, the Association for the Study of Persianate Societies, and the Symposia Iranica Conference at the University of Cambridge. I am thankful to all participants and organizers of these events and panels for creating spaces for exchange and collaboration and for engaging with my work. Much of this book developed in and through the proceedings of a Wenner-Gren workshop I co-organized, The Sacred Social: Investigations of Spiritual Kinship among the Abrahamic Faiths, in Charlottesville, Virginia. I remain indebted to Todne Thomas, Asiya Malik, Susan McKinnon, Don Seeman, Carol Delaney, Gillian Feeley-Harnik, Fenella Cannell, Joëlle Bahloul, Fred Klaits, Naomi Leite, and Guido Alfani for a workshop that continues to inspire me in my academic career.

This research was funded by a National Science Foundation Doctoral Dissertation Research Improvement Grant, a Wenner-Gren Dissertation Fieldwork Grant, an Albert Gallatin Graduate Research Fellowship, an Iran Heritage Foundation Academic Grant, and a scholarship from the Mount Holyoke College Alumnae Association. Writing was funded by a Charlotte W. Newcombe Doctoral Dissertation Fellowship and by the Sharmin and Bijan Mossavar-Rahmani Center for Iran and Persian Gulf Studies at Princeton University, which funded my position as a postdoctoral research associate. Most recently, I am deeply grateful to my fellow faculty at the University of Michigan-Dearborn, who have been instrumental in helping me prioritize this project and encouraging me to publish. I'm especially grateful to Pamela Aronson, Carmel Price, Sally Howell, John Chenoweth, Nadine Anderson, Patrick Beauchesne, Jonathan Smith, and Rachel Buzzeo. I am also very much indebted to my wonderful editors at the University of California Press, Kate Marshall and Enrique Ochoa-Kaup.

A few more words of thanks remain. My mother, Irene Wellman, has been an incredible source of light, encouragement, and insightful reading and copyediting during this process. I am also thankful to my father, Donald Wellman, for believing in me. I am thankful to Mamanjun and her family. Most of all, though, I am thankful to my dear husband, Naser Alijabbari, who has been a stalwart support through it all.

Note on Translation and Transliteration

Unless otherwise noted, all of the translations in this book are my own. Persian (Farsi) terms appear first in English and then in italicized Persian, with phrases and compound words appearing in quotes for clarification. I use a modified form of the Persian transliteration system of the *International Journal of Middle Eastern Studies*. Consonants are consistent with this system, but with the exception of the aleph, diacritics are not used to distinguish letters that have the same pronunciation in Persian. Short vowels are transliterated with the closest English equivalent; this means that I use *e* and *o*, rather than *i* and *u*. Long *ye* is rendered as *i*, and *vav* is written as *u*. Final *heh* is written as *eh*. *Ayn* is indicated by an opening single quotation mark ('), and the *hamza* is indicated by a closing single quotation mark (') (Olszewska 2015a, xviii). The IJMES Word List provides transliteration of commonly known words and the names of historical figures such as Imam Husayn. Certain Arabic words are transliterated according to Arabic rather than Persian conventions. Others are so common in English that they are not italicized. I do not italicize people or organizations and use common spelling conventions where appropriate.

Introduction

KINSHIP, ISLAM, AND THE STATE

Nushin's grasp is warm and firm. She pulls me through a crowd of women on the street, only a few feet from a similar group of men. I estimate that there are hundreds, if not thousands, of people gathered here on Fars-Abad's main street in Fars Province, Iran.[1] I use my free hand to clasp my black chador at my chin as I attempt to keep pace with Nushin's steady progress.[2] But the pressure of bodies increases as we near the slow-moving flatbed trailer pulled by a truck inscribed with the words "Yā Husayn."[3] I lose her hand in the crowd and call out. She nods briefly in apology but continues on. Nushin is now only a few feet away from the trailer containing two wooden caskets wrapped in Iranian flags. Inside the caskets lie the bodies of two unknown martyrs (*shahid*), fallen heroes from the Iran-Iraq War (1980–88).[4] Their bodies have been brought here from the border of Iran and Iraq during the Week of the Sacred Defense, an annual commemoration of the war, and will be reburied in fresh graves in the town park.

Nushin has already, for just a second, managed to reach out and touch the wooden side of the trailer. Above and around her, other women throw the scarves that they have brought with them from home to uniformed male guards riding next to the martyrs. The guards in turn brush the scarves on the caskets, infusing the fabric with the blessing of the martyrs' bodies and blood, before throwing them back. Behind us on the street's median, Reza, Nushin's teenage son, a budding computer scientist, is filming the proceedings with my camera. The footage he captures shows town officials, including the mayor, the droning of a military band, hundreds of townspeople, and a plethora of local media makers participating in the procession. The martyrs are on their way to their final resting ground, the town's park.

The next Friday, the town's prayer leader and local representative of state religion, the "Friday Imam," holds a prayer and votive meal at the site of the new graves. I sit cross-legged on the ground next to Nushin and the other women while he introduces a "prayer giver," who reads the Supplication of Kumail, a fifteen-minute prayer for the protection against the evil of enemies and for the forgiveness of sins. After the prayer, uniformed male soldiers distribute to the hundreds of men and women in attendance cups of yogurt, juice boxes, and plates of freshly cooked "lentils and rice" (*adas polow*) from giant metal vats located on the outskirts of the gathering. This food is paid for by the Foundation for the Preservation of Heritage and the Distribution of Sacred Defense, a parastatal group that had organized the multiday commemoration.[5] As we eat the blessed fare, the Friday Imam speaks: "Because this martyr is unknown, we the people are his brother, his sister, his mother." He calls on all of the attendees to think of themselves as the kin of martyrs, a kinship that is enacted in real time as the uniformed soldiers and townspeople call one another mother, father, brother, or sister in thanks as they receive and pass along food.

What aspirations compel Nushin and her fellow townspeople to reach out and touch the unknown martyrs' caskets, attend their commemorative prayers, and eat blessed food at the site of their burial? What is the significance of this heartfelt participation in state ritual? And how does it relate to the everyday experience of living as kin in the Islamic Republic of Iran?

This book draws from a year and a half of ethnographic research among Shi'i state–supporting families in the provincial town of Fars-Abad, the city of Shiraz, and Iran's capital, Tehran, in order to understand how ideas and practices of kinship and religion are linked to state power. I ask: What can an analysis of home life and everyday piety tell us about contemporary nation-making? Answering this question requires an investigation into the metaphorical and analogical resonances between the intimate spaces of the home and the state. It also requires an on-the-ground exploration of how the substances and practices of kinship—from blood, to food, to family prayer—are being deployed in state rituals to create ideal citizens who embody familial piety, purity, and closeness to God.

This book is for anyone interested in reimagining the interstices between kinship, religion, and the nation-state. It is about the hopes and dreams of ordinary Iranian supporters of the Islamic Republic. And it is the first account of these supporters outside of Iran's urban centers since the 1979 Revolution.

· · · · ·

Despite hegemonic narratives of modernity that position kin-based societies as prior to modern state-based societies, kinship has a persistent power in modern nation-making. In the same way, religion has not receded into the confines of the private sphere in the manner assumed by liberal theory. It continues to shape diverse local, national, and transnational political allegiances and affinities. This is particularly apparent in Iran, where since the 1979 Revolution a cohort of religious scholars and intellectuals has argued that the nation's authentically Islamic interior—composed of virtuous Muslim brother and sister citizens—has to be (re)generated while resisting a spiritually vacant, "Westernstruck" exterior. Supporters of the Islamic Republic, like Nushin, her husband, and her children, are on the front lines of these efforts. They are members of the Basij, Iran's paramilitary organization, and they claim that other Iranians have forgotten the sacrifices of the martyrs. They worry that their society is losing its morals in favor of the frivolity of urban and middle-class life. Postwar Iran seems no longer to aspire to the revolutionary values of simplicity, piety, and self-sacrifice to the Supreme Leader of Iran that they uphold (Sadeghi 2009).

Faced with these perceived challenges, state elites, including provincial town officials, and ordinary state supporters, such as Nushin, are deploying ideas and practices of kinship and religion in very tangible ways to configure citizens as Muslim "kin" while reinforcing the Revolution's values. To regenerate and sanctify the Iranian nation, its citizens, and its landscape, the state displays the blood of kinship, spilled from the veins of Iranian citizens, throughout the country. This blood appears on street signs, in graveyards, and in ongoing ritual commemorations of Iran-Iraq War martyrs. It organizes the bodies of Iranian subjects around the paradigmatic martyrdom of the grandson of the Prophet, Imam Husayn, at the Battle of Karbala (680 CE). Imam Husayn's martyrdom is thought to have kept Islam alive and has become an inspiration for fighting injustice, including during the 1979 Revolution and the Iran-Iraq War.[6] At the same time, the Islamic Republic and its supporters draw from ordinary and extraordinary acts of making pure kinship at home—acts such as the sharing of food—to bless citizens and create divinely sanctioned relationships in the wider sphere of the nation-state. Indeed, a full spectrum of material substances, immaterial qualities, acts, and processes of kinship in Iran is being deployed in the grand rituals of state power to create and legitimize an ideal society organized by the revolutionary values of pure kinship, piety, and closeness to God.

Comprehending the precise ways this occurs requires an investigation not only of how kinship and nation can transform each other via shared ideas and metaphors, but also of how kinship's more subtle substances, ineffable qualities, acts, and processes appear in state ritual to create convincing concordances between the intimacies of family life and the nation. Home life and piety connect to state power in multiple ways. Even as common kin-based tropes such as blood and law give a sense of coherence, legitimacy, and inevitability to nation-states, other locally salient aspects of kin-making—such as sharing blessed food in public commemorations—provide vital means of creating and shaping moral, pious, and familial relations among citizens.

SACRALIZING KINSHIP, NATURALIZING THE NATION

Kinship is often deeply entangled with contemporary nation-making. Indeed, the two fields share similar forms of inclusions and exclusions, hierarchies and equalities, as well as shared essences and essential differences

(McKinnon and Cannell 2013, 24; Schneider 1969). In Iran and elsewhere, these cross-connections are not lost on state elites, who strategically use notions of kinship, including gender, reproduction, and marriage, to naturalize dominant ideologies of patriarchal authority, race, class, and religion (Heng and Devan 1992; Joseph 1999; Yanagisako and Delaney 1995; Yuval-Davis and Anthias 1989).

Perhaps the most striking way that kinship informs nation-making in the contemporary world is through shared ideas of ancestry, origins, genealogy, procreation, and blood (Alonso 1994; Bear 2013; Bryant 2002). As imaginations of the biological or "the natural," these concepts help make sameness and difference seem inevitable with respect to a nation, "race," or ethnic group (Nash 2008, 10). Blood is an especially compelling medium in this regard. Simultaneously a substance and a metaphor, blood is powerfully involved in notions of kinship, life and death, nurturance and violence, and connection and exclusion (Carsten 2013). It further has a special capacity to participate in and flow among domains that scholars often presume to be distinct, such as kinship and economics or kinship and politics (Carsten 2013).

In Iran, blood is strikingly visible in both home life and politics, participating in and flowing between these seemingly distinct domains. It appears in commemorations for martyrs as a substance of kinship and as a reminder of the sacred history of martyrdom and prophetic genealogy. Indeed, the resonances of blood as a "natural" and "sacred" substance pile onto each other, increasing its power to shape citizens, thus adding both a naturalizing and a sacralizing dimension to blood in the political project of regenerating the Islamic Republic (see chapter 3).

Yet blood, law, genealogy, and ancestry are not the only traditional aspects of kin-making that inform the nation. Kin relations can be formed through materials such as food, land, hearths, and houses, and they can be constituted through "processes of doing" such as care, nurturance, feeding, exchange, and making choices (Bahloul 1996; Carsten 1995; Labby 1976; Weston 1991). Kin relations can further be created via immaterial, ethical, or sacred acts and qualities that work alone or alongside the substances of kinship (Wellman 2017b; Cannell 2013). In Iran, this may include cooking the right food, praying, memorializing, remembering, moving through sacred space, or participating in a ceremony or event. Kinship is not a stagnant formula but a process: constantly shifting and forming through ongoing (pious) action, affect, and context.

Indeed, Iranian kinship is fundamentally constituted, not only by ideas of blood and Islamic law, but also through acts such as cooking, feeding, and prayer—acts that imbue relationships with divine blessing and shape the purity of the household. Women, in particular, orchestrate food to purify kin relations and shape relationships among family members. And these *other* kinship practices *also* appear in the grand rituals of the Iranian state, to powerful effect. State elites, Basijis, and other supporters of the Islamic Republic strive to fashion and authenticate pure and "religiously permissible" (or halal) relations among citizens through cooking, feeding, and prayer. In the same way that Nushin and I sat on the dusty hill in the park eating the blessed food offered by soldiers in Fars-Abad, shared food and prayer appear across Iran at state-funded martyrs' commemorations and national-Islamic holidays, a means of imbuing citizens with divine blessing while emphasizing a common Shi'i Islamic kinship.

This book focuses on how and why state elites and supporters are creating convincing concordances between the intimacies of home life and state power. I explore the multiple ways kin are discerned, protected, and shaped and how this full range of kin-making appears in the grand rituals of state power. And I examine how kinship (and religion) help make configurations of citizenship seem convincing, inevitable, and God given.

FIELDWORK

When I arrived in Tehran to begin fieldwork as a British American in 2010, unrest over the disputed 2009 presidential elections was gradually dissipating due to a strong government clampdown. Despite the decreased street turmoil, a general feeling of wariness pervaded the streets of Tehran. Tensions ran particularly high in the universities. Fearing unwanted government attention, many professors and academics were reluctant to help me secure a research visa. I heard stories of frequent faculty firings, especially in the social sciences. Fortunately, through the help of several professors and officials affiliated with the Department of Anthropology at the University of Tehran, the sheer persistence of Haleh, the college-educated daughter of my Tehrani hosts, and the aid of my British passport, I was able to obtain an official research permit at the Iranian Ministry of Foreign Affairs. Soon after, I began my fieldwork in the home of a family of state-supporting, card-carrying Basijis.

The family—including Mahmud, a veteran of the Iran-Iraq War; his wife, Parvin; and their four young adult children—lived in Ekbatan, a middle-class suburb of Tehran. Mahmud earned a living as a taxi driver. Parvin worked part-time as an accountant in the Tehrani suburb of Ekbatan. They owned their small apartment but lived frugally, especially when Mahmud's cough worsened, a result of being exposed to mustard gas and nerve agents during the war.[7] When I began my dissertation fieldwork in 2010, I had already known this family for three years. In the summers of 2007 and 2008, I had lived across from them in the apartment of an Iranian American friend and had accompanied them on outings to parks, restaurants, and food shows, as well as to national religious sites such as the Mausoleum of Ruhollah Khomeini and Zahra's Paradise, Tehran's largest graveyard. Sitting in the back of Mahmud's green taxi with Haleh, his daughter, in 2008, I had also visited their hometown of Fars-Abad, a provincial location approximately two hours from Shiraz and a ten-hour car or bus journey from Tehran. When I returned to Iran for long-term research in 2010, I chose this family, and specifically their home town of Fars-Abad, as the site of my research. This was the provincial home of Mahmud's mother, brothers, nephews, and nieces.

My experiences in Fars-Abad in the household of Ahmad, Mahmud's brother and another veteran of the Iran-Iraq War; Ahmad's wife, Nushin; and their four children, together with their immediate neighbors and extended kin in Tehran and Shiraz, form the heart of this ethnography. Both Ahmad and Nushin were retired teachers and had been directors of the local schools (boys' and girls' schools, respectively). They were landowners and now supplemented their pensions by farming and renting their land to extended kin. I lived in their home for nearly a year through many changing circumstances: a move to a new house, the death of a cousin, the days and nights of Ramadan, and the Iranian New Year celebrations. On most nights I slept in a room with their daughter Maryam. I cooked with Nushin, washed dishes, taught English to their teenage children, and spent hours conversing (in Persian) with family members and visitors. In different ways, all three of Ahmad and Nushin's young adult children—their fourth child was newly married and less often present in the household—became my research assistants and escorts for research interviews around town.

In the middle of my fieldwork, my hosts moved to a new home across town that had been under construction. Our first residence had been in an alley in the center of the older portion of town and was the home of Ahmad's kin. There, his family members lived together in a row of adjacent houses occupied by Ahmad's (and Mahmud's) recently widowed mother, Hajj Bibi, a woman stooped over by time and wrapped in a blue cotton chador; Qassem (the other, mutual brother of Ahmad and Mahmud) and his family (his wife Farah and their two young adult children); and Qassem's oldest child, his wife, and their infant daughter. In the alley, there were frequent visitors, including Ahmad's patrilateral cousins and his cousins' children. Ahmad's wife's kin also visited regularly. These included Nushin's wise elderly mother, Goli-Mehrebun; her four sisters and brothers, their affines, and their children; and finally, on occasion, her half siblings, the numerous children of her father's second wife.

In the new house, in contrast, with the exception of Nushin and Ahmad's eldest daughter, who lived a block away, we were surrounded by a very different set of nonkin neighbors: a local "descendant of the Prophet" (*sayyed*), his wife, and their son; two married couples with young daughters; and a family who had recently moved from Shiraz. We also lived closer to Nushin's niece and her husband, who lived in a nearby apartment complex. As in the alley, however, the larger "extended families" (*qowm-o-khish*) of both Ahmad and Nushin frequently visited us. Indeed, especially in the first few weeks after the move, we had visitors almost every evening.

The people and social relationships surrounding both the old house and the new house shape this research in different ways. For my hosts, the new house was better: "the air (*havā*) is better and cooler," they said, commenting on its location closer to the edge of town and near the park. Most importantly, the new house created a future living space for Ahmad and Nushin's two sons and their future wives.[8] Yet despite its practicality and the relative proximity of the new house to the old, the move was difficult. My hosts missed their elderly grandmother, Hajj Bibi, who could not walk the kilometer that separated the two locations. In addition, the increased physical distance of the new house, combined with my living arrangement in one of the four brothers' houses and not the others, amplified preexisting tensions between Ahmad and Nushin's household and some of Ahmad's patrilateral kin.

"Almost Mahram," "Almost Daughter"

Through unspoken mutual agreement, I began my stay in Ahmad and Nushin's home in Fars-Abad by dressing modestly with long sleeves and covered legs but without a headscarf while inside. Although he was a devout Muslim, a member of the Basij, and a veteran, Ahmad said that he did not see my veiling as an obligatory act given my different religious and cultural background. Yet while his children were laxer, offering me the occasional high-five or hand shake, Ahmad never allowed physical contact unless by accident. At a typical meal, he sat across from me rather than next to me to help ensure this distance. At more formal meal occasions, however, such as when we were hosting guests, he often inserted himself as a buffer between the visitors and me. Compared with the guests, he explained, I was "almost *mahram*" (*taqriban mahram*), meaning that I was almost a close relative rather than a potential marriage partner who should, therefore, veil. "You are a member of the household," he said on numerous occasions; "You have shared food and salt at my wife's 'dining cloth' [*sofreh*]."

Amid these negotiations of home life, my presence as an American researcher was also becoming known in the wider community. Townspeople began to notice my presence with the family in the street or in the family car, and they mistakenly wondered whether I was a new bride of one of the sons. To prevent such gossip, Ahmad and Nushin started asking me to keep a headscarf ready in case guests arrived unexpectedly. This, Nushin explained, was a matter of maintaining the family's reputation and esteem (*āberu*). It helped to signify to curious onlookers that the household was halal and pure.

My research was colored in both positive and negative ways by this position. On the one hand, I was there when Nushin worried about her painful back or when her teenagers argued. I was there when the family prepared to attend a wedding or a funeral. Indeed, by living with Ahmad and Nushin and getting to know their extended families, friends, and acquaintances as part of their family unit, I was able to understand the comings and goings of town life in a way that I might never have done if I had merely rented a room. (This scenario would not have been possible in Fars-Abad, in any case.) On the other hand, I was constrained by local officials and family members who were concerned with both my safety (from street violence or assault as an obvious foreigner) and their own safety vis-à-vis the state and local elite, who might misinterpret my presence and scrutinize their family. They required that I conduct research with an escort. Ahmad at one point emphasized this point and made my stay in his home more official by introducing me to the mayor of Fars-Abad, who reiterated that I should not leave Ahmad's house without an escort "for my own protection."

Finally, the intensity with which my hosts practiced Islam and strove to emulate Islamic values also shaped my research. My hosts saw me as a person who was "learning" about Islam. God was showing Islam to me, they said, encouraging me to convert. Why else was I witnessing Shi'i prayers and devotion or learning to read the Qur'an? Why else had I wound up in Iran to begin with? "You are lucky to have been exposed to Islam," they often told me (see Harding 1987, 171 for a similar experience). This reasoning molded my time in Fars-Abad. I was an object of potential conversion. Indeed, the words of the Qur'an were becoming ingrained in my mind through the daily prayers I did with Nushin when she invited me to her room in the morning after drinking tea. There with Nushin, kneeling and supplicating on her beautiful prayer rug, I would try to find a space between my methodological agnosticism and Edith Turner's (1993) powerful and political call for a recognition of the reality of spirits. Before I returned to the United States, my hosts sacrificed a henna-painted sheep and distributed it among their kin to bless my departure. They filled my suitcases with homemade pomegranate sauce and quince lime syrup.

SUPPORTING THE ISLAMIC REPUBLIC: AMBIVALENCES AND ALIGNMENTS

"Down with America, down with England, down with Israel!" Ahmad yelled these words into a megaphone as he rounded a corner on Khomeini

Street in the center of Fars-Abad. Only a few minutes before, I had come out of the door of the town "meeting house for Imam Husayn" (*hosayniyeh*) with Ahmad's wife, Nushin, in a state of relative shock. I had had no forewarning that, on that day, the Friday Imam would call for a rally following the usual prayer sermon. It was the summer of 2010, and the rally was one of many erupting in Iran against fundamentalist pastor Terry Jones, who was threatening to burn hundreds of copies of the Qur'an in Gainesville, Florida (Cave 2010; Worth 2010). The chadored women around me were excited, whispering directions to each other as they hurriedly put on their shoes. For many in the crowd, this was an exhilarating opportunity to participate in politics and help defend Islam.

Almost before I had fully processed what was happening, Nushin and I were whisked along with the other women near the back of a well-ordered procession that stretched about two hundred meters in each direction. Walking in rows of four or five, I noted that some women next to us were beating their chests in the style of mourning for Imam Husayn. Nushin and I were more sedate, but we couldn't help glancing at each other on occasion, sharing quick, nervous smiles. We had walked in this manner for about half a mile in the dusty August heat when Ahmad and the other men took a sharp turn around the roadway's median so that they now faced those of us closer to the end of the procession. There was just enough time for Ahmad to look up from his prominent position at the head of the rally and nod in my direction. The irony was palpable. He was leading the town rally with the words "Down with America," and I was a guest in his home, an American.

Later, when we returned to the house, Ahmad and Nushin tried to gauge my reaction. Chuckling wryly, Ahmad commented, "I only mouthed the words 'down with America' into the megaphone." He further sought to clarify, as he would on many occasions, "We mean down with the government, not the people. It's just a saying. We are used to this expression."

As previously noted, many of my hosts—with the important exception of a few teenage children—supported the idea of Iran as an Islamic Republic and its foundational legislation that is enshrined in the "guardianship of the jurist" (*velāyat-e faqih*), a concept expounded by the late Ayatollah Khomeini that gives political leadership—in the absence of a divinely inspired Imam—to the jurist (*faqih*). Khomeini, as the leader of the 1979 Revolution, successfully advanced this position as a model for Iran and was succeeded by the current Supreme Leader of Iran, Ayatollah Khamenei.[9] For Ahmad in Fars-Abad, support for these leaders and their ideas began during the Revolution and was fueled by his belief in Khomeini's special relationship to God and to Imam Mahdi—the prophesized redeemer of (Shi'i) Islam, also known as the Twelfth Imam. Ahmad said that he modeled himself on Khomeini, whom he called the "Imam," aspiring to the same selfless relationship to God, not only for his family but also for the Islamic Republic and beyond.

Notably, although Ahmad and many of his neighbors and relatives also backed the presidency of Mahmoud Ahmadinejad (2005–13) because of his apparently greater attention to the infrastructure of provincial areas of Iran such as Fars-Abad, others did not.[10] Ahmadinejad's election was dramatically contested in Iran in 2009 by "Green Movement" (*moj-e sabz*) protesters, who challenged the election results and sought increased freedoms and a reformed Islamic democracy. In June 2009, for instance, when members of the Green Movement took to the streets to protest Ahmadinejad's second-term election victory over the incumbent, Mir-Hossein Mousavi, Haleh (Mahmud's daughter in Tehran) wanted me to understand something important. She wrote in an email (7/22/09): "We, too, are afraid of the police [the militias in the street]." Haleh argued that although she was a Basij and ideologically committed to the Islamic Republic, she did not condone the recent turn of events, violence, and suppression of protests. "What has your media been saying about us?" she asked me. She excitedly described how, outside her family's apartment, the suburb of Ekbatan was filled with the voices of people chanting "God is Great" in support of the protesters. At the same time, she added, "I cannot stand to see effigies of the Supreme Leader desecrated. When they tore up his picture, I turned away from politics." Haleh here reveals competing ideologies within the Basij about the role of the organization and its values. Not all members of the Basij, she argued, participate in this kind of violence. Nevertheless, her and her family's memberships in the Basij shaped this research in numerous ways.

The Basij

Ahmad and Mahmud (and their children, including Haleh) are members of the Basij, Iran's voluntary paramilitary organization (Sāzmān-e Basij-e Mostaz'afin; literally, the Mobilization of the Oppressed). As Ahmad himself explained, the Basij was founded by Khomeini in 1980 to "help protect the moral values, unity, and self-sufficiency of the Islamic Republic and its constitution."[11] Often translated as the "people's militia," the term "Basij" is the name of the force, while "Basiji" refers to an individual member. Members of the Basij are often described as the original revolutionaries, who participated in the "Sacred Defense" of Iran during the Iran-Iraq War and were the first to go to the front and be martyred. At its inception, Khomeini construed the force as a potential "twenty million man army," on call to defend the Revolution from internal and external threats (Nazemi 1993; Golkar 2015). By the late 1980s, approximately three million Iranians had become members of the Basij, with one-third of this number fighting on the front lines of the Iran-Iraq War (Bajoghli 2019, 10).

In addition to its military activities, segments of the Basij participate in intelligence gathering, law enforcement, the organization of public religious ceremonies, the provision of social services, and perhaps most famously, the moral policing of Iranian citizens (Bajoghli 2019; Golkar 2015). They are involved in the production of proregime media and propaganda, intended to confront what they describe as a "soft war" or "cultural invasion" waged by the West and the Iranian diaspora against the Islamic Republic (Bajoghli 2019). At the same time, the Basij provides a large voting bloc and a state apparatus with thousands of bases stretching across neighborhood branches, universities, factories, and workplaces (Bajoghli 2019, 10; Golkar 2015). They are the self-proclaimed vanguard of revolutionary morality (Golkar 2015, 68,75), and they are one of the most important sites of state power and citizen participation in Iran.

The Basij, notably, is subsidiary to and different from the Islamic Revolutionary Guard Corps (IRGC), which is currently designated a terrorist organization by the United States, Saudi Arabia, and Bahrain. Khomeini formed the IRGC in 1979 after the Revolution, in part because he did not trust the regular Iranian military (*artesh*), which remained loyal to the shah (Bajoghli 2019, 30). While Iran's military would defend the borders of Iran, the IRGC would defend the Revolution.[12] The IRGC recruited the Basij from mosques and schools around the country. Volunteers in the provinces signed up and were sent to a local training center. There, many learned how to fight in various environments and were given specialties. Ahmad often described his sense of brotherhood and equality during this training as well as on the front lines. "We were all the same," Ahmad related. "We called each other brother," evoking his sense of kinship with other soldiers. However, he told me that Basijis were paid less than revolutionary guards. Indeed, its founders conceived of the Basij as a less professional force (Bajoghli 2019, 33). Moreover, in contradistinction to the IRGC, the organization included more men and women from lower socioeconomic classes (Noori 2013, 129).

In postwar, post–Green Movement Iran, the Basij's leaders continue to claim mass membership, with most units falling under the supervision of a neighborhood mosque or community center. During the presidency of Ahmadinejad, for instance, the numbers were allegedly at 13.6 million, about 20 percent of the population of Iran. Of this given number, 5 million were women and 4.7 million were schoolchildren (Aryan 2008).[13] There are three main categories of membership in the Basij: regular, active, and special.[14] Regular members, like my hosts, obtain a Basij card when they are at least eleven years old and have passed very minimal training. (Indeed, my hosts' young adult children—both males and females—were given cards because of their fathers' memberships and connections and had not participated in formal military training.) In contrast to regular members, active members are more carefully vetted and must be at least age fifteen. Applications are reviewed by the "Deputy of Confirmation of Ideological Qualification," a branch of the "Representative of the Supreme Leader," and by the "Counterintelligence Bureau" (Golkar 2015, 48).[15] The third group, "Special Basij," have undergone much more extensive military and ideological training and are technically members of the IRGC (Golkar 2015, 50; Bajoghli 2019, 38). Members of this latter group serve full time and receive a salary. It is some cohorts of this Special category who appeared on the streets to violently dampen 2009 Green Movement protests.

As "regular" members, my hosts were not active in Basij meetings during my research. Ahmad and his brother, however, continued to have ties to provincial officialdom as a result of their service in the war and membership in the Basij. Perhaps even more importantly, their life experiences, beliefs, and aspirations had been shaped by the Revolution and by their active volunteerism during the war. They participated in state-sponsored religious events more than other Fars-Abadis. They also received limited benefits from their membership, including the potential to access loans and discounts to certain venues as well as political connections and clout. For instance, Ahmad was personally acquainted with the town's mayor as well as with its local, government-appointed imams. Even further, he himself had been mayor of Fars-Abad soon after the Iran-Iraq War, and he maintained friendships with people in local government.

WRITING BASIJI LIVES

It is important to note that I did not set out to write about the Basij or call my interlocutors Basiji in my notes or writing. It was only when I had returned to the United States and had begun describing my research and fieldwork to an American audience that these terms began to emerge. In the beginning, I oscillated between "supporters of the regime" and "pro-Khomeini Shi'i Iranians."[16] I needed to somehow specify that my fieldwork was not about the urban secular Iranian reformists or the ayatollahs and state elites we tend to hear about in the news. I also needed to specify that my hosts were different from the Revolutionary Guard. In the end, I chose to use the word Basij because it was the term that my interlocutors used to describe themselves, and it helped make clear their particular positionality vis-à-vis the Islamic Republic. (On at least three occasions my hosts' sons and daughters proudly showed me their Basij identity cards.) However, this was not the only term they used to describe who they were. They also called themselves "good Muslims" or people "from the provinces" or, even more simply, "Fars-Abadis." This is particularly significant in that several of the young adults I came to know admitted that they held different political views from their parents. Occasionally, too, I came across an extended family member who did not believe in the vision of an Islamic Republic in the least and questioned its ideological foundations.

Even my host Ahmad—perhaps the person I knew the best, who most strongly supported the late Ayatollah Khomeini's vision for an Islamic Republic as well as the current Supreme Leader, Ayatollah Khamenei—once told me that he had made an explicit decision to turn away from politics after he had completed his term as mayor of Fars-Abad in the 1980s and become a teacher. He said that he valued learning, knowledge, and Islam, above all. Indeed, Ahmad's unique stance was obvious in that he took an American researcher into his home. Moreover, he was comfortable openly criticizing some of the more innocuous positions of one of Fars-Abad's two government-appointed Friday Imams. For instance, he argued that there is no need to replace a rug made impure (*najes*) by a child's urine (which he said was pure), and that it was not necessary to avoid prayer on a carpet with birds and animal designs (Ahmad thought these were beautiful). He also critiqued the apparent need to build courtyard walls exceptionally high to make it impossible to see into a neighboring home, thus creating *mahram* spaces.[17] Ahmad's leanings may in part clarify why he agreed to host a foreign researcher. Yet his continuing membership in the Basij and ties to local officialdom also help explain why he felt that he could *safely* host an American in the sensitive years after the 2009 election protests. If he had not been so positioned, he may have endangered his family, bringing them unwanted and intense state scrutiny.

That said, I must emphasize that throughout my research, the support for the Islamic Republic that Ahmad, Nushin, and many of their family and friends articulated was neither mere political opportunism nor a performance for an American guest. They believed in the framework of the Islamic Republic. And with the exception of a few of their young adult children, they did not privately desire "Western freedoms" (Manoukian 2012, 103). The family members I interviewed, including many youths, were sincerely motivated to achieve a better world for themselves and their children vis-à-vis an Islamic state, one organized by the religious and moral values articulated by Khomeini, and they awaited the return of Imam Mahdi. They were striving to change "what is" into "what should be" for their families and communities: a harmonious, virtuous, orderly, and authentic Muslim society linked to God (see also Manoukian 2012). Although this striving did involve the careful editing (and control) of public appearances at times, it was not insincere. What was at stake, they said, was the defense of the Islamic Republic from spiritual and moral corruption while ensuring the spiritual and bodily health of their kin and their reckoning on the Day of Judgment.

Regardless, the term "Basij" and the organization itself provoke strong reactions. To many Iranians both in Iran and abroad, members of the Basij are hypocrites, opportunists, or agents of the state, and they are often looked down upon by the country's secular and educated elites. One left-leaning Tehrani university student explained: "A big reason secular Iranians dislike the Basij is the perks. They have homes in nice suburbs. They get jobs guaranteed in a society with a lot of unemployment. Their college entrance exams are graded on a better curve and their military service is reduced." Political scientist Saeid Golkar (2015, 182), for instance, argues that "only a small number join the Basij purely for ideological reasons" and points to incentives such as the "educational privileges" that certain members receive.

At the same time, a large number of overseas journalists (e.g., in the BBC News, the *New Yorker*) depict the Basij as the negative foil for a promising new generation of "modern," secular, educated, middle- or upper-class urban youth. Indeed, as the keepers of the Islamic Republic's "official speak" and the epitome of "culturally repugnant others" (Harding 1991), "hardliners," and "fundamentalists," few categories of person attract a more powerful and unmixed opprobrium in the liberal US popular view. They are a kind of "cultural 'other,' apart from, even antithetical to, 'modernity'" (Harding 1991, 374). And in contrast to the secular urban youth, they are conceived of as backwards, literal, and bigoted.

For many people, then—including many Iranians—members of the Basij seem opposite to those who valiantly resist the regime and take to the streets in protest or pursue creative self-expression despite its strictures. But we need to be careful of these binaries (Mamdani 2002). They have resulted in a scholarly and journalistic focus on elite urban youth and in a lingering impression of a deep rift between a totalizing Iranian state and a population disengaged from the domain of power (Olszewska 2013; Adelkhah 1999). We imagine Iran as a regime set against the masses. But as my hosts attest, this seeming rift is not everywhere present. A large cohort of Iranians are participating in the religious ideology and rituals of the state. The families I interviewed, as regular members of the Basij, their friends, and their relatives reveal how this participation occurs for those who occupy a kind of middle ground: people who are not elite officials but who support the values of the Revolution.

Scholarly Accounts of the Basij

A scant but excellent assortment of work on Iran similarly unsettles typical, monolithic portrayals of the Basij (Tawasil 2015; Bajoghli 2017; Sadeghi 2009; Wellman 2015). Anthropologist Amina Tawasil (2015), for instance, examines the lives of opinionated and highly educated Basiji seminarian women in Tehran who seek to strengthen the Islamic state by increasing the availability of Islamic jurisprudent research and education concerning women.

In a different vein, Narges Bajoghli (2017, 2019) examines Basij media makers in Tehran and their efforts to cultivate a new generation of regime supporters through modernized, nationalist, and paternalistic propaganda. She contends that, contrary to popular belief, opinions within the ranks of Basij media makers are much more diverse than one would think, particularly across generations. According to Bajoghli, the first generation are those who fought in the Iran-Iraq War. The second generation are those who joined the Basij in the 1990s, and the third joined in 2005, approximately when Mahmoud Ahmadinejad became president. She explains that many members of the first generation are critical of the later generations, who were trained under the Supreme Leader and seem to advocate more hard-line politics. Indeed, it was this younger generation of active and special Basijis who were called upon to suppress the 2009 Green Movement (Bajoghli 2019, 34) and whose brutality was feared by my hosts' teenage Basij children during those same protests. Nevertheless, Bajoghli argues, what unifies members of the Basij is their belief in the protection of the regime. For the most part, the urban Basij media producers she spoke with were stalwart supporters of the framework of the Islamic Republic (although not necessarily of current state actions, representatives, or officials) (Bajoghli 2019, 13).

I here offer a perspective on a very different population: a rural, regular, non-elite Basij, a group that is only tangentially connected to the state and is removed from the urban centers.[18] I specify that my interlocutors are Basijis when this designation is relevant to the ethnographic text and when it is possible to parse out what is distinct about my hosts vis-à-vis their membership. At the same time, I use terms like "Fars-Abadi" when I am writing about town life more generally or about persons and family members of my hosts who were not affiliated with the Basij.

This is thus an account of provincial Basijis as supporters of the Islamic Republic, their family life and piety in the context of postrevolutionary Iran; it is an investigation of the ways in which the intimacies of home life shape and are shaped by state power. But it is also an account of family and religion in provincial Iran, more broadly.

CONTOURS OF AN ISLAMIC/REPUBLIC

In post-Revolution, postwar, and post–Green Movement Iran, the precise relationship between Islam and the nation-state has been a continuing matter of tension and debate. Early revolutionaries were initially internationalist: they sought to export their Islamic Revolution to other Muslim countries and called for liberation and solidarity for the whole Islamic world (Zubaida 2004). Ayatollah Montazeri's statement in a post-1979 Tehran Friday prayer sermon is typical of this early sensibility: "The Iranian nation doesn't want one span of Arab soil. . . . [I]nstead we want Islam, which doesn't know borders" (Montazeri, 5/10/79, quoted in Ludwig 1999, 190). Similarly, Ayatollah Mutahhari, a close aide to Khomeini and the chairman of the Revolutionary Council until his assassination on May 1, 1979, was a firm critic of nationalism. He argued that nationalism was inadequate in comparison to the positive aspects of Islam, which provides a transnational framework of potentially global reach. Further, he adamantly dismissed definitions of the nation based on the individual, race, ethnicity, or even place, regarding nationhood as a myth constructed by governments. The Pahlavi state's ideology of Iranian national identity, modeled on Ataturk's nation building in Turkey, exemplified these deficiencies (Fischer and Abedi 1990, 191). Even the Persian term for nation was a philological mistake. Mutahhari contended that nation, or *mellat*, is a Qur'anic word, which means a path that the Prophet offers for people, not a nation (Fischer and Abedi 1990, 192).

Yet despite an early anti-nationalist and anti-territorial focus on the "Muslim community of believers" (*ummah*), the new Islamic Republic of Iran was never strictly pan-Islamic. From its inception, the 1979 Constitution fused democratic and theocratic principles and institutions (Mir-Hosseini 2010; see also Schirazi 1997).[19] Early revolutionaries, moreover, largely failed to export the Revolution elsewhere, and the subsequent Iran-Iraq War led many of those in power to refocus on the territorialized (Muslim) nation-state as the category of import (Ansari 2007; Ludwig 1999). State elites thus imagined a *republic* that was established and founded on the spirit of Islam (Paidar 1995, 175). As political scientist Mostafa Vaziri relates: "The relationship between Islamism and Iranism—their boundaries of consciousness, their authority and sentiment—however, remained a gray area until the 1979 Revolution (and indeed continues to be one today, under different circumstances)" (1993,189).

Today, the simultaneity of being an Islamic/Republic is visible in how women are participating in religious and legal interpretations of their rights and roles (Osanloo 2009). They employ Islam as a source to render individual responsibility and social accountability *and* utilize liberal ideas to claim status as rights-bearing citizens (Osanloo 2009). Yet how, precisely, these two categories should coexist is often the subject of debate (Osanloo 2009). Indeed, what the precise contours of Islam and the nation-state should be was a frequent and heavily politicized subject of conversation among my state-supporting hosts and others in Fars-Abad and Tehran. Mehdi, a Tehrani cousin; Ahmad, my host; and Zahra, another cousin, each provided a different interpretation of the relationship between Iran and Islam.

Mehdi

Mehdi, a young Basiji computer scientist living in Ekbatan, Tehran, and the son of Mahmud, my Tehrani taxi-driving host, sat on the family sofa and answered my questions over the background noise of the television. I asked him to explain the notion of an Islamic republic. He answered: "In Iran, religion supersedes nationalism. There are two things: Islam and 'Iranian culture' (*farhang-e Iran*). The chador is Iranian but wearing hijab is from Islam." He continued, "Islam is adapted by different 'cultures' (*farhang-hā*) differently.... Religion comes first, then culture." When I asked him if the citizens of Iran feel a connection with each other, he responded: "Yes, we have a connection in Iran. We are good to each other. We are brothers, sisters, mothers, and fathers of Islam.... Religiosity (*mazhabi*) is very important in Iran."[20] Mehdi here and elsewhere also explained that he employs terms such as mother, father, and brother when referring to other Iranians because he and his fellow citizens share the same religion, the same emphasis on purity, religiously permissible family relationships, trustworthiness, and closeness to God.

Ahmad and His Brother-in-Law, Haji Nazari

Several months into my fieldwork in Fars-Abad, I asked my host, Ahmad, and his brother-in-law, Haji Nazari, whether they regarded Iran as a religious entity based on Islam or as a territorial entity based on land (*khāk*). Their debate grew increasingly intense, almost to the point that I worried I had caused a family feud. Haji Nazari was in his fifties and was a member of the Azeri Turk minority and had a fondness for poetry, Nescafé American-style coffee, and Persian translations of William Blake. He argued that Iranians are connected by the land. "The nation and its borders come before the religious aspects of life," he said, and then added: "People in Iran have different religions. If something helps someone in Iran, it helps the people of Iran, not the religion of Islam." Ahmad adamantly disagreed. He argued, as had his nephew Mehdi, that Islam and religion come first. He said that he counts the Palestinians and other Muslims as his brothers and that helping them is helping Islam. "The commands of Allah," he explained, "extend beyond Iran's borders. Islam 'established' (*ijād kard*) the Republic. Khomeini [the founder of the Islamic Republic] believed (*mo'taqed budan*) this from the beginning." His brother-in-law responded: "First comes a house that you can pray in. Being Iranian means having a house that you can pray in. It means respecting the air, the soil, the mountains, and the forests."

Haji Nazari's argument that the nation and land are like a house, a container that must provide the land, air, soil, mountains, and forests for prayer and religion, was, although not uncommon, a controversial position in conservative-leaning Fars-Abad. Here were two distinct understandings of how to interpret national and transnational solidarity as well as martyrdom (as an Islamic or national enterprise), and each had differing and consequential perspectives on who is counted as "us."

I could sense the disquietude of the room as the two men argued. Other family members grew quiet as the debate continued, aware that this topic was political (*siāsi*) and heavy (*sangin*), as well as dangerous to both the harmony of their own social relations and their positions within the state.

Zahra

A young Basiji woman in Tehran named Zahra shared yet another position in this debate. She was working as a researcher for a professor while studying political science and had invited me to come see her workplace. We were sitting in the office on a rainy day in the winter drinking tea, when I asked her why or for whom she prays and practices Islamic charity. She responded with her views on the relationship between Islam and Iran:

> We say the "Islamic Republic of Iran," first "Islamic" and then "Iran." Do you know what I mean? They [the media and government] say that, for example, Islam and Iran together are one. This means that it must be both Islamic and Iran. They are one and the same. Their value is equal. It is really important that they say it this way. Because, for example, when we fight in a war, it is because of Islam that we fight. Both because of the nation (*vatan*) and because of Islam.... They say that if Iraq attacks Iran, if it takes the country, Islam will die. Shi'ism will be destroyed.... We fight both to protect Islam and the nation.[21]

For Zahra, the nation and Islam, meaning "Shi'i Islam," have roughly the same shape and the same boundaries, and they incorporate the same people. As she argued, if Iran as a nation is destroyed, Islam will also be destroyed. Nevertheless, she insisted, people should accept the existence in the country of certain other non-Muslim and non-Shi'i Iranians, such as Zoroastrians, Jews, and Christians. Iranian diversity exists and can be appreciated within the model of an Islamic republic.[22] But the nation is an *Islamic* nation, guided by Islamic principles.

The precise relationship between Islamism and Iranism remains a matter of debate in contemporary Iran, though the card-carrying Basijis I spoke with most often supported their coevalness and equivalence. In chapters 3 and 4 I show how they reinforce these connections through such tangible work as the continuing burial of martyrs from the Iran-Iraq War and the regulation of (halal) food products at national borders, emphasizing the sacred defense of a pure *national* space, bounded by territory yet built with the spirit of Islam: an Islamic nation-state.

BROTHERS AND SISTERS OF ISLAM

The other guiding principle of the Islamic Republic, according to my hosts, is kinship. Since the time of the Constitutional Revolution (1905–11), which produced Iran's first constitutional monarchy, the trope of kinship has been integral to Iranian nation-making. During and after this revolution, the family was recontextualized as the foundation of a nation or *mellat*, a unit composed of daughter and son citizens who were to care for a mother homeland or *vatan* (Kashani-Sabet 2014). Men and women, moreover, were called brothers and sisters (Najmabadi 1997, 463), evoking an affective bond that was also a basis for political solidarity. Notably, too, the (pure) female homeland of Iran was in need of protection from transgression or *tajāvoz* (both in the sense of rape and the invasion of territory) (Najmabadi 1997, 459).

More recently, since the 1979 Revolution in Iran and subsequent Iran-Iraq War (1980–88), the call for citizens to relate specifically as an "*Islamic Iranian family*" or as "brothers and sisters of Islam" has been a driving force in national politics (see also Sadeghi 2009).[23] On *'Ashura'*, the tenth day of Muharram, December 11, 1978, for instance, the late Supreme Leader and founder of the Islamic Republic, Ayatollah Khomeini, rallied millions to participate in demonstrations with the words: "Sisters and Brothers be resolute. Do not show weakness and lack of courage. You are following the path of the Almighty and his prophets. Your blood is poured on the same road as that of the (martyred) prophets, Imams, and their followers" (Khomeini 1999).[24] Later, on September 16 of the same year, Khomeini continued to emphasize this vision of the nation as an Islamic brother- and sisterhood:

> One of the most significant effects of this movement [the Revolution] is the change brought about in all of you, in the ladies, in the brothers and

sisters alike. That change is the sense of duty that we all now feel, a duty to our country, a duty to educate, to educate people in those things that will be useful to them in religious and worldly affairs. ([1979] 2001, 71)

Khomeini here regarded national citizens as brothers and sisters who share a duty to educate people in religious and worldly affairs. This shared duty, moreover, was linked by Khomeini and others to the concept of a "social being," a person who is active and committed to others in the public arena while maintaining piety and respectability in private life (Adelkhah 1999, 5; see also Olszeweska 2015a, 19).

Today, the Islamic Republic and those who most vigilantly support it continue to aspire to a kindred Islamic/nation, centered on a sometimes pan-Islamic, but often simultaneously nationalistic, brother- and sisterhood.[25] Indeed, according to the Iranian Constitution (1979; revised in 1989), the family is "the fundamental unity of society." During my fieldwork, I found that evocations of "brothers and sisters of faith" or "brothers and sisters of Islam" appear in contexts as diverse as weekly Friday prayer sermons (both in Tehran and in the provinces) (Wellman 2015), the "official speak" of organizations such as the Basij and "Sister's Basij" (Basij-e Khāharān), the materials of Islamic seminary schools for men and women, and Islamic-national rituals commemorating martyrs or the birth and death days of Imams.

For supporters of the Islamic Republic, moreover, the trope of kindred religious nationhood is polysemic. It requires participants to strive for the values of purity and simplicity of the family of the Prophet, evidenced in such feats as the sacrifice of Imam Husayn at the Battle of Karbala (680 CE) or the heroism of his sister, Zaynab. It further calls on participants to remember, protect, and renew the mass solidarity that was felt among protesters during the 1979 Revolution. Finally, the continuing aspiration for an Islamic brother- and sisterhood interpellates its participants as gendered citizens with differing male and female roles and responsibilities in public and private, including lawful (halal) interaction, comportment, behavior, and modesty.[26]

According to Partha Chatterjee (1989), these critical symbols of religion and family life are common to the construction of an "inner," "spiritual" domain of sovereignty in anti-colonial nation-states (such as Iran), even as the "outer" domains of statecraft and modular nationalism persist. My research has shown me that there are many competing and shifting narratives in Iran about the construction and relationship of Islam, kinship, and Iran as a state. Most recently, for instance, the media producers for the Revolutionary Guard and Basij have sought to promote Iranianness over religion in their propaganda efforts to create feelings of nationalism among Iran's youth (Bajoghli 2017). They have also been heavily promoting notions of national kinship. For instance, in newer propaganda they are focusing on the valorization of Iranian masculinity and paternal protection (Bajoghli 2017). As one of Bajoghli's (2017) media-producing interlocutors noted: "You don't have to pray to be a hero to your cousin." For many of the Revolutionary Guard and Basij leaders, this approach is a kind of necessary dissimulation, required to convince young and increasingly secular Iranians to join the Basij and defend Iran in the event of an attack by a foreign nation or body, such as the Islamic State of Iraq and Syria (ISIS) (Bajoghli 2017).

But as my fieldwork attests, this ploy is not universal. In Fars-Abad, state elites such as mayors and officers, as well as everyday citizens, saw Islamic piety and national continuity as deeply interconnected. Moreover, they sought to use these connections to garner support among their pious constituents. Chapters 3 and 4 explore this continued emphasis, not only on religion and the sacred in provincial Iran as a means of state making, but also on the religious family as a model for the state.

OFF THE BEATEN PATH: FARS-ABAD, LANDSCAPE, AND HISTORY

As one takes the road that leads north beyond the outlying suburbs of Shiraz and the famous Shiraz "Qur'an Gate," the landscape quickly changes to a mixture of irrigated green farmland and dry yellow desert. The road is speckled with towns, some big and some small. Viewed from a bus or car traveling from Shiraz, key road signs point out the city of Marvdasht and the turn to the famous ruin and tourist destination, Persepolis, the capital of the Achaemenid Empire (550–330 BCE). The Rustam Relief from the Achaemenid and Sassanid periods appears on the side of the highway, red-orange rock monuments cut into the cliff. Finally, the road, which ultimately stretches on to Esfahan and then Tehran, passes near Parsargad, the tomb of King Cyrus (founder of the Achaemenid Empire), and an array of smaller towns and villages.

Fars-Abad is one of these smaller towns, located only a few kilometers from these historic sites. In the 2006 Iranian state census, the town's population was 14,095 persons forming 3,375 "families," with 4.2 persons per household.[27] In 2010, Fars-Abad was known locally for its relative conservatism. Taxi drivers in Shiraz would often gloss Fars-Abadis as "the good ones/children" (*bache-hā-ye khub*). In contrast to the metropolitan centers of Shiraz and Tehran, and even some neighboring towns, in Fars-Abad the black chador was required street attire for women, and men rarely wore T-shirts, favoring long-sleeve garments. The local Friday Imam was said to be strict (*sakht-gir*); in general, religiously permissible interaction between males and females was maintained in public and private.

Located in the northern region of the Fars province, Fars-Abad is on mostly flat land irrigated by underground water tables and well systems. It is surrounded by rolling hills on which shepherds herd their sheep. A single main street, Imam Boulevard, connects its three neighborhoods. The first neighborhood is called "the valley of the river of the birds" and is the site of the mansion of the former ruler or khan and of the local pickling factory (one of the town's major employers). The second and most central neighborhood is the town's shopping and ritual center, called by the town's name, "Fars-Abad." The third is poorer and is known by locals as the Arab district. Quiet on a typical midday, Imam Boulevard springs to life with heavy traffic in the late afternoon: Pekans, Peugeots, farm trucks, semitrucks, and motorcycles fly past in all directions carrying teenage boys, families, and old men. (Women never drive motorcycles but they do ride them, and they sometimes drive cars in town.) On the sidewalks, middle-aged women in black chadors and men in white or light blue collared shirts walk to and fro or wait in line. They carry plastic bags of bread or milk, stopping at tiny convenience stores, bakeries, butcher shops, and fruit or vegetable markets. Male teenagers assume the most risqué attire and postures, occasionally gelling their hair and wearing short-sleeve shirts and stylish jeans (Shahshahani 2008). At dusk, the Muslim "call to prayer" or *azān* blares out from the speakers of the meetinghouse for Imam Husayn.

Figure 1. View of Fars-Abad, Iran, from the town park

In the old section of town, near the center, families live in narrow brick- or cement-walled alleys that radiate from the wider main street. The mosque and meetinghouse, along with the nearby educational center and graveyards, form a local ritual center. In 2010, while the mosque was under construction, the meetinghouse was the focal point of town religious affairs, holding events as diverse as Friday prayers, commemorations for dead martyrs, and funerals.

Older streets wind and crisscross around the mosque and meeting house. These streets resemble the neighborhoods of South Tehran and are often the width of a single car. Short alleys extend from these streets to household units, often housing two or three homes occupied by the families of male siblings and their parents. This was the kind of alley I moved into when I first arrived in Fars-Abad.

In Fars-Abad, too, most homes have a gated front-facing courtyard but no more than three or four rooms. Showers and bathrooms are in separate

Figure 2. Alley, Fars-Abad, Iran

"outhouse"-style facilities within each family's courtyard space. Inside, intricate red Persian carpets cover the floors, and bright red cushions line the walls for leaning and sitting on the floor. (Very few homes had tables or chairs of any kind during my fieldwork.) Typically, homes also include a central skylight, under which people keep an array of household plants. The kitchens have a refrigerator, a stove, cabinets, a sink, a meat grinder, and a teakettle, but no microwave. In 2010 there were still a few houses in town that had a separate kitchen with its own door, located in another part of the courtyard.

A large number of homes in the oldest parts of town are made of decaying mud and clay or a mixture of mud, clay, and brick. These homes have high mud walls and flat roofs of mud and straw supported by wooden rafters. The new housing structures, such as the one my hosts moved into during my fieldwork, stand in direct contrast both to the older-style homes and to the alleys and narrow streets in the older center of town. These detached homes, designed for single families and perhaps their parents, are made largely by manual labor from brick and iron rod fixtures. They have a garage-style car park and walled courtyards in the back. A new collection of apartments, made of the same material, provides dwelling places for young families. Outside the town center, several multistory, gated apartment complexes reach up to two stories high. Finally, the richest of the town residents—mostly factory owners or those who had connections with the previous king or his stewards—have large homes, both old and new, enclosed on all sides by gardens filled with fruit trees and flowers, patios, and shallow pools. During my time in Fars-Abad, I visited only three or four homes in this style but saw several more from afar.

Finally, Fars-Abad has several parks for recreation and picnicking, two frequently visited graveyards, a major industrial pickling factory, a small Islamic Azad university providing associate degrees, a grade school, and a high school. The parks offer recreation, exercise equipment, flowing water, and the shade of trees. An older graveyard in the center of town is the resting place of the town's martyrs from the Iran-Iraq War. A newer graveyard on the edge of town is the site of present-day burials and commemorations. Schools are sex-segregated until high school, after which they become coed.

Outside these living and ritual spaces, family-owned orchards extend to the north and west. Arranged as plots of land with high mud walls and tiny paths between them, these gardens grow an array of fruit trees and shrubs: apricot, plum, apple, walnut, almond, and grape. Often the gardens include cement platforms for sleeping or spending the afternoon. These gardens are an important part of family life and are regularly used as places for family picnics or for the enjoyment of fresh fruit. Finally, farmlands skirt the town, with fields growing wheat, barley, tomatoes, cucumbers, and saffron, among others crops. Several farms raise cattle or other animals for slaughter. Itinerant nomads herd sheep and goats on the town's outskirts, often passing by or through the town's parks.

Locals describe the edge of town as a desert (*kavir*). For town dwellers especially, the desert is the place where settled, agricultural land ends. As such, the agricultural outskirts of town are considered a kind of in-between place, beyond which is a "wild land" replete with mountain spirits or jinn. Outside of Fars-Abad, however, the desert is not entirely barren. Green plants, grasses, and trees grow around small streams and rivers, and the surrounding rolling hills have copious amounts of scrub vegetation. Neighboring settled Basseri nomads frequently camp out at night in the desert, collecting plants and herbs or hunting wild animals such as hogs, which they eat, considering them different from the forbidden pig.

In general, people in Fars-Abad describe the plain on which they live with pride. "This is the plain chosen by King Cyrus the Great," they say, in reference to the good agricultural lands, streams and underground water tables, and proximity to his tomb. At the time I was doing my research, they had experienced three dry years in a row, and water (even from the underground tables) was becoming increasingly difficult to access, a scarce resource.

Then and Now

Fars-Abad's past remains an active part of living memory in contemporary town life. The remnants of the castle or fortress (*qal'eh*) that stood at Fars-Abad until around 1975 and once enclosed it are still visible in several places. "Before the meetinghouse for Imam Husayn, there was a fortress in the center of town," remembered Goli-Mehrebun, Nushin's eighty-year-old mother. Born in the 1930s in Fars-Abad, Goli-Mehrebun was the first wife of her husband, an affluent man of royal ancestry. She was in the process of raising her first two of five children when her husband took his second wife, with whom he had four more children, my host mother's half siblings. According to her children, Goli-Mehrebun was always respectful of this other wife, who lived in a separate dwelling, but she described herself as much more proficient at raising and educating her children. Goli occasionally smoked opium to calm her aching joints but was intelligent and alert. In the style of the town's older generation, she wrapped her body and head in a dark-colored cotton chador decorated with tiny flowers. She moved slowly and methodically, always commenting on the state of affairs in the town and overseeing her family.

Goli and her son Sami, Nushin's brother, were in the process of recounting Fars-Abad's past when my host sister and I came to visit near midday on a hot summer day. She offered us tea from her tiny pot in her one-room home, located within the same courtyard as the home of her son. A fan whirred in the background.

"The walls [of the fortress] formed a gated, twenty-meter-tall enclosure, and were designed to keep thieves out," she said.

> Within, there were one hundred and fifty household complexes with one or two floors, each with between five and ten members. In the center of the fortress was a market that divided into dozens of narrow alleys. Some of them had corners and twists. The doors of homes opened to the alleys, which were very narrow because there were no cars. Only donkeys crossed them with hay on their backs. The first floor of the homes stored this hay and people lived on the second floor. Next to the fortress was a tower. At night they went into the tower and watched over people with guns.

Goli and others I spoke with explained that those who were there "from the beginning" had bigger homes, and many residents were extended family. This social mapping continues in Fars-Abad today, with the original families, such as Nushin's family, still surrounded by large extended networks of kin, numbering in the hundreds. Those who came from the outside villages built small homes in the corner of the courtyard of a larger home.

Before land reform took place in Iran in 1962, Fars-Abad had a ruler or khan, a relation of the Qajars (a dynasty that ruled Iran between 1785 and 1925). In this system, the khan controlled access to agricultural land and other means of livelihood. Farmers had traditional rights to land as shares, but not to ownership of specific tracts of land. They kept half of the harvest, and the khan received the other half. Although this history of kingship has largely been erased from public town history, town residents I spoke with remembered their particular khan as a good person. They described him as "literate" and "cultured" and specifically mentioned his university degree in architecture. They further emphasized that he did not oppress people as khans in other townships did. Rather, he helped them by giving them medicine.

Local Class Politics

During the 1960s land reform of Iran, the land of Fars-Abad was divided, but supporters of Shah Mohammad Reza Pahlavi took or bought the majority of good farmland, while the peasants and the recently settled nomads were allotted next to nothing. As a result of the 1979 Revolution, the land was again redistributed. Fars-Abadis remember how people filled the streets in protest, entering the khan's former living quarters and beautified, tree-filled gardens with the intention of ousting his supporters. My hosts described this fight as one for social equity. They proudly remembered the role of Nushin's father in this political movement and his fight for a more equitable distribution of land. He fought, they said, for the inclusion of the more peripheral settled nomads and Iranian Arabs into Fars-Abad's community. In rural Fars-Abad, my hosts, their friends, and their neighbors continue to describe this hope for greater equity as a reason for their continuing support for the Islamic Republic (see also Hegland 2013).[28] They believe that the regime is more just than the khans of the past, and they point to positive changes in infrastructure since the Revolution.

The 1979 Revolution did bring about numerous changes to life in Fars-Abad, changes that were accompanied by rampant population growth and urbanization.[29] The development of rural Iran was one of the Revolution's imperatives (Salehi-Isfahani 2019), and rural areas saw a visible expansion of basic services, including electricity and pipeable clean water (Hooglund 2009).[30] Another dramatic improvement was an increase in roadways and connection to a national highway system. Before the Revolution, there were only 4,790 miles of rural roads, and most were dirt tracks. By March 1999, however, the Construction Jehad (Jehād-e Sāzandegi)—a key organization formed in 1979 only two weeks after the IRGC—had built approximately 36,660 miles of two-lane rural roads, including paved and graded gravel roads, bridges, and tunnels (Hooglund 2009).[31]

Relatedly, the pro-poor and pro-rural policies of the Revolution precipitated a sharp reduction in abject poverty and an expansion of health care and education in rural areas, including health clinics, primary schools, secondary schools, and "Islamic open universities" (Hooglund 2009; Saleh-Isfahani 2019). The number of students participating in higher education across Iran soared, rising by 80 percent from 2005 to 2015 (Saleh-Isfahani 2019).

My hosts sometimes reflected on these changes, arguing that people in Fars-Abad had shifted from being simple and illiterate followers of a khan to more independent wage earners with better education. As Ahmad's aunt, Nistdar, explained, "After the Revolution, the situation got better. We had been illiterate. Life was simple. But after the Revolution, people's 'reasoning/knowledge of God' (*'aql*) improved. People progressed. Because of the Revolution, people got land, and then they got salaries. Slowly, they began to become independently wealthy."[32]

Iranian women benefited in numerous ways from these intertwined changes in education and health care in particular (Bahramitash 2012). Their life expectancy rates increased with the improvements in health care, and they saw a decrease in infant mortality (Bahramitash 2012). At the same time women's widespread use of state-sanctioned family planning following the Iran-Iraq War led to lower fertility rates, a shift that allowed even more women to pursue higher education (see also Tober, Taghdisi, and Jalali 2006). In rural areas, for instance, the average age for marriage increased from the mid-1960s, from 14 to 23.4 years (Bahramitash 2012, 53).

Yet despite some advances, my hosts (and particularly their young adult children) still bemoaned a general "lack of available opportunity" in the town and beyond. Young Fars-Abadis, even members of the Basij, were struggling to find suitable employment amid Iran's high youth unemployment rate, a deficit that some economists argue derives from the country's slow growth in the private sector and ongoing dependence on oil profits (Salehi-Isfahani 2019). According to the 2016–17 census, for instance, unemployment in Iran for men (aged twenty-five to twenty-nine) was 34.6 percent, and for women of the same age the unemployment rate was 45.7 percent (Saleh-Isfahani 2019). Thus, even though by most measures absolute poverty has decreased in postrevolutionary Iran due to government and private assistance programs for low-income households, it is still a serious problem. Writing in the early 2000s, for instance, sociologist Mostafa Azkia noted that around 50 percent of rural households were at or below the minimum annual income necessary to provide food, clothing, housing, and utilities for a family of four (Azkia 2002, 101–3).

And while postrevolutionary policies have led to a dramatic increase in people receiving education, growth remains slow in the private sector, leading to a large group of young, educated, and dissatisfied "would be middle-class people," particularly in the urban areas (Olszewska 2015b, 27). In contrast to this cohort, my hosts in Fars-Abad, Tehran, and Shiraz might be described as part of a new "regime class," ideologically aligned with the state and benefiting from these ties by way of better loan rates, connections, and so on. According to anthropologist Zuzanna Olszewska (2015b, 27), "the consequences of these contradictory movements seem still to be playing out, both in everyday life and on the national stage, and they are as much cultural as they are economic." My hosts' support for the Islamic Republic is thus deeply entangled with their location in rural Fars Province, their position in this regime class cohort, and the ways in which their livelihoods improved in the context of postrevolutionary Iran.

OUTLINE OF THE CHAPTERS

This book has this introduction, four ethnographic chapters, and an epilogue, and it makes two crosscutting comparisons. The first comparison concerns the mutual structuring and transformation of kinship, nation, and religion as interrelated social domains and the literal flow of kinship-related substances and pious acts between the intimate spaces of the home and the nation. The second comparison shows how two different kinds of sacred materiality—inheritable bodily substances such as blood and food—play out in Iranian sociality.

Chapter 1, "Blood, Physio-Sacred Substance, and the Making of Moral Kin," examines the everyday religious and moral experience of being kin in (provincial) postrevolutionary Iran. It begins by describing the key debates about the shape of the family and correct gender relations in Iran and investigates how blood and the other shared substances of kinship channel "physio-sacred" qualities along lines of descent. The chapter then explores how the physio-sacred "stuff" of kinship is mutable and can be developed as an object of prayer, protection, and ethical work. In the context of a society that is seemingly "losing its values" and that is fraught with problems—ranging from "lack of familial trust" to drug addiction—women's and men's everyday pious acts, such as praying and visiting kin, are part of an ongoing effort to protect the pure inside relations of family and household from outside and possibly corrupt kin, in-laws, or strangers. These acts infuse the vulnerable bodies and souls of kin with blessing and purity and protect children and other family members from outside physical and/or spiritual harm. In so doing, they reveal kin-making to be an embodied, sacred, and ethical process.

Chapter 2, "Feeding the Family: The 'Spirit' of Food in Iran," investigates how pure and moral kin, as well as the inside spaces of household and family, are constituted and protected through a range of ritual and everyday food practices. Food in Iran is more than a means of providing nutrition. Rather, it is an agent of transformation and a vehicle for channeling divine blessing, whether directed inward to the pure family core, which is materialized by the cloth upon which the family meal is spread (*sofreh*), or directed outward, for the spiritual nourishment of extended kin. This chapter further explores how acts of fasting and participating in ritual meals shape and protect correct and ethical kin relations. It also discusses how conservative state politics can infuse everyday family life.

Chapter 3, "Regenerating the Islamic Republic: Commemorating Martyrs in Provincial Iran," analyzes how provincial state supporters and elites mobilize the bodies and blood of martyrs to sacralize the post-Revolution, postwar national landscape. Since the 1979 Islamic Revolution, a powerful cohort of religious scholars and everyday citizens has emphasized the need to (re)generate the authentically Islamic interior of the nation while resisting an immoral, "Westernstruck" exterior. A significant part of this sacred defense against a Western cultural invasion has been the exhumation of bodies of Iran-Iraq War (1980–88) martyrs from the battlefront for reburial and commemoration at sites across the national landscape. This chapter investigates these ongoing practices of reburying and memorializing martyrs. It argues that these exhumations and reburials of martyrs are strategic religious practices that organize the bodies of Iranian subjects around key reference points, specifically the martyrdom of Imam Husayn at the Battle of Karbala, the 1979 Revolution, and the Iran-Iraq War. In addition, it shows how acts of commemorating martyrs emphasize the sacrificial blood of male citizens, a bodily substance that draws further symbolic efficacy from its associations with the life-giving blood of kinship (see chapter 1). This is the first ethnographic account of how martyrs are interred and commemorated in provincial Iran.

In contrast to chapter 3, chapter 4, "Creating an Islamic Nation through Food," examines how Iranians employ food to articulate, shape, and contest the making of an Islamic nation. Like the family, the nation is organized by the imperative to create and contain inner purity within its borders. Indeed, as an *Islamic* republic, the Iranian nation-state depends on the continual regeneration of a pure, Islamic interior composed of the right kind of virtuous (*bātaqvā*) kindred citizenry. This chapter foregrounds an analysis of food and food rituals not only because of their unique ability to forge, circulate, and internalize these "right" virtues and qualities into and within the nation, but also because of the powerful analogy between food sharing at home and food sharing for the nation. Here, my argument builds on chapter 2 to suggest that, for my interlocutors, food sharing works in tandem with other means of making (national) religious kinship in Iran, such as prayer and martyrs' sacrifice, to relate Muslim citizens both to each other and to the divine.

The epilogue to *Feeding Iran* makes explicit the mutual constitution of kinship, nation, and religion in the Islamic Republic. Challenging the conventional academic separation of kinship from politics, it underscores not only how the family can be a model for the nation but also how the literal flow of kinship-related substances and acts between the intimate spaces of the home and of the nation can infuse the grand rituals of state power. Here, the meanings, feelings, and substances of kinship are critical to legitimizing the state and making it appear natural. The conclusion also revisits the problematics of "writing Basiji lives" in light of popular media portrayals that depict the Basij as fundamentalists and hard-liners who stand in opposition to liberal modernity. It calls for a more nuanced, humanistic understanding of these non-elite, provincial state supporters' aspirations and values. Finally, it explores how conservative state politics are made to seem natural and legitimate by those in power.

1   Blood, Physio-Sacred Substance, and the Making of Moral Kin

Oh Zaynab!
They killed Husayn.
His thirsty lips.
Dear Zaynab, help us.

Protect our families
I vow to the family of the Prophet
God, grant our wishes.

Help our children.
Help the addicts and the sick.
Help those who cannot come home.
Those who cannot sit with their mothers and fathers
   and eat lunch.
Oh Zaynab, help us.

—Women's prayer gathering, Fars-Abad, 2010

Nushin and Ahmad spoke in hurried whispers. They had just received news of Ehsan's death. They told us to go upstairs and get ready to leave the house. Ehsan was Nushin's nephew, and his father, Nushin's brother, would be expecting us. Maryam and I ran to our room to put on our chadors while the boys hurried ahead. I vividly remember the silhouette of Nushin's back as she walked a few steps ahead of us in the alley, her steps kicking up dust and her frame shuddering in shock. Fatemeh, Nushin's married daughter, with her baby Setayesh on her hip, found us in the street and walked with us the next few blocks to the gated door of

Ehsan's home. Passing under the black cloth of mourning that hung over the alley and through a group of men sitting in the small walled courtyard, we entered the home's living room, its walls lined with women who had somehow already arrived and were tearfully praying. At the door, I held Setayesh while Fatemeh adjusted her scarf. Marjan and Farrin, Nushin's nieces (Ehsan's sisters), were sitting on the floor crying, surrounded by several groups of women. Marjan, Ehsan's eldest sister, rocked back and forth sobbing: "My brother, my brother, my brother . . . for the love of my father, my father!" Marjan's mother wailed next to her now brotherless daughters, sometimes being hushed by the other women. Nushin went over to hold her hand.

. . . . .

Ehsan was only in his twenties when his body was found, bloated from several days in the sun, in the desert outside of Fars-Abad. He had died on the Holy Night of Power during Ramadan, they said, of a drug overdose, probably heroin.[1] Nushin told me later that the drugs had likely been trafficked "from Afghanistan and were ultimately the effect of US foreign policy there." But it was unclear how his body had gotten to the desert, and there were unsubstantiated rumors going around town that his death was not an accident. When news of the family's calamity spread in the town, neighbors, close friends, and kin filled the house of his parents, offering their condolences: "May God have Mercy on Him" (*khodā rahmat-esh koneh*), they said.

Ehsan was buried on the Thursday after his death (his burial had been delayed a few days due to ongoing investigations into the circumstances of his passing). He was brought to the cemetery by ambulance in a wooden casket, and his close male relatives carried him up the hill to the earthen gravesite. Nearly one thousand people attended the burial and the subsequent funeral. His immediate kin, both male and female, formed the first circle of black-clad mourners around the still open grave and then covered it with fresh earth. His sisters and mother cried and prayed. After the burial, they and their cousins distributed dates, fruit, and *halvā* (a sweet wheat paste made from browned flour and butter, rose water, sugar, and saffron) to the attendees. Then the mourners, in a long car chain, followed the sound of recitation of the Qur'an, broadcast from a truck decorated with a picture of Ehsan wreathed in flowers, to Fars-Abad's meetinghouse for Imam Husayn. Inside the large, carpeted hall, the Friday Imam spoke on the loudspeakers about the Day of Judgment to the male and female mourners.

What can Ehsan's tragic death and funeral tell us about how supporters of the Islamic Republic, their neighbors, and extended family members are experiencing kinship in provincial Iran? How do events like these reverberate in their lives, shape their prayers, and change their relationships, both with each other and with the state? And finally, what can we learn about their aspirations to create households that embody familial piety, purity, and closeness to God in the context of what they see as increasing societal corruption despite the promises of the Revolution?

A few months after Ehsan's funeral, Nushin and I sat together drinking tea in her home in Fars-Abad. She folded her flowered cotton chador over her knees and confessed that she was worried about her two sons (aged nineteen and twenty-three). What if they became drug addicts like Ehsan and died in the desert too? What if her husband also became an opium addict as he grew older, like Ehsan's father, her brother? (Ehsan's father, Nushin's brother, was a brilliant poet but smoked opium throughout the day.) Nushin's concerns were not limited to the high rates of opiate addiction in Fars-Abad and elsewhere in Iran, though.[2] Family tensions were simmering for other reasons. Her young adult children, teenage brothers and sisters, were arguing too much. What was more, she felt that she could not trust one of her husband's relatives, who lived in the family's old complex close to the center of town. "It is especially ugly when people belittle each other," she said, speaking about the tension between herself and one of these extended family members. "You have to be very good so that you can change yourself or someone else for the better. It's very difficult, with your own good behavior, to change the bad behavior of others into good behavior." Then she added, "In the past, people's lives were simple. They didn't have electricity or refrigerators, but they weren't stressed and they weren't quick to anger (the way we are today).... There was more trust." Yet Nushin, perhaps because she supported the regime and her husband and children were card-carrying members of the Basij, did not fault the Revolution for what she saw as an increasing fragmentation of kin relationships and Islamic family values in her society: "This is not because of the Revolution—Khamenei and Khomeini are good," she told me on another occasion as we walked in the local park. "The problem is that others have surrendered hope."

This chapter explores the everyday religious and moral experience of being kin in postrevolutionary Iran from the perspective of the Islamic Republic's provincial state supporters. I explore how Nushin and her family as well their extended kin and neighbors conceive of kinship as both a threat and a resource, employing their prayers and actions to protect and delineate their family households. Not surprisingly, and despite their allegiance to the state, however, my interlocutors' experiences of kinship sometimes conflicted and sometimes converged with notions of Islamic legal kinship as shaped by inheritance laws and "marriage exclusions."[3] Although they organized their families with regard to these Islamic laws, they also held that blood and the other shared substances of kinship channel and contain not only a set of connections or relationships across generations but also "physio-sacred" qualities such as purity and piety.[4] The "descendants of the Prophet" (*sayyeds*), they told me, transmit divine light, purity, and "closeness to God" (see also Ho 2006). But even for non-*sayyeds*, immaterial or sacred qualities such as purity and blessing help determine who counts as kin and/or who might be conceived of as a potential marriage partner.

Even more, they often talked about how their family members' shared qualities of temperament, character, blessing, and purity could be lost or developed. And this physio-sacred "stuff" of kinship was always shifting, an object of prayer, protection, and ethical work. For state supporters like Nushin and her family, this protection was all the more important in a society pervaded by a "lack of familial trust" as well as by problems of divorce and premarital sex. This was a society in which people like Ehsan died in the desert—a result of US meddling in the Middle East. It was against this backdrop that women's and men's everyday pious acts such as praying, visiting, and sharing food (see chapter 2) were essential to maintaining and creating pure and moral kin relations. These "acts of kinship" infused the vulnerable bodies and souls of kin with blessing and purity, protecting children and other family members from outside physical and/or spiritual harm. After all, what was at stake for my state-supporting hosts was not only the spiritual and bodily health of kin but also their reckoning on the Day of Judgment and the future of the Islamic Republic.

SACRALIZING KINSHIP

This chapter is premised on an approach to kinship in the Middle East that does not confine understandings of kinship to a genealogical grid, notions of biology and DNA, or formalized laws. I view kin-making as an embodied, sacred, and ethical process (Cannell 2013, 2017; Wellman 2017b). The immaterial, *sacred* acts and qualities of kinship may work alongside or in dynamic tension with other ideas of blood, law, or genealogy, but they are no less important for doing so. This point warrants particular emphasis because kinship has traditionally been regarded as a secular affair (Cannell 2017; Delaney 1986). Schneider, for instance, examined religion as a second-order phenomenon in his work on the meanings of "blood" and "law" in American kinship and largely neglected the particular religious formations that constituted American modernity (Cannell 2013; Feeley-Harnik 1999). In *The Seed and the Soil: Gender and Cosmology in Turkish Village Society*, Carol Delaney (1991) began a challenge to this partitioning of kinship and religion (and of politics) by illustrating how concepts of monogenetic human procreation are linked to monotheistic understandings of divine creation in which God is the Father of creation. But too often, scholars continue to analytically separate the somatic or physical aspects of incorporation into kin groups and the nonphysical acts and qualities that create kinship (Johnson et al. 2015, 7). They rank the nonphysical, immaterial, or ritual acts of kin-making as "pseudo" or "fictive" and therefore miss how such understandings may be fundamental to local kinship(s).

New research, however, shows that there are many examples of sacred and/or sacralized kinship (Thomas, Malik, and Wellman 2017). For instance, Fenella Cannell explores the American Mormon "recognition" of past and future kin to show that kinship can occupy a "third space" in which it rests on neither biogenetic substance nor man-made law/convention, but rather on something spiritual, immaterial, and ineffable (2007, 6; 2013). Indeed, people may participate in the holy "by caring for their kin" or they may "care for their kin through participating in the holy" (Sered 1988, 130).

Scholarly research of Muslims in the Middle East has similarly begun to explore kinship as a process. Families in locations as diverse as Lebanon, Morocco, or Iran may be organized not only by blood and law but also by ideas of "closeness" (Clarke 2007b), by the sharing of houses (Bahloul 1996), and through active and shifting networks of relations (Shahshahani 1990). Shared breast milk and suckling in Islam can be a source of kin-making (Parkes 2005; Clarke 2007a).

This research lays the groundwork for understanding how my Basiji hosts conceived of kinship in Fars-Abad and beyond: as a religious and ethical process of becoming the right kind of moral and pure kin. This process of making the right kind of kin, moreover, was deeply connected to the hope of embodying the values of the Revolution and thus of protecting the Islamic Republic. This chapter attends to a full spectrum of acts and processes of kin-making—including the immaterial qualities and ritual actions that shaped my hosts' relationships. I begin, however, with a brief overview of how they understood Islamic family law, gender, and divine creation in relation to their support of the regime.

ISLAM AND KINSHIP IN FARS-ABAD

In Islamic legal discourse, both Sunni and Shi'a, there are three main categories of kinship: consanguinity (*nasab*), affinity (*musāharah*), and milk kinship (*ridā'*) (Clarke 2007b, 381; Haeri 1989). A relative of any of these types is considered to be a "close" person and is owed certain rights and has corresponding duties (Clarke 2007b, 381). As part of this framework, Islam delineates a set of relatives who are "forbidden in marriage" (*mahram*). These include parents and children, aunts and uncles, nephews and nieces, and siblings, as well as some affines, but not cousins. Those who are forbidden to marry are considered to be "close" and intimate, explicitly contrasting with those for whom marriage is an option and who are "strangers" or "foreigners" (Clarke 2007b, 382–83).

Gender difference is another key element of kinship in Iran. Gender and sex are tightly connected and are premised on the categorization of male and female bodies into anatomically and hormonally opposing types (Najmabadi 2013; Torab 2007, 13). Moreover, gender and sex is conceived of as naturally fixed and God-given; even in the case of hermaphrodites, the surgeon's role is to discover the "real" sex, not create it. This seemingly natural fixity of gender spills into ideas about family roles and responsibilities. For instance, according to Ayatollah Morteza Mutahhari (1920–79), one of the most important Islamic scholars connected to the 1979 Revolution and a disciple of Khomeini, "Familial relations are quite different from other forms of association. By their very nature motherhood and fatherhood create duties and obligations which are anchored in natural laws. Given that men and women are biologically different and have different natures, so their familial duties and obligations too are different" (quoted in Afshar 1998, 143).[5] Here, God-given "laws of nature" regulate the differences between the sexes as well as family duties, roles, and responsibilities (Haeri 1989, 27; Mir-Hosseini 2004, 6).[6] And further, although women are equal to men in creation and do not depend on men for attaining perfection, women and men are created differently (Mir-Hosseini 2004).[7] The distinction between male and female is due to the inherent biological and psychological differences described in the Qur'an, in which women are typified as more emotional and men as more rational, a difference that is both given by God and natural (Paidar 1995, 175).[8] In this framework, the most important duty for women is motherhood, and a woman's "natural activities" should ideally occupy her inside the home.[9] Indeed, divine creation and "natural law" (*ain-e fitrat*) specify a particular kind of gendered family that is at once divinely ordained, biologically determined, and immutable.[10]

Most of the Basijis I interviewed, including my hosts and a majority of their young adult children, upheld these views, describing Ayatollah Mutahhari as one of the most highly respected Islamic scholars on issues of gender and family. In their everyday lives, they recognized kinship and inheritance through blood, milk, and marriage, and they carefully navigated the boundaries of whom they considered to be marriageable and whom they did not according to the rules of *mahram*. One of Ahmad's nephews, a thirty-year-old, who was also a member of the Basij, enjoyed debating these concepts with me during my time with his family in Tehran. On one occasion, he used Mutahhari to defend his position that "females are made by God to be more concerned with family and the household" and "men can better work outside the home" (even as he acknowledged the increasing need for two-income families in contemporary society).[11] On another occasion Maryam, my host sister in Fars-Abad, clarified her understanding of gender roles and responsibilities for me by directly citing some of Mutahhari's writings, which she had first read in her local high school.[12] By means of Mutahhari, moreover, my hosts often told me that it was the "divine creation of nature" that was the ultimate foundation of kinship and procreation.

In what follows, I explore the cultural logic of procreation, gender, inheritance, and divine creation in Fars-Abad and beyond. I then discuss how my hosts—as members of the Basij and vanguards of the Islamic Republic—expressed the need to embody the "right" kind of "pure" family, modeled on the family of the Prophet.

A Local Teacher of Islam: Procreation as God's Creation

Nushin and I cleaned the house for Mr. Hosseini's visit. She swept the carpet with a long straw brush while I helped make tea. Ahmad, who had finished his morning prayer, was pacing back and forth. He had already turned off the TV and satellite, which received BBC Persian and numerous other "Western" channels. Better that Mr. Hosseini not see the satellite, he muttered, a little on edge. Mr. Hosseini was the first formal guest we had had in a while (most of our guests were extended kin or neighbors) and the first guest to come to talk about Islam. Watching Ahmad pace, I again wondered why he had asked Mr. Hosseini to come to the house. My sense was that he felt that this visit would be good for the family and good for my research on Islam. After all, Mr. Hosseini was well known in town for his ability to answer questions about religion. He had given talks at gatherings in Fars-Abad before and was well liked. It was good timing as well. Neither of his sons would be in their computer classes today, and his daughter was taking a break from studying for her college entrance exams.

When he finally arrived, we wondered what Mr. Hosseini would say, but he began almost immediately: "God is limitless," he said. "Relative to God, we are but a glass in his ocean. We are limited, limited with respect to understanding (*dark*) and knowledge (*'aql*). . . . God created this world

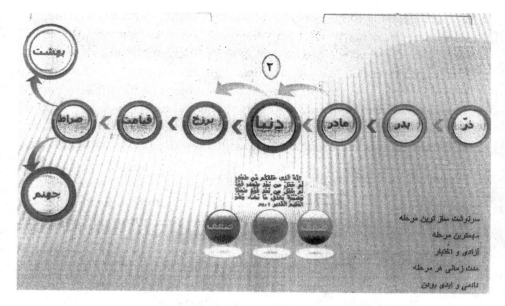

Figure 3. Mr. Hosseini's diagram of the course of human existence

for us and he created us for worship." With the patient and slow voice of a teacher, Mr. Hosseini explained that it is ultimately God's command that causes a creature to be born. He then turned to a page in a spiralbound course packet he had developed for his students. On it, he had charted the course of a human life from before birth to after death. He showed us the diagram: "To understand Islam," he said, "you must first understand three questions: 1) where were you? 2) where are you ? and 3) where are you going?"

From right to left the circles depict the course of human existence. As he explained, the answer to "where were you?" reads, "particle" (*zar*), a word also associated with the Qur'anic concept of "the world before creation" (*'alam-e zar*); next comes (your) "father" (*pedar*) and "mother" (*mādar*). Next, the "world" (*donyā*) denotes where you are or your present location. Finally, the chart shows from right to left where you will go after your death: first to "limbo" (*barzakh*), then to "Judgment Day" (*qiyāmat*), then to the "path" (*sarāt*), and finally to either "heaven" (*behesht*) or "hell" (*jahannam*). He added, "We were a fetus in the womb (stomach) of our mother. Before that, we were in the existence of our father. Before that, we were in nature, in the earth. We were in foods. Every person was in a piece of food, apple, or bread. This builds (makes) blood and this blood makes a "male seed, sperm (*notfeh*)." He continued, "If you ask a ten-year-old what he was ten and a half years ago, he would say, I was a fetus (*jenin*) in my mother. If you ask that same child what they were eleven years ago, he would say that I was blood 'in my father's backbone' (*posht-e pedar budam*). This means that I was in the existence/body of my father." Mid-conversation, Ahmad, who had been paying close attention to all of this, interrupted Mr. Hosseini and, looking over at me and his sons, stated: "Of course it comes from the mother too. This is recognized!" But Mr. Hosseini continued his lesson as if he hadn't heard Ahmad's comment.

In addition to Ahmad's and Mr. Hosseini's differing notions about the gendered contributions to procreation (Ahmad had been a schoolteacher and had some knowledge of genetics, eggs, and sperm), what is notable about Mr. Hosseini's notion of procreation is its divine temporal framing (e.g., questions such as Where were you? or Where are you going?). It emphasizes the movement of physical and substantial materials of humans through a divinely ordained timescale. According to Mr. Hosseini and his chart, we are from God.

The question of gender, God, and procreation came up on several more occasions during my research. Our neighbor in Fars-Abad, for instance, explained: "Those who give God a gender are mistaken. God does not have a body (*jesm*). God is not limited by the capacities of man or woman. We can't fathom God. God is something beyond." Similarly, Mehdi, Ahmad's Tehrani nephew, described God as spirit (*ruh*) or energy (*enerzhi*), holding that God breathes spirit into the fetus approximately forty days after conception. "God is the ultimate Creator and Sustainer, the provider of human conception and procreation," he said. When I asked for more clarification, he and my other hosts usually offered the following verse from the Qur'an: "Surely we created you of dust, then of sperm-drop (*nutfa*), then a blood clot ('*alaqa*), then a morsel of tissue (*mudgha*), formed and unformed, so that we may make clear to you [the creation and development of the child in the womb]. We establish in the wombs what we will, till stated term, then we deliver you as infants, then that you may come of age; and some of you die, and some of you are kept back unto vilest state of life, that after knowing somewhat, they may know nothing" (Q. 22:5; Arabic translated by Sachedina 2009, 102). This passage makes an analogy between human procreation and God's creation. On one occasion, Ahmad's niece, Atefeh, and her cousin, Leila, attempted to explain this to me, pointing out the verse in their household Qur'an. Conception, Atefeh said, begins with the sperm or semen (*notfeh*), transitioning to the "blood that has not yet formed into a shape, not hands, not feet, hardly anything" (*'alaqeh*). "It is something" the cousin explained, "that is coming into being." The next part of the process is the forming and thickening, with the "faintest shape apparent." This phase is described as the *mudgha* (Arabic) and denotes the formation of the blood package (*khun basteh*) or "meat." "In the *azam* stage," the same cousin continued, "the bones are formed and the *lahm*, or flesh. Finally, God 'gives spirit' (*damidan-e ruh*) to the fetus."

Here, and regardless of gendered contributions to life, God is the ultimate Creator and Sustainer (the foundation of both creation and procreation). These Qur'anic understandings of the divine creation, people told me, also underlie notions such as descent, gender, and marriage. Kinship depends on God's will and gift of spirit. It rests solely neither on biogenetic substance nor on man-made law/convention. Rather, it is premised on the divine. And as we will see, it also involves the channeling and containment of qualities that are sacred, immaterial, and ineffable between generations (Cannell 2013).

Gendered Substances, Inheritance, and Procreation

We were still living in the old house at the end of the alley when I asked Ahmad's niece, Fariba, a thirty-year-old married woman with a four-year-old son, to explain how the family is shaped. We sat kneeling in a semicircle on the bright red Persian carpet with several other women from her extended family, including Mona (Fariba's mother), Atefeh (Fariba's sister), and Marjan and Farrin, Nushin's brother's daughters. Fariba led the conversation while the others nodded in agreement.

"We call it the *qowm*, as in the term you've probably heard of, *qowm-o-khish* (relatives, kinsmen)," Fariba said. "We have a relationship of 'same blood' (*ham khun*). It begins with the (male) grandparent, who we call the 'ancestor' (*jadd*). From the grandparent, we count the children (*farzand*), the grandchildren (*naveh*), the great-grandchildren (*natijeh*), the great-great-grandchildren (*nabireh*), and the great-great-great-grandchildren, or the 'unseen offspring' (*nadideh*), so called because the great-great-great-grandparents will never meet this generation." She continued as her sister, Atefeh, brought a piece of paper and pen from her room. "The family is like a tree (*shajareh*) with branches (*shākheh*)." "The mother's line is called the 'milk line' (*khat-e shir*)." Atefeh wrote this down for me. Fariba added, "The father's line is called the 'backbone' (*khat-e posht*)." I asked which line was more important, the mother's or father's. She responded, "The mother is a foundation (*asli*)." "But the father," she emphasized, "is the foundation of the foundation (*pedar asli-ye asli ast*)."

The Fars-Abadis I knew described the entire extended family as a *qowm-o-khish*, a group of relatives who claim a common origin and relation through bilateral—patrilateral *and* matrilateral—ties (on *qowm*, see also Shahshahani 1990, 245; Naef 2017). This intergenerational unit had six linear generations (*nasl*), stemming from the "ancestor or line of descent" or *jadd*, most often a grandfather. Indeed, the term *jadd* was a metonym for the totality of intergenerational, lineal relationships, roughly a line of descent or lineage. People attended to these lines of ancestry very carefully. As one woman explained, "If the line of descent of a person is good, I [their descendant] will also be good." These generations were primarily interconnected through inherited blood, or what people refer to as the "being of the same blood" (*ham khun*). Indeed, blood is a central way of conceiving relatedness in Fars-Abad and elsewhere in Iran. Fariba described a six-generational model of blood relations, but she and others also recognized very distant blood connection between patrilateral and/or matrilateral ascendants and descendants. As the Basseri brother-in-law of Ahmad's nephew put it to me with pride, "We [the Basseri] are a society of the same blood." This kind of relation is also sometimes described as being "of the same body," an image of bodily/physical continuity that appears in commemorations of the "five bodies" (*panj tan*) of the household of the Prophet.[13]

But relations could also be traced through "male backbone" (*posht*) and female "breast milk" (*shir*). Male backbone refers to the father's line or lineage and is the "main foundation" (*asli-ye asli*) of intergenerational relationships. For Fariba, Atefeh, and their relatives, this line was imagined as the inheritance of backbone or vertebrae. "To be of someone's backbone" (*az posht-e kasi budan*), Fariba said, "is a patrilineal relationship, the relationship between father and son or between grandfather or great-grandfather and a son." In the past in Fars-Abad, as well as in other towns in Iran, some men could recite up to seven patrilineal generations in this fashion. Moreover, in everyday conversation, *posht* refers to an emotive tie and is evocative of the love and mutual support of lineal male descendants. The "back" may be filled or emptied as an expression of grief or joy. When Ahmad recalled his grief at the time of his father's death, for example, he said, "It was as though my backbone had been emptied." More than inherited family identity, then, the concept of inherited backbone provides a sense of familial love and support. In addition, *posht* was sometimes a gloss for "male seed." The phrase, "the backbone of the father took in the womb" indicated that a woman had become pregnant.

Yet although inherited male blood and bone are the essence or "central foundation" (*asli-ye asli*) of the intergenerational family, Fariba and the other women also recognized what they called the "milk line," or the mother's descent line, as another "secondary foundation" through which one can trace ancestry. On the one hand, the "milk" line was a gloss for matrilineal descent via female blood. Both the men and women I knew in Fars-Abad recognized these female links. A son might trace the ancestry (*jadd*) of his mother's father and other matrilateral kin and link it to himself. Similarly, a grandmother is recognized as "another ancestor" (*jadd-e digar*) and is linked to her descendants, even if she herself is formally part of her father's family tree. Thus, although male descent lines are privileged, ancestry is also frequently reckoned through female links, and both males and females transfer blood and identity to the fetus.[14]

My hosts told me that matrilateral relationships are more relaxed and "closer" than relationships with their patrilateral kin. They spoke of the characteristics they had inherited from their mother's father and said that they were related to these ancestors by blood. Correspondingly, they saw qualities of these ancestors in themselves. "Like my mother's father, I am giving and care about others," explained Ahmad and Nushin's son Reza on numerous occasions. He and others kept track of the physical, emotional, and spiritual characteristics they held in common with their mothers' ancestors.

On the other hand, the "milk line" refers to "milk kinship." It is not only female blood that is transferred to children across generations, but also breast milk. In Islam, shared milk through suckling at the breast creates a sexual taboo between a baby and his wet nurse's lineal kin, leading to a series of marriage prohibitions (Parkes 2005; Q. 4:27). This kin relation, described in Persian as *ham-shir*, has been referred to in the literature as "foster parentage," yet does not confer the inheritance of property (Parkes 2005; Clarke 2007a). Today, it is stipulated in Shi'i law that a child must be breastfed at least fifteen times by one woman before foster parentage is created (because that entails the strengthening of the bones and the building of the flesh; Clarke 2007a, 298). However, in addition to forming a marriage exclusion, Fars-Abadis emphasized how people inherit personal characteristics from the women who nursed them, whether they are their mothers or not. The person, they said, "is formed by milk," whether this is the milk of one's mother, the milk of another relative, or both.

Milk kinship is not necessarily a generationally deep tie, but it can be if one is nursed by one's own mother, who was in turn nursed by her mother, and so on. For example, in conversation someone might say, "Of course X is a good person, s/he drank milk from Y who is of known personal esteem (*āberu*)." The power of milk to make kin or shape kin is strengthened generation after generation. In Fars-Abad, people paid close attention to breastfeeding and regarded it as far superior to using formula. They claimed that bodily substances such as blood and breast milk have the capacity to transmit or accrue qualities such as purity, emotion, faith, or corruption across generations. Nushin, for instance, once confessed her belief that if a baby consumes the breast milk of a female descendant of the Prophet, or *sayyedah*, he or she will become a *sayyed*. Ahmad, who was with us in the room during our conversation, said that he disagreed.[15]

Despite this recognition of matrilateral kinship, the handwritten diagrams that people drew for me emphasized patrilineal descent. In these "kinship maps," female family members did not at first include any of the wives, or even any of the daughters of their family. "Do you want me to include the daughters?" Atefeh asked me one day as an afterthought after having already populated the chart with men. This perplexed me. I knew that she saw her matrilateral relations as kin by blood and milk. Why had she, an educated twenty-one-year-old Fars-Abadi woman, now working outside the home in a neighboring village's elementary school, neglected the daughters of her own family, including herself? I realized that the family members she had drawn were the male kin: those who would pass on their last names to their children. With the daughters, the line stops. The act of writing had shifted her into the territory of more official kinship charting and naming. After all, children in Iran take their father's last name and not their mother's father's last name. (Women in Iran do not take the names of their husbands when they marry.) National identification cards similarly privilege patrilineal descent, listing the father's first name and last name instead of the mother's.

Nevertheless, same blood, male backbone, and female milk are the "foundations" of kinship in Fars-Abad, a configuration with important consequences for the characterization of family relationships and procreation.[16] These substances shape the immediate family, including those who are deemed "unlawful to marry" (*mahram*). *Mahram* persons include, for instance, the father and mother, grandparents, and great-grandparents; the brothers and sisters; and the children, grandchildren, and great-grandchildren. They also include affinal relations such as fathers- and mothers-in-law, sons- or daughters-in-law, the stepfather, the stepmother, and the stepchildren (Haeri 1989).

Yet according to many of the people I spoke with, blood and the other shared substances of kinship are more than mere material substance.[17] Blood from the veins, a Tehrani cousin and Basiji explained, carries spirit (*ruh*), energy (*enerzhi*), and life (*jān*).[18]

MORE THAN SUBSTANCE: BLOOD AND PROPHETIC GENEALOGY

The lineage of the Prophet epitomizes these immaterial, sacred qualities of blood and their intergenerational transmission, and it may be called on for its protective, fertile, and vital qualities. This lineage is composed of *sayyed*s, or descendants of the Prophet, who are seen as pure and close to

God. For Nushin and other Fars-Abadis I spoke with, these vital qualities were made evident by a local baby who had been protected by his pure ancestry:

> A *sayyed* from the line of the Prophet's family was living here in Fars-Abad. A small baby, he was coming home with his mother from Shiraz in the car. His name was Sayyed Allah Al-din. Right here in Fars-Abad, he was being held by his mother when the car crashed. Although his mother died, he fell into a bush in the desert. . . . They said that his ancestral line protected him. His mother died, but he lived. We say that *sayyeds*, because they are in the doorway, at the threshold of God's presence, that they have a lot of *āberu* [the water of one's face, here meaning esteem and purity]. They are in God's threshold. We seek help from them the way we do from the other family members of the Prophet Muhammad. We say, "Pray for us. You are *sayyed*s. Please request your ancestors' line to help us."[19]

In this story, which was told to me on a number of different occasions by my hosts and other Fars-Abadis, a *sayyed* infant was protected by his "proximity to God" in a tragic car crash that killed his own mother. The infant's purity, locals said, was inherited through the lineage and *blood* that he shared with the Prophet. As one neighbor related, a *sayyed* is a person who is "of the same blood" as the Prophet (570–632 CE) and "who can trace their ancestry to his holiness Imam Husayn, to his holiness 'Ali." As such, they are a source of protection and help.

On the "prophetic genealogy" of the *sayyed*s Enseng Ho (2006) writes: "Genealogy provided a sublime form of identity that could hold both pure Prophetic essence and create human substance without contradiction" (187). Similarly, for Shi'as in Iran, Prophetic genealogies do not oppose spirit and matter, divine light, or blood. Rather, they flow together between generations. Such light is also referred to as "divine grace" (*barakat*). In the postrevolutionary Islamic Republic, this divine light is depicted in murals and other votive art. It emanates from the faces of the family of the Prophet and their descendants and is further understood as a vital, life-giving essence that animates the world and its creatures (see also Aghaie 2004). For my hosts, however, even those who are not *sayyed* can inherit immaterial qualities such as purity, religiosity, and esteem through blood. Here, blood is at once a substance, material, metaphor, and medium. It is powerfully involved in life, death, nurturance and violence, connection and exclusion, and kinship and sacrifice (see also Carsten 2013; Wellman 2017a).

Fars-Abadis frequently emphasized the purity (*pāki*), simplicity (*sādegi*), and particular esteem (*āberu*) of *sayyeds*.[20] Recalling examples of *sayyeds* in Fars Abad, Atefeh, a cousin of my hosts, indicated: "Some of them can't sin. They are so pure that they don't know how." Another cousin explained: "God doesn't give them the knowledge (*'aql*) to hurt others or sin ... some of them.... They are so pure that they don't even know how to do bad things." These assessments resonate with the Qur'an, which similarly mentions purity as a quality of the *sayyeds* (Khuri 2001, 34).

According to my hosts and their extended family, the descendants of the Prophet can trace their lineage through a patriline (*sayyed*), a matriline (*sayyedah*), or both, a practice that is fairly common in Iran. When a person can claim that both of his or her lineages link to the Prophet, he or she is considered "even more pure" and is conceived of as "closer" to the family of the Prophet than a person who can claim *sayyed* status through a patriline alone. Similarly, albeit controversially, many Fars-Abadis I spoke with recognized the inheritance of *sayyed* status through one or more female links.

The logic of the purity and esteem of *sayyed* lineage has implications in everyday life. Following names such as "mir," indicative of *sayyed* status, or other listed honorifics, my hosts in Fars-Abad and Tehran chose *sayyed* medical doctors in Shiraz to treat their medical conditions. *Sayyed*s, they said, might have a special perception into illness because of their trustworthiness and purity. They and their kin also completed local pilgrimages to the tombs of the town's *sayyed*s. For instance, on our almost regular Thursday trip to the local cemetery, Nushin always walked to a *sayyed* grave at the top of the hill, where she prayed to protect the esteem of her family. The grave was covered by windswept green parchment held in place by tiny rocks. She recited the first verse of the Qur'an, Surat al-Fātihah, and gently knocked on the grave to communicate to the buried *sayyed*'s soul that she was praying there, an act she also did for her own deceased kin.

It was also a frequent practice to donate sacrificial meat to poor *sayyed*s in town. During the summer of 2010, I helped distribute meat from a sacrificed sheep to local *sayyed*s with Ahmad, Nushin, and their children. We

Figure 4. Nushin praying at the tomb of a *sayyed* in a graveyard, Fars-Abad, Iran

drove around the narrow alleys of the old neighborhood and knocked on doors that made up the locally known geography of *sayyed* homes, many of which were still built with clay walls, indicating that the occupants had not upgraded their homes to newer brick. Nushin and Ahmad said that they gave meat to *sayyeds* who had "roots" of particularly "good standing" (*mo'tabar*). "They are closer to God," Nushin remarked as we returned to the car. "Did you see how simple that woman was?" According to Nushin, some *sayyeds*, in action, deed, and visible simplicity, show themselves to be more directly connected to the Prophet than others. She often spoke about the lineages of local *sayyeds* in this manner, assessing and valuing certain local families of *sayyeds* as particularly good and pure.

In addition to their protective and life-giving qualities, the lineage of *sayyed*s was also thought to offer fertility. Aunts, wives, mothers, grandmothers, and even young brides told me that they make supplications to the line of the (local) *sayyed*s specifically to protect and bless their marriages and give them children. One woman explained, "We sometimes make a vow for a problem of my child. . . . We bring them [the *sayyed*s] money and ask them to pray because of their ancestral line." Her sister responded, "They don't always take money. They are so good and pure." Relatedly, several Fars-Abadi women told me that female *sayyed*s are more fertile than non-*sayyed*s, have more children, and reach menopause in their sixties, which, they added, normally occurs between forty-seven and fifty years. One of Nushin's friends, a teacher from the local school, insisted that such later menopause is a good thing, explaining that "menstruation is cleansing and problems like high blood pressure and blood sugar begin when it stops." When I asked why *sayyed* women had late menopause, she and Nushin agreed that this was "because God wants the line of the Prophet to multiply."

The associations between the *sayyed*s and fertility may have been more pronounced in Fars-Abad before the Revolution. As Nistdar, an elderly aunt, recalled, "In the past, they [people in Fars-Abad] danced for three days at weddings. During that time, the bride and groom would go to the cemetery to change their clothes because the [graves of the] *sayyed*s were there. They would do this so that the lineal ancestry (*jadd*) of the *sayyed*s could help them."[21]

The immediate family of the Prophet and his near descendants are an even more potent source of fertility. On the sixth day of the month of Muharram (the month that commemorates the martyrdom of the pure Imam Husayn and his family at the hands of the corrupt Yazid), several of my female host family members participated in a ceremony, locally called milk-suckling (*shir-khor*). The ceremony centers on Ali Asghar, the youngest child of Imam Husayn, a milk-suckling, six-month-old infant who was martyred with his father at the Battle of Karbala. In this ceremony, mothers bring their young babies and toddlers to the local meetinghouse for the Imam Husayn.

They dress them in bright green, black, or white cloth and wrap bands, inscribed with the words "Yā Husayn, Yā Abolfazl, or Yā Hazrat-e Zahrā" around their foreheads. Alternatively, they cover their small infants' heads with a white shroud, a cloth normally reserved for the deceased. One participant explained: "Imam Husayn took Ali Asghar in his hand on the sixth day of the battle. He said to his enemies, 'Have mercy on this six-month-old, even if you do not have mercy on us.' But he [the tyrannical Yazid] did not have mercy on him and did not give him water. Without water, without milk, they pierced his throat and sent him to martyrdom." [22] In the meetinghouse, the ceremony's female participants listen to speeches and eulogies about the Battle of Karbala and the martyrdom of the tiny infant, Ali Asghar, who was still suckling from his mother's breast. They mourn, crying and beating their chests. They sing, for example:

> Oh, my [dear] Asghar,
> Oh, my blameless infant,
> The calm of my soul,
> The sweet of my tongue.

At the ceremony, some women specifically made a vow with Ali Asghar; for example, one woman said, "If I become pregnant, I will cook and distribute 1,000 kilos of votive rice." By making this vow and attending the ceremony, Nushin explained, "They believe that Ali Asghar can intercede with God and help with pregnancy." She continued, offering me evidence of this potency:

> One year, there was a woman who had not been able to get pregnant for 14 years. Another came who had not been able to get pregnant for 12 years. The doctor told them there is nothing else she can do: "You will never conceive." But they had sought help (or intercession, *motavassel shodan*) from Hazrat-e Imam Husayn and Hazrat-e Ali Asghar [his son]. Because of this, their wishes for pregnancy were granted. Hazrat-e Ali Asghar received their wishes to become pregnant. One of the women picked up her child, and showed it to the women. She said that after 12 years of infertility she had become pregnant.[23]

In this and other examples, the potency, fertility, and purity of the descendants of the Prophet can transform the fertility of women through prayer and vow making. More than a matter of substantial relations, kinship is sacred, emerging from and contoured by concepts of the divine and the intercession of the Prophet's family and descendants.

When I talked with Ahmad about *sayyeds*, he used the opportunity to discuss the Prophetic descent of the current Supreme Leader of Iran, Ayatollah Khamenei. "Those who are *sayyeds* have traced from their ancestry (*nasl*) and have figured out which Imam they come from. Sometimes they frame this [on their wall]. Some of them are called Mousavi, others Hosseini, some of them have names that indicate *sayyed*-hood in other ways, but some of them don't. In Fars Abad, the Friday Imam claims to be a *sayyed*, Mohammad Hosseini. Our leader is also a *sayyed*. *Sayyed* Ali Khamenei. Many of those who are spiritual leaders are *sayyeds*."[24]

However, it is not only the lineages of *sayyeds* that are hierarchically valued for their spiritual qualities, although they are considered the closest to God and the most vital. During my research I noted that my hosts fashioned differential evaluations of the lineages of non-*sayyeds*. In particular, they regarded qualities such as goodness, purity, temperament, or evilness to be qualities inherited through non-*sayyed* lineages. Unlike the *sayyeds*, however, within whom purity is innate (the quality of which is dependent on the directness of their link to the Prophet), they said that these qualities among non-*sayyed* families stem from the acts of ancestors. Mohadeseh, a Fars-Abadi aunt of my hosts, explained: "We don't have any descendants of the Prophet in our family, but our roots (*risheh*), my father's ancestral line, accepted Islam. It is now our family religion. I am happy that I have Islam because it provides me with inner peace." In this example, Mohadeseh implicitly acknowledges that her ability to be a good Muslim stems, in part, from the inheritance of her father's lineage's acceptance of the faith. She argues that she is a (good) Muslim both because she learned to be one and because she was born a good Muslim.

The families of martyrs also exemplify this dynamic. As I address in more detail in chapter 3, for many of my Basiji hosts, in particular, the blood of martyrs is holy, life giving, and purifying. It is associated both with the martyrdom of the Shi'i Imams, especially Imam Husayn, and with the martyrs of the Iran-Iraq War. Indeed, in popular martyr iconography, spilled red blood is associated with the growth of red tulips and with regeneration. My hosts and other state supporters tend to regard the families, and even the lineages, of martyrs, who have sacrificed their blood for Islam and the nation, as inherently more pure or good than others.

Through the act of spilling blood on the battlefield, these martyrs receive the power to intercede with God on behalf of their loved ones. They give their descendants a connection to the divine, a connection which, as Atefeh and several other Fars-Abadi women told me, may be passed on to the martyr's descendants, "if they also act with piety and faith."[25]

Finally, and perhaps most surprising, my hosts and their friends frequently distinguished the lineages of provincial rulers (hereafter khans) from those of others as especially worthy of respect and esteem. For example, my host mother's patrilateral kin had been khans and had had a lot of influence on village life in the past. Today, when townspeople speak of her family, they often mention its good roots, ancestry, and descendants. In the same way, Ahmad and Nushin admitted that their now son-in-law's royal ancestry had played an important role in their decision to allow him to marry their eldest daughter, Fatemeh. They considered the marriage mutually beneficial, even though the son-in-law was not well off monetarily. (He had taken a large loan from Ahmad in order to work selling ice cream from a truck to neighboring towns, a job of relatively low pay.) Nushin explained: "Their root is good. They were a respectable family. Their lineage is good. They used to also own a lot of land. But there were two brothers and one became an opium addict and sold all the land. His [Fatemeh's husband's] mother bore 12 children. He is the youngest. She is now more than 70 years old. People back then lasted longer. They were healthier. Their lives were simple. They didn't have electricity or refrigerators. But they also didn't have depression or temperamental problems. It is now the opposite. We live comfortably, but we are stressed."[26]

The neighbors talked about Mohammad, who lived in the apartment next door, in the same way. Even though he was also addicted to opium, unemployed, and in a troubled marriage (his wife had recently left their home and had returned to the household of her parents, a practice called *qahr kardan* or "estrangement / ritual avoidance"), he was consistently given the benefit of the doubt because of his good and noble family lineage.

Across these examples, my hosts saw kinship not as a secular or materialist phenomenon (Cannell 2013) but as a process of channeling physio-sacred substance. Bodily substances transferred spiritual qualities such as

Islamic purity and ethics across generations. These immaterial qualities were seen as God given and innate (as exemplified by the esteem given to the descendants of the Prophet). These God-given qualities, moreover, can be a source of authority and leadership in claims to Islamic knowledge (and state power). Ayatollah Khamenei, the current Supreme Leader of Iran, for instance, claims *sayyed* status, as did Ayatollah Khomeini.

In the following section I turn to the ways in which these qualities of kinship could also be created and protected through pious acts within and across the homes I visited in Fars-Abad, Shiraz, and Tehran. In part because of their ties to officialdom, but also because of their aspirations to a pure Muslim society, my Basiji hosts often articulated a heightened need to epitomize the right kind of pure family, modeled on the family of the Prophet, and they vigorously attended to the pious acts that could shape the spiritual and physical health of those in the household. They were explicit in connecting the protection of the family to the defense of the Islamic Republic, a charge that is central to the Basij (Golkar 2015, 116).

But maintaining a pure and pious family was no easy task. For Nushin, who seemed to carry much of this burden, it was a matter of constant tension, debate, and prayer. After all, she lived in a world in which a beloved nephew could die in the desert of a drug overdose and many of her fellow citizens seemed to have diverged from Islamic family values.

BEYOND BLOOD: FAMILY AS AN OBJECT OF ETHICAL AND RELIGIOUS CULTIVATION

> Imam 'Ali, said, "Have a relationship (*peyvand*) of 'coming and going' (*raft-o-āmad*) with your relatives, even when they have cut relations."
>
> —Nushin, Fars-Abad, October 20, 2010

In her work on the Islamic Revival Movement in Egypt, Saba Mahmood builds on Aristotelian concepts of ethical cultivation to explore how the (pious) self emerges through embodied practice. She asserts that "bodily form . . . does not simply represent the interiority, but serves as the 'developable means' (2005, 149; see also Asad 1993) through which certain kinds of ethical and moral capacities are attained" (Mahmood 2005, 148). Similarly, Jarrett Zigon illustrates how Russian Orthodox women pray in a specific way "to be, or to create, the kind of person who has this kind of relationship with God" (2008, 57). These approaches usefully focus on the actions and processes by which persons accrue and embody ethical or pious capacities (Lambek 2010, 16).[27] Yet although these scholars highlight performativity and action—whether these acts are conceived as complete and irreversible or processual over time— they have too often focused on the analysis of the individual subject-self (Wellman 2017b).[28]

The case of Iran—and of ordinary state-supporting, Basiji families in particular—points to a different object of ethical cultivation: the family unit or relationship (see also Wellman 2017b; Seeman 2017; Faubion 2001; Lambek 2010; Khan, Wellman, and Tawasil 2013). It is the relationships *between* family members that are the most central objects of ethical work. Individuals seek to create not only virtuous selves but also virtuous families through pious and relational acts of prayer and food sharing. And they are constantly in the process of "expanding, maintaining, repairing, or even disentangling from constitutive relationships" (Zigon 2014, 27). After all, they are trying to raise "good" and "pious" children in what they see as fraught and uncertain circumstances (Mattingly 2014).

Inner Purity and Outer Corruption: Forging the Family Household

Nushin leaned against the wall in her home, sipping from a glass of golden tea before returning it to the flowery tray next to her on the carpet. "'Ashura' [the day of mourning for the martyrdom of Imam Husayn] has great meaning for us," she said. "We say that Imam Husayn brought Islam to life. Specifically, he brought to life 'the promotion of virtue and the prevention of vice.' He accomplished this with his act [of martyrdom]." She explained that this means that we must both do good and "reject evil and ugliness" (*duri az badi-hā o zeshti-hā*). It means that we must act from within (*bāten*) and garner "inner purity" (*safā-ye bāten*) to "forbid the indecent."

Sitting beside her, I could tell that Nushin hoped to spark my empathy for the sacrifice of Imam Husayn at the hands of the evil Yazid during the

Battle of Karbala (622 CE), an event that continues to be a key symbol for and of life in the Islamic Republic. But she followed her description of the sacrifice of the Imam with a deeply connected concern: the need to promote virtue among her own family and protect them from harm, particularly her own vulnerable teenage sons.

My conversation with Nushin reveals some of the ways in which religio-politics infused her home life. Indeed, even as she spoke of her sons, she echoed Ali Shari'ati's notion of the "prevention of vice" (*nahi az monkar*), a revolutionary act directed against social injustice, "cultural imperialism," "Westernstruckness," and corruption from outside of Iran. Today, Article 8 of the Islamic Republic's Constitution continues to emphasize the obligation of every Muslim to guide others toward goodness and save them from evil. It describes this act as a "mutual duty" that shapes how people should relate to each other and to the government. This is in accordance with the Qur'anic verse, "The believers, men and women, are guardians of one another; they enjoin the good and forbid the evil" (9:71). For Nushin, this desire to create and protect a pure inner person and family household against a dangerous, corruptible exterior was a matter of constant attention, prayer, and caring labor.

Other pious, state-supporting women I spoke with in Fars-Abad, Shiraz, and Tehran repeated these aspirations. As Nushin, Ahmad, Parvin, and others explained to me on numerous occasions, it is important to "do good" and "reject evil and ugliness" by acting from within. By cultivating inner purity, one can forbid the indecent. Very often the "indecent" they were seeking to forbid was right on their doorsteps: drug addiction, dating, and premarital sex. Fariba, one of Nushin's nieces, explained to me how this worked. She described how, when she was followed on her university campus once by a strange young man, she recited a verse of the Qur'an for her protection; he realized she was a good Muslim and did not touch her. She told me how her mother prayed every day for her and her brothers, asking God for them not to become addicts. Indeed, Nushin, her family members, and their neighbors were vigilantly trying to maintain the "inner purity" of their households. They linked this inner purity to the model of the family of the Prophet and sought to cultivate "religiously permitted" or halal, harmonious, and pure relationships in their homes.[29]

Persons and Households

In Iran, the person is composed of a pure, moral inside (*bāten*) and a corruptible, appetite-driven outside (*zāher*) (Beeman 2001; Bateson 1979). The ideal "right" or "complete" person is someone whose exterior expresses his or her interior virtue. Crucially, rather than a rigid set of distinctions, outside qualities and actions consistently penetrate the inner core, and inside qualities and actions are also subject both to outside contamination and redefinition (Beeman 2001). The family and household are similarly conceived. While the inner space (*andaruni*) of the household is the enclosed location of inner purity, "permitted family relations," physical intimacy, and devotion, the outside (*biruni*) is the location of possible corruption, "unrelatedness," physical restrictions between sexes, and spiritual vacancy (Khosravi 2008). My hosts and their extended family were always reinforcing these spatial distinctions by delineating between what was appropriate inside the home (the location of relative freedom) and outside it (the location of societal control and self-control).

Yet my hosts also often lamented the immense difficulties of fashioning a pure family household. On the one hand, both Nushin and her Tehrani sister-in-law Parvin, for instance, were acutely aware that certain others in their immediate family's vicinity did not fulfill their ideals for purity and rightness and were negatively influencing the inner purity of their family. These others were sometimes extended kin (aunts, uncles, cousins, second cousins, etc.). On the other hand, they also blamed the larger political context, war, and foreign intervention for these problems. People in their thirties, whom they called "generation two" (*nasl dovvom*), had been damaged by the war with Iraq. Ahmad estimated that 50 percent of this generation was addicted to opium.[30] Even worse, he believed that this rampant addiction was a method the United States was using to subdue Iran. He described the third generation, those who had been raised after the 1979 Revolution and, for the most part, after the Iran-Iraq War, as "a lot better," adding, "They have grown up in the Islamic Republic, a different society. They are much more stable, the true products of the Revolution." But they were still in need of protection. Nushin, Ahmad, their cousins, and others engaged in intensive efforts to create and sustain pure and halal kin relations as a defense against a range of "dangerous" afflictions, including drug addiction, premarital or extramarital sexual relations, and the general encroachment of Western "moral decay" (see also Khosravi 2008; Bajoghli 2019). Indeed, some of the Basijis I spoke with felt that these efforts were part of their duty to protect the values of the Revolution and defend the Islamic Republic.

With all of these concerns, it is not surprising that although Islamic understandings of inheritable bodily substances helped determine kinship, these same understandings did not predict how relations unfolded, shifted, or were actively protected and shaped by family members. Rather, what was salient in the unfolding of relations was the contingent and changing location of kin—and especially extended kin—on a continuum between inner family purity and outside corruption. Interlocutors demarcated inner circles of moral and trustworthy kin relations through acts of visiting, literally, "coming and going" (*raft-o-āmad*), and they indexed those who were external to these relations through tactics of kin avoidance.

Family Tensions

Kobra, one of Nushin's married nieces, lived less than a kilometer away from her parents in a tiny apartment that she shared with her husband and daughter. She spent long hours every day taking care of her baby and relieved the stress and monotony of daily life by bringing her six-month-old daughter to her parental home, which I visited frequently. She often stayed for hours, spending time preparing food, eating lunch, or showering while her mother or I babysat the infant. Her younger brothers, still "legitimate" members of the household who were studying at the local university, were becoming more and more unhappy with Kobra's frequent visits. "She is making our mother's life unpleasant," they said. "Where is her husband? Why doesn't he take care of the baby? Why doesn't he know how to change diapers? Why isn't he around? Why doesn't he tell her to stay home?" Their father, Jalal, laughed, "Even I know how to change diapers," pointing out that Kobra's husband never engaged in this simple task. There was also the minor issue of a loan that Jalal had given Kobra's husband a while back that had not yet been repaid.

One day Kobra's youngest brother, Sami, had had enough. He said that his mother was stressed and unwell and that the baby was taking up too much of her time. His mother had been sick and had been seeing doctors for stomach pain. Kobra swore at him and accused him of being full of himself and of conducting himself immorally. She left, angry. After the fight, Kobra and Sami did not speak for several months; they danced around each other, an act of ritual avoidance. But Abbas, the eldest son, was searching for answers. He had tried sitting everyone down to talk rationally and calmly. He had said the *salavāt* hundreds of times (the *salavāt* is a formulaic greeting to the Prophet and his descendants). He had read two pages of the Qur'an every day and had burned wild rue in the house to cleanse the home. He had even obtained some esoteric knowledge from a pious elder that apparently required burning hot peppers in the garden. When these did not heal the rift, Abbas asked his father for advice.

His father's answer came from a book in his small library in the room he slept in with his wife. The book, entitled *[Divine] Healing and Remedy with the Qur'an*, had a chapter on the healing benefits of the Qur'an. The writer, Mojtabi Rezai, draws on comments by Imam Sadeq (700 or 702–65 CE), the sixth Shi'i Imam, and recommends writing a specific piece of Qur'anic verse on paper and performing three steps: (1) sending a formulaic greeting to God and his descendants, (2) writing the special prayer with saffron ink and pure intention, and finally (3) mixing the prayer with water and drinking it. The book in which this prayer could be found was in a small library that also included a copy of the Qur'an, a heavily read volume of Khomeini's *Islamic Government*, and the *Peak of Eloquence* (*Nahj Al Balāgheh*) by Imam 'Ali. On their request, I consumed this mixture with the family, internalizing the word (and protection of God). We were trying to heal the family tensions by incorporating the sacredness of the Qur'an directly into our bodies, bringing us closer to each other and to God (see also Boylston 2014).

Unfortunately, despite these efforts, the fight lingered on for quite some time. It only began to abate after they conducted a prayer gathering to purify the household (similar to the one I describe in chapter 2). By the end of my research, the two siblings were again on speaking terms. Everyone was relieved; after all, such discord was more than unpleasant. It was sinful, starkly contrasting with Islamic ideals of respectful (and thus moral) relations between kin.[31]

Saving Family "Face"

Another important way that Nushin and others endeavored to manage the tensions of kin relationships was through "daily prayer" (*namāz*). Nushin prayed every day for the health and well-being of her children, and she asked God to protect family esteem (*āberu*). I knew this because she often invited me to accompany her when she prayed, carefully laying out her prayer mat and clay tablet from her pilgrimage to Mecca, then handing me her extra mat and tablet.

The concept of esteem or *āberu*, literally "the water of one's face," is similar in some ways to the sociological term "face," or "collective reputation."[32] *Āberu* can be garnered or lost by the family as a whole, rather than by the individual. It can be exchanged, poured, or mixed between persons, and it can be lost. For instance, *āberu* can be spilled (*rikht*), carried away (*bord*), or "made unclean" (*gand zad*). It can be "brought into the hand" (*be dast āvardan*), or it can "be protected" (*hefz kardan*). And, like liquid, the tiniest drop of soil can contaminate it, and the tiniest hole can empty it (see also Shahshahani 2004). *Āberu* is precarious. It is made and lost through actions.

Ahmad explained, "My wife and I have worked very hard to bring *āberu* to our family over many years. We have not bothered others unnecessarily, and we have worked in this town as teachers and directors of the local school. We have helped others when we can, and we have been good neighbors and kinsmen." Part of the family's general esteem, moreover, had been garnered by Ahmad's service in the Iran-Iraq War. It had been won by his wife's willing support of his service and by his later service as town mayor (in the late 1980s). But as Ahmad's son, Ali, told me, this patiently garnered *āberu* can be lost very easily. "When a son becomes an addict, like Ehsan, for example, or when a daughter becomes pregnant before marriage, the family's *āberu* can be lost." Ahmad explained: "Because we are in a small city, if someone has a good job, we are happy. But if someone is an addict, like a cousin, this is bad for us. It is difficult."[33]

Brothers, Sisters, and Secrets

Hagar, another of Nushin's nieces and a high school student studying for the college entrance exam, kept the fact that she had a cell phone completely hidden from the watchful eyes of her two brothers and her father. This was no easy feat. She would sit with it hidden behind her knees on the couch, texting with her friends and pretending to watch TV while her unsuspecting brothers sat across the room. When she used the phone to make calls, she did so only in the late hours of the night or when her brothers were absent. Her intrigue went so far that she kept her small phone in her pocket when she slept (so they wouldn't come in her room and find it); as an extra precaution, she erased each text and call record from the phone after making it. Amusingly, almost everyone other than her brothers and father knew about Hagar's cell phone and collectively kept the secret. Even when her father eventually found out, he said that it didn't worry him. He trusted her.

One evening at the park Hagar explained to me why she went to these great lengths to hide her phone. The first reason was that her older brother, Hassan, was full of "(religious) zeal and pride" (*gheirat*). Such zeal, notably, is most often gendered male: a man who has *gheirat* has guarded his family's honor. In so doing, he has also guarded his own "male honor" (*nāmus*) by protecting the purity/chastity of his closest female kin: his mother, sister, wife, or daughter.[34] In some ways, Hassan was the sibling Hagar most respected and feared. Her younger brother Hossein, she said, was slightly more relaxed. But would they think she was texting a boy? If she was, I knew, she needed to be careful. One of her cousins, a young woman, had been forced to move away from Fars-Abad to Tehran and marry a "stranger" when word got out that she had been in a car accident with a young man who was not *mahram* to her.

In Fars-Abad, people defined brother and sister relationships by the need to protect each other from losing *āberu* and thus from losing the esteem of the larger family. One day in the heat of Fars-Abad's summer, Hagar and her younger brother, Hossein, began talking about how they saw siblingship. Hossein began, "The job of the brother is to protect his sister. Her *āberu* is more easily lost. Brothers and boys can get away with a lot more.... But the whole family is always concerned about sisters and daughters, especially in small communities [such as Fars-Abad] in which esteem is easily lost." As he spoke, Hagar nodded, seemingly in agreement.

For Hossein, the need to protect *āberu* legitimized his watchful and potentially disciplinary "protection" of his older sisters. Similarly, a sister also protected her brother through acts such as bringing her sibling's inappropriate behaviors to the attention of their parents. In the end, and despite her having successfully kept her cell phone secret, Hagar's younger brother became increasingly suspicious that something was going on. When I asked her how she put up with this kind of treatment, she said simply, "I'm used to it." Hagar, not complacent, retaliated by watching her brother Hossein's activities more closely and criticizing his behavior. At the same time, she told me that whoever her brothers married would be lucky. "Because," she said, "they are good, trustworthy young men."

In her writings on the brother/sister relationship in Arab contexts, Suad Joseph (1994, 55) describes how "the security, identity, integrity, dignity, and self-worth of one is tied to the actions of the other." This was the kind of intensity of relationship that Hossein and Hagar had as siblings. Their individual notions of self-worth, security, and dignity were tied together. Notably, this relationship was further heightened for families affiliated with the Basij, such as my hosts. There was as sense that, not only was this relationship pivotal to the protection of family morality as a whole, but it also was being surveilled by the state and by others in the community.

Nevertheless, the kind of secrecy surrounding Hagar's cell phone was common in Fars-Abad. Other sisters and brothers whom I met kept similar secrets from each other: a visit with a boy, a phone conversation, or a trip to the salon with their mother to pluck their eyebrows before marriage. But secrets meant much more than the mere withholding of information. Family members often told me that having secrets and collectively protecting family esteem is what differentiates the immediate family from extended kin or outside others. As my Tehrani host, Haleh, put it when she described her Fars-Abadi kin: "Here we have secrets between us. They [my extended family in Fars-Abad] don't know our secrets [the secrets of my immediate family]. [In contrast, my family] knows about my feelings about what I do. My mother knows what things I like and what things I don't. They [the Fars-Abadi cousins] don't know to that extent. I also don't know about them. One night or two we are together then we go. There are many things I don't know. My mother knows more. Here I am comfortable" (3/1/10). For Haleh, true intimacy and the sharing of secrets was confined to the immediate family, those who had the same blood and living accommodations.

Yet my hosts' extended family members and friends were very conscious of the fact that *āberu* was relative to their community's conventions and explained that these expectations are "imposed by society" and not by their family or even by God. Nushin's husband Ahmad, for instance, philosophized that although *āberu* is a kind of regulatory agent that creates limits on actions, it was still necessary to abide by them. He explained to his teenage children that every society has boundaries and that they must follow the boundaries of their locality and positionality as state supporters in Fars-Abad. These boundaries included such things as women donning the black chador, men and women praying while at work, and young men avoiding wearing short sleeves. But these boundaries were often contested. Nushin often lamented the watchfulness and carefulness necessitated by the "small environment" of Fars-Abad, contrasting it with bigger cities such as Shiraz or Tehran.

Degrees of Kinship

Against this backdrop, Fars-Abadis also recognized varying degrees of (blood) kinship. Family of "degree one" or *darajeh yek*, they said, are immediate kin. This group was also described as "the small household" or *khānevādeh-ye kuchik*, and includes the husband and wife and their children. As one cousin explained, "*khānevādeh* are those people who were with me from the beginning and still with me and who are my relations.... [W]hen we leave [the house], we leave together and when we come back, we come back together. We share our lives." In Fars-Abad, people also included grandparents in this designation. But this category was not stagnant. Daughters, like Nushin's married daughter Fatemeh, who leave the house when they marry, are no longer considered part of the family household, although they remain "degree one" kin. Similarly, I am an example of someone who had become a member of the household, an American/foreigner/sister who was ultimately privy to most goings on, and as my host Ahmad once called me, "almost mahram (*taqriban mahram*)" (Wellman 2018).

"Degree two" kin (*darajeh do*), in contrast, includes the wider circle of uncles, aunts, cousins, and their affines as well as more extended relations vis-à-vis grandchildren and great-grandchildren and so on. But one's relationship with second degree kin is much more flexible. Depending on mutual trust and perceived family purity, degree two kin might frequently visit each other or might rarely do so and only when necessary. Together, these two degrees of kinship form what in practice is the main circle of intimate extended family, entailing reciprocal kinship obligations. Their contours are most visible at funerals and weddings. For a funeral, according to Nushin's daughter Maryam, "Visitors show up at the house before the funeral. They visit afterwards. But close family, 'degree one' kin, don't fix their eyebrows, and they continue visiting every day. Sometimes for hours and hours." Following Ehsan's passing, Nushin, whose own brother's family was affected, her daughter, and I did not get a haircut for forty days. Furthermore, to mark the end of Ramadan, Nushin and Ahmad's family mourned by not celebrating the festival of Eid. We also did not attend several weddings that we had been invited to following the month of Ramadan. This, my hosts said, was their obligation to degree one kin.

Visiting Extended Family: "Having a Relationship of Coming and Going"

> It is good to have a relationship with your extended family. Why? Because they are the same blood (*khun*), the same roots (*risheh*), and the same origins (*asl*). Even the television talks about this . . . the Islamic scholars. We don't like to have to be estranged from family members in Iran. This is *seleh-e rahem*, the significance of having a "coming and going" relationship with close relatives.
>
> —Nushin, Fars-Abad, October 20, 2010

Seleh-e rahem, the concept referred to here by Nushin, is mentioned in the Qur'an and the hadiths and denotes a bond of kinship that does not break or that opposes breaking. In both Arabic and Persian, "*rahem*" literally means womb or shared womb and is a linguistic cognate of Allah, Al-Rahim, The Merciful. It denotes "those who are close" (*nazdikān*) or "those who are related" (*bastegān*). In Arabic, it is pronounced *silat al-rahim* and translates literally to "the tie of the womb," although it is not limited to matrilineal kin (Clarke 2007b, 381). In Islamic jurisprudence, however, *rahem* refers to lineal, descent relations—not relations of marriage—whether male or female, "permitted relations" (*mahram*) or "illegal" (*nā-mahram*), Muslim or heretic, or from the mother's side or the father's side. *Seleh*, in contrast, means a gift or a favor, implying a relation accompanied by love and kindness that opposes "distancing" (*duri kardan*) and the breaking of relationships. One of our neighbors explained the concept by referring to a question asked of Imam Sadeq (~702–65 CE), the Sixth Imam and a descendant of the Prophet. The question goes: "Some of my relatives do not have the same views as me. Do they have title/right on me?" The Imam responded: "Yes, the right of closeness (*qorbat*) and relationship (*khishāvandi*) cannot be broken. Even further, if relations lead to human harm, humans still do not have the right to sever the link (*peyvand*)."

For Nushin, her neighbor, and others, *seleh-e rahem* thus implied the necessary maintenance of "blood" relations through visiting and acts of care despite the struggles inherent in doing so. It was often brought up when people felt conflicted about their Muslim obligation to maintain family relations and their equally significant effort to protect themselves and their children from outside, immoral kin and in-laws, and strangers. In practice, this translated into tense decisions about who family members should visit on any given night and why.

At night the streets of Fars-Abad fill with families engaging in the practice of "night visiting" (*shab neshini*). They walk from house to house or travel together on motorcycles along Fars-Abad's narrow streets. I participated in visiting with Nushin, Ahmad, and their children, as often as three or four times a week. We would walk down alleys, passing bustling shops and the meetinghouse for Imam Husayn on our way to the gated courtyard of an extended kinsperson: Nushin or Ahmad's aunt or uncle, a sister or brother, perhaps even a cousin. Often arriving unannounced, we sat on their carpeted floor, leaning against the wall, while they presented us with cushions, hot tea, sweets, and other hospitality. When I first arrived, I wondered why my host family visited certain homes of their extended relatives and not others. In particular, I wondered why Ali, the pious and vigilant older son, often warned his parents to avoid the homes of certain extended kin. I once heard him warn his mother explicitly: "You can eat with such and such person, but not with so and so. Don't go to their house. Don't drink their tea."

It soon became clear that family visits were purposeful and carefully thought out (see also Hegland 2013). Here, and although Nushin and Ahmad strove to visit both sides of their family, they favored visiting Nushin's siblings, whom they described as closer and more cultured and pious. There, they were comfortable and chatted in relaxed postures, their legs spread out as they sat on the floor, drinking tea and eating fruit and other items. These were the kin with whom they had a relationship of "coming and going." They were less trusting of certain members of Ahmad's kin and therefore visited them more sparingly. When they did visit, they stayed for a shorter time and tried to refuse food and drink.

Over time, I learned that there were several reasons for this avoidance of certain family members and their food. First, Ahmad and Nushin did not wish to create reciprocal visiting obligations with kin who might negatively influence their own family members by modeling unethical or impious actions such as drug addiction, fighting, or "prayer-taking" practices (*do'ā gereftan*, esoteric prayer with intention to cause harm). Second, they did not wish to share the possibly contaminated tea or snacks of immoral family members, the consumption of which was a ritualized necessity of all night visiting. In these circumstances, when they did visit with such untrusted kin, they made a great effort to refuse food and drink or only consumed a bare minimum, unfortunately often alerting the host of their suspicions. So great were the complexities of visiting that Nushin was constantly anxious about whom the family should visit, how they should visit, or who planned to visit her home.

Significantly, and despite the risks, some amount of visiting with untrusted kin was necessary, if only to ward off retaliation in the form of casting "the evil eye" or from "prayer-taking." As family members explained to me hesitantly, and only after I had spent several months in their home, prayer-taking was a sinful process undertaken by those led astray from true Islam, over foods such as tea. The results were immediate or latent physical and spiritual sickness, fighting, and/or psychological ailments such as depression (see chapter 2 for more details).

As a member of the household, I too was swept up in the danger of visiting. One day, having consumed the food of a particular extended family member, I returned to the house feeling unwell. When I told immediate family members, they warned: "When you go there in the future, don't eat anything. Actually, it's better if you don't go there at all." I later gathered that my hosts were worried that the food I had consumed was cursed and that it would pollute not only me but the entire family, causing fighting or disrespect between parents and children. I return to this subject in chapter 2.

Regardless, for Nushin, Ahmad, and Ali, acts of visiting helped distinguish and develop an inner and trusted circle of kin relations. These kin were "closer" and were described as having a relationship with the family. They were explicitly contrasted with potentially impure others who could not be trusted and who did not model "correct" and halal relations. Indeed, everyday ethical and religious life was deeply entangled with the work of sorting, maintaining, and protecting shifting circles of trusted and correct kin relations. More than a set of substantial relations enshrined in Islamic law, kinship for my interlocutors was sacred, a matter of vigilance and ethical work. Importantly, however, knowledge of whom one had a "coming and going" relationship with was not made public. Only those in the household knew who made up their family's circle of most trusted kin. They often talked about who was in and who was not, and they vigilantly kept this information secret from others.

EHSAN'S BURIAL

During the funeral that followed Ehsan's burial in the cemetery in Fars-Abad, I sat in a circle of my hosts' female kin while other such circles formed across the great hall. Although the imam was talking about the Day of Judgment over a loudspeaker, the women hardly listened to him. They were speaking about Ehsan, about what had happened, and about the difficulty of his sudden death for his family. They were also discussing the relative auspiciousness of the night of his death, one of the Nights of Power in the holy month of Ramadan. As we sat there, Ehsan's female relatives passed out lemon drink and dates, a silent request for us to pray for him. Then, on a Thursday a week after the burial, Ehsan's degree one and two family met again at his family home and traveled together again by car to his gravesite. They spread a carpet on the fresh dirt and put a tray of dates mixed with *halvā* and walnuts on its soft surface along with containers of pastries and fruit, before sharing the food with attendees.

For my hosts, Ehsan's death was a tragic and visible sign of the societal corruption still present in postrevolutionary Iran. Protecting children and other kin, they said, was difficult and pertinent work. They intensely strove to develop and maintain what they called halal, harmonious, and pure relations through ongoing everyday and ritual acts such as prayer and visiting. Thus, while blood and other shared substances of kinship channel "physio-sacred" qualities of purity along lines of descent, pure and halal kin relations are additionally constituted through a range of everyday and ritual acts, acts that not only infuse the bodies and souls of kin with blessing and purity but also delineate the inner space of the household from outside corruption.

My hosts, as supporters of the Islamic Republic and members of the Basij, were particularly vigilant in this active delineation compared to some of their neighbors and extended kin. In part, this vigilance may have been related to Ahmad's increased visibility in the community as a prominent Iran-Iraq War veteran and former mayor, but this did not make it any less sincere. Their experiences of kinship were complicated, interwoven with Iran's history of revolution and war and with their personal experiences of loss and also inseparable from local cultural logics of family piety, religion, and socioeconomic status. Yet uniquely, one of the threads that did consistently seem to shape my hosts' family life was the need to construct the right kind of pure family as a means of protecting society, in this case the Islamic Republic.

My hosts' intense striving to create the right kind of pure kin necessitates renewing our attention to the religious and ethical dimensions of kinship, to how kin relations can be formed through embodied, sacred, and pious acts, in this case against the backdrop of state power. We need to consider not only the given or natural connections between kin formed through substances such as blood (where they exist) but also the malleability of those connections and the ways in which the religious purity of the connections themselves may shift and change according to context, politics, and ritual actions. Finally, we must attend to not only the "recognition" of kin through acts such as visiting but also its ethical constitution through these acts and processes. We must further ask how such notions of ethical kinship and the vigilance it requires are linked to the shoring up of state power and authority.

Chapter 2 continues this inquiry, with a focus more specifically on how food shapes kinship's lived boundaries. Basiji families in Fars-Abad employed combinations of food and prayer to purify and cleanse the "inside, intimate spaces of the home" while defending against incursions of immorality from those beyond or "outside" the immediate kin group (e.g., from certain in-laws, extended kin, neighbors, strangers, or the West). In chapters 3 and 4, I turn to how my interlocutors' experiences of kinship inform and intersect with the making of the nation-state.

2 Feeding the Family

THE "SPIRIT" OF FOOD IN IRAN

Ali had to do something. He was fighting with his brother and his sister, who were also fighting with each other, almost to the point of violence. Reading the Qur'an over the noise of their arguments did not seem to help. Burning wild rue (incense) to ward off the evil eye did not help. There were other troubles, too: the recent death of his cousin Ehsan in the desert, for one. But Ali, a twenty-year-old computer major, believed he had found an answer: a *ziārat-e 'āshura'*, a ritual prayer and votive meal in honor of Imam Husayn, the grandson of the Prophet who was martyred in the Battle of Karbala. He convinced his mother and father that this was what the household needed. "Having the prayer at the house," he said, "will make it clean (*pāk*) and fill it with angels." The next morning he and his mother, Nushin, made a list of invitees and a list of foods needed for the prayer meal. They explained to us that their main intention (*niyyat*) was to rid the house of evil and spiritually heal the family. They said that the inner purity of the household had been breached and the evil eye had struck.[1]

Ali guessed that the person responsible was a jealous aunt or neighbor. But regardless of who it was, it was highly likely that *someone* had struck them with the evil eye and also engaged in harmful prayer-taking, a kind of negative prayer form, over the tea that one or more of us had consumed. This was what had caused the unusual escalation of tensions between the siblings as well as between parents and children. Such discord, Ali explained, was more than unpleasant. It was sinful, starkly contrasting with Islamic ideals of harmonious and "religiously permissible" or halal relations between family members. He and his parents hoped that the prayer would reverse this trend by cleansing the home of evil, encouraging reconciliation (*āshti*) between kin as opposed to estrangement (*qahr*), and by restoring the purity of the family and its relationships.[2] A key ingredient for this transformation, he and his family emphasized, was the mutual incorporation of blessed food, in this case homemade "saffron rice pudding" (*sholeh zard*). I explore how this event played out at the end of the chapter.

My field notes are peppered with examples like this in which food, imbued with occult power, is either a source of the contamination of families and households or a means of regenerating and purifying kin relations. During my time with Ahmad and Nushin, the family held and participated in numerous events involving the cooking and distribution of blessed food, each with scores of guests. In Iran, this sharing of blessed food is called *nazri*, and it is usually a part of the fulfillment of a vow to a Shi'i Imam.[3] Some of these public votive meals and rituals are performed for specific reasons, such as praying for the health of a divorced son or ensuring a daughter's successful marriage. But almost all are explicitly linked, in one way or another, to the healing, purification, or protection of kin.

Everyday family meals at home have similar import. "Maybe in America it is not this way," Ahmad explained as we sat at the family's lunch *sofreh*, an intricate spread of stew, rice, salad, fresh herbs, and yogurt, prepared by Nushin, "but we Iranians have to make it such that both our children's souls and bodies are right and complete. We say that food makes our children happy. Food changes the soul. It affects it." On this occasion, the meal we were about to eat was a delicate pomegranate and walnut stew called *fesenjān*. It had been shaped, Ahmad said, by Nushin's skill as a cook, her mindfulness of Allah, and her pure intention to nourish her family. Sitting across from him, I examined the tasty concoction before me with its rich brownish purple sauce flavored with stewed meat, pomegranate, and walnuts. I was beginning to learn that these flavors and colors were the outward expression of the meal's more important moral and sacred qualities, qualities that were necessary for the family's spiritual and bodily nourishment.

Indeed, by the time this meal arrived in front of us on the *sofreh*, family members had carefully vetted its ingredients for their blessing (*ne'mat*), spiritual purity (*pāki*), lawfulness (halal), humoral balance (*tab'*), localness (*mahalli*), strength (*moqavvi*), and overall rightness (*dorosti*). The meal was the end result of several hours of Nushin's hard work cleaning vegetables, cooking, and washing, and it was also the result of her pure intentions, her prayers, and her careful selection of pure and halal ingredients obtained from painstakingly selected sources.

Food helps constitute not only the shared substances of kin but also the "right" kind of kindred Islamic spirit for families who support the Islamic Republic. From before a child is born until the Day of Judgment, pure, trusted, and halal foods are seen as critical to nourishing both the body and soul.[4] More than nutrition, food—and food accompanied by blessings in particular—is an agent of transformation and a means of channeling divine blessing (*ne'mat*), whether inward, to the pure family core, embodied by the lunch *sofreh*, or outward, for the spiritual nourishment of extended kin, neighbors, and community. Yet while food is understood both explicitly and implicitly to "change the soul" and shape ideal qualities for both individual kinsmen and the family as a whole, for my Basiji hosts in particular, this "right" sense of kindred spirit (*ruh*) is precarious and permeable to the failing morals of postwar Iranian society.

Certain foods, in particular, have the potential to harm the family via their consumption at the *sofreh*, influencing generations to come. My hosts made careful distinctions between foods that are halal, pure, home cooked, and locally grown and produced versus foods that are unlawful (*harām*), impure, or of foreign origin, the latter of which have the potential to spread spiritual illness in the form of family infighting, sinning, and sickness.

Yet while many Iranians believe food has the potential to "change the soul" and shape ideal qualities for both individual kinsmen and the family as a whole, my Basiji hosts emphasized the ways in which food could influence the *purity* of their family members and of their interfamily relationships. They mobilized their food in alignment with the values of the Basij to create the right kind of moral, pure, and halal family. And they were particularly vigilant in all aspects of food procurement, preparation, and feeding, especially when foods originated from sources outside their home, town, region, or country and were incorporated into family meals. After all, food was a vital part of infusing the vulnerable bodies and souls of kin with blessing and purity and of protecting children and other family members from physical and/or spiritual harm.[5]

ENTANGLEMENTS: FOOD, RELIGION, AND KINSHIP

Arguably an embodied practice, food is very often a medium of relationality and religiosity. It is, as Mary Douglas emphasized, an encoded message "about different degrees of hierarchy, inclusion and exclusion, boundaries, and transactions across boundaries" (1972, 61). Everyday acts of feeding and living together may influence which persons count as kin (Janowski 2007; Carsten 2004; Weismantel 1995). For instance, Malays on the island of Langkawi incorporate new kin both through ties of inherited substance *and* through everyday acts of feeding and living together in a house (Carsten 2000). Similarly, Zumbagua people in the highlands of Ecuador become parents by feeding and caring for children over extended periods of time rather than in the moment of procreation. Food and cooking may also be directly likened to procreation. For the Bangangté of Cameroon, for instance, pregnancy is seen as a "cooking process," or a process of heating, cooling, and the mixing of "ingredients" (Feldman-Savelsberg 1996; see also Ott 1979). As Appadurai relates on the subject of the bio-moral cosmos in India, "Food, along with blood and semen, is a particularly powerful medium of contact between persons and groups. In a cultural universe that sets considerable store by a host of heterogeneous persons, groups, forces, and powers, food (whether "hot" or "cold," raw or cooked, sacred or sullied) always raises the possibility of homogenizing the actors linked by it, whether they are husband or wife, servant or master, worshiper or deity" (1981, 507).

Here, food is more than a medium of contact or of embodying sameness through commensality. It is also deeply connected to religious ontologies (Feeley-Harnik 1995; Bynum 1997). Religious charity efforts, prayer, and life-cycle and calendric events frequently feature food, and it appears in offerings to the divine, in rituals, or as a vehicle of blessing or of religious purity, altering the body and soul of the consumer (see Bynum 1997). Indeed, "food is not just a symbol or metaphor for social and cultural processes (e.g., in its transformation from raw to cooked) nor simply a signifier that reflects or embodies aspects of culture. Food is not only transformed, it is transformative" (Fajans 1988, 143).

For pious families in Iran, food is deeply connected to both religious practice and kinship. It is critical to what Sered calls "relationship oriented religiosity" (1988, 131): the processes wherein relatives care for each other through everyday acts such as feeding and blessing. For my hosts, in particular, women's (and sometimes men's) acts of feeding "the proper way" or building the "right" substance in kin are a critical part of discerning, creating, and protecting the physio-sacred family. At the same time, food choices and preparation are inseparable from the life histories of my hosts and their politics, including participation in the 1979 Revolution, membership in the Basij and service in the Iran-Iraq War, or the everyday contingencies of living as a "regime class" in rural Fars Province. Indeed, for my hosts, the ethical work of creating and consuming the right food at the home *sofreh* is a bulwark not only against family schisms, accidents, and illness, but also against the fading morals of Iran's postrevolutionary society.[6] Food is religio-political, a kind of "daily revolutionary practice" (Sutton et al. 2013).

I focus on three main contexts in which food infuses the vulnerable bodies and souls of kin with blessing and purity: (1) everyday food at home, (2) fasting, and (3) ritual and votive meals for Shi'i Imams that frequently overlap with life-cycle events as well as seasonal and Islamic calendars.

KINSHIP AT THE *SOFREH*

Early in my stay in Fars-Abad, Nushin, her son, and I visited the home of Nushin's eighty-year-old mother, Goli-Mehrebun. She lived near the town's main street less than a half kilometer away in a two-room apartment located in the courtyard of Mahmad, her son and Nushin's brother.

Our intention was to visit Goli, but when we arrived, Mahmad's wife, Fariba, unexpectedly invited us to lunch, which she had almost finished cooking. As I would soon learn, our acceptance of her invitation was highly unusual; with the exception of key ritual events and holidays, my hosts and extended kin most often had lunch in their own homes, choosing to decline other invitations. We took off our shoes in the outer courtyard and entered the house. Fariba's two daughters and daughter-in-law were helping her prepare an eggplant stew: they were chopping vegetables and laying out plates, cutlery, glasses, serving dishes, bread, salads, and herbs on a square plastic table cover or *sofreh* that was spread on the living room floor. When the food was organized in a symmetrical array of colorful food and plates, we joined them on the floor—men and women both—and began eating, some sitting cross-legged and some kneeling. After lunch, the women got up and went to sit comfortably on the kitchen floor while the men remained in the main living area. We began to talk about the meaning of "family," and Fariba's voice rose above the rest, "Family," she said, "are those people who sit around the *sofreh* together."

In Iran, the phrase "spread the *sofreh*" (*sofreh ro pahn kon*) means something like "set the table." However, the term *sofreh* can also stand for the entire meal or even the "votive offering of a meal" (*sofreh-ye nazri*) to family, neighbors, or the poor.[7] The *sofreh* is also a metonym for intimacy. A *sofreh-ye del* translates to "a dining spread of the heart" and entails confiding one's innermost thoughts and feelings to one another (Shirazi 2005). Here, the *sofreh* is explicitly linked to the *del*—the heart, stomach, or belly—and is associated with the ability of the *del* to contain emotions, desires, thoughts, memories, and passions.

In other contexts, including the everyday, the term *sofreh* evokes a feeling of blessing (*ne'mat*). As a Tehrani nephew of Nushin's explained to me, "When people look at each other and sit in a circle at the *sofreh*, they receive blessing and it brings [them] more pleasure." Accordingly, those who sit together at the *sofreh* correspond with and delimit those who share blessing, intimacy, and trust. The daily meal *sofreh*, in particular, marks the contours of the permeable, yet distinct, intimacy of the immediate family, or what my interlocutors often termed "the small family" (*khānevādeh-e kuchik*).

Figure 5. Votive *sofreh* featuring *kāchi* (flour cooked with butter and oil, saffron, and turmeric), a food associated with pregnancy and fertility, Tehran, Iran

I first noted this interrelationship of the *sofreh* and family on the thirteenth day of the Iranian New Year (Sizdar Bedar) in 2010.[8] I spent the crisp spring afternoon with my hosts and their extended family of about one hundred people beside a small, tree-lined river near Fars-Abad. On this celebratory day, all the members of either the husband's or the wife's extended family join each other outside at a park or on a riverbank to cook kebab and a votive soup dish, play games, dance, and sing. This year my hosts had elected to spend the day with Nushin's side of the family—their matrilateral kin—a group that numbered more than one hundred individuals because Nushin had eight brothers and sisters and many nephews, nieces, and cousins. People arrived together crammed into cars or on motorcycles.

However, what was most striking about the gathering was that each smaller family unit (usually a mother, a father, their children, and, potentially, their grandparents) created their own small area on the grass and spread their own rectangular *sofreh*, thus forming an array of small units that stretched out around trees and up the grassy hill. At lunchtime, each small family sat around their own specific *sofreh* to eat their meal (food such as rice, chicken, etc., had been cooked at home) and drink tea provided by their own mother/wife. The only food substance that crossed the lunch *sofreh*s of these small units was the grilled kebab, which had been cooked by collectives of "degree one" male relatives.[9] As the kebab was passed around, it demarcated who was included in this "degree one" category, which in this case included a particular subset of pure and moral kin who had been invited to share the kebab (an array of first cousins, aunts, and uncles who were also deemed trustworthy and right). As Nushin explained, these kin were neither the small family nor the extended network of kin. They were close (*nazdik*) and they were "good people." I noted, for instance, that Nushin's half sisters from her father's second wife were excluded from this circulation. The lunch *sofreh*s on the thirteenth day of the New Year thus not only made visible a spectrum of kinship, inclusions, and exclusions, but also those who were seen as trustworthy and pure. The circulation of home-cooked food demarcated those persons whom the family deemed to rank as moral and good kin and distinguished them from others implicitly deemed to lack those qualities but who were nevertheless family.

After lunch, family members invited one another for tea at their respective *sofreh*s and shared sweets in the exact same way that family home visits are conducted throughout the year. As they strolled through the sea of dining cloths, family members employed the Iranian conventional politeness (*ta'arof*) in the same way they would at other times of the year to invite passing friends or relatives into their family homes.[10] For example, as I walked with Maryam, Nushin's daughter, among the array of *sofreh*s, people would say, "Welcome! Please join us inside!," to which we replied, "Thank you very much. We won't bother you," only to be invited for a second time and a third time, as is customary: "Please sit with us. Have just one glass of tea, just one. We have just poured it. Come in." When we accepted, which we did on only two occasions and only with "degree one" kin, our hosts followed the same pattern of serving tea that is common at most home visits. This act of food sharing brought us within the threshold of the temporary house, here the *sofreh*, and required that we act as guests.

I learned later that family members took great care to only share tea at the *sofreh*s of those they considered to be good and moral kin: those whom they trusted. The tea, in such settings, is brewed at home from loose-leaf black tea and is brought outside in a large thermos. It is never offered in disposable cups but is instead poured into clear glass tea cups, so that its brilliant golden color is visible. On the thirteenth day of the Iranian New Year, acceptance of tea at a family's *sofreh* indicated a positive moral evaluation of that family and the existence of a relationship. Refusal, in contrast, had the potential to either signal or create a schism of relations. I noted that the women around me, including my hosts and their cousins, were carefully tracking the movement of people and tea through the gathering, making mental notes of each encounter.

The care taken in such movements and acts of tea commensality stemmed in part from the potency of the tea itself and its two opposing uses. On the one hand, the sharing of tea, brewed by a mother or daughter and shared among intimates, neighbors, or friends, signifies hospitality, reciprocity, and trust. On the other hand, and although this is rare, tea may also be used for ill purposes. Specifically, tea over which prayers are "taken"—a kind of negative prayer form derived from esoteric knowledge of the Qur'an—can cause people to become injured, to sin, or to act immorally. It is therefore incumbent upon tea drinkers to carefully evaluate tea brewers and their kin and to avoid consuming suspect tea when possible. As Bloch (1999, 145) notes on the subject of such commensality, "the better food is as a conductor that creates bodily closeness, the better it is as a medium of poison." In Iran, tea is such a substance.[11]

Interestingly, when night fell, the pattern shifted dramatically. The entire group gathered together to eat votive soup that was prepared outside in a large single vat over a gas stove. The traditional votive soup or *āsh* consisted of stewed herbs, noodles, and vegetables. The cooking was supervised by Goltab, one of the most respected of Nushin's sisters.

Nushin told me that the soup was full of blessing, that it would make us pure and heal our ailments. On another occasion, she told me that the food we ate at the *sofreh* at home had a similar kind of blessed quality, especially when it was prepared in the right way, with the right ingredients. More than a symbol of intimacy, the *sofreh* was a means of (re)constituting, protecting, and demarcating family.

(IN)CORPORATING FOOD INTO THE *SOFREH*:
INTIMACY AND PROTECTION

In Fars-Abad, three *sofrehs* organize the daily comings and goings of family members: breakfast, usually eaten between 6:00 and 9:00 a.m.; lunch, eaten between 2:00 and 3:30 p.m.; and dinner, eaten between 8:00 and 10:00 p.m. Each is linked to a different kind of intimacy and thus has different import for the family. As a well-known proverb relates: "Eat breakfast alone, eat lunch with loved ones, and eat dinner with enemies" (*sobhāneh tan hā bokhor, nahār bā dustān, va shām bā doshman*). In Iran, lunch is the most important and the most intimate meal of the day. Breakfast, in contrast, may be eaten alone and is a time of personal sustenance. And dinner, while normally shared with immediate family, is relatively open to visitors such as neighbors or relations; as the proverb indicates, it may be strategically shared with "enemies."[12]

In the framework of these three meals, there are several overlapping ways my hosts, their extended kin, and their neighbors evaluate how food at the *sofreh* affects individuals and families. Most generally, they judge all foods on a scale of quality or virtue (*khāsiyat*). For example, someone might say, "We made the saffron rice pudding because of its particular virtue." The qualities of virtue here referred to are multiple. While the most valued foods are blessed (*ne'mat* or *barakat dārand*), trusted (*qābel-e e'temād*), lawful (halal), pure (*pāk*), or homegrown (*khānegi*), other foods are valued for qualities of potency (*moqavvi*), healthfulness (*salāmati*), and hot and cold "humoral balance" (*tab'*). Additional evaluations determine whether foods are sound or healthy (*sālem*), unsound or unhealthy (*nā-sālem*), tasty (*khosh-mazeh*), disgusting (*bad-mazeh*), whole (*kāmel*), or packaged (*basteh-bandi*), as well as whether they are natural (*tabi'i*) or unnatural (*shimiāyi*), foreign (*khāreji*) or local (*mahalli*).

Other foods are entirely avoided: food that is untrustworthy (*bi-e'temād*), either because of its ingredients or because it has been touched by an untrustworthy person; food that is unlawful (*harām*), such as meat that is improperly slaughtered, pork, and alcohol; and food that is impure (*najes*). These three types of food can cause both bodily and spiritual illness. As a female law student and member of the Basij told me with great seriousness as we walked in Tehran's Imam Khomeini Square: "Impermissible foods can affect a person's character. They can cause a moral person to sin." Accordingly, food can provide both physical and bodily nourishment and malnourishment, and it can influence one's actions. The religious, nutritional, and aesthetic elements of food are inseparable (see also Harbottle 2000, 151).

Because of the numerous qualities and significance of food, Nushin, Ahmad, and their children carefully vetted which items would be incorporated into the breakfast, lunch, and dinner *sofrehs* as well the people who touched, prepared, and shared food. While they rejected certain foods and persons, they incorporated others into the intimate circle of the *sofreh* to help create a pure and halal family, modeled on the family of the Prophet and connected to God. Here, while many of my hosts' kitchen practices were typical of pious Iranians across the region and in Iran more broadly, the precise way in which they saw food as a potent vehicle for danger, transformation, protection, and resilience was shaped by their location in a small factory town surrounded by farmland; their personal metaphysical beliefs about food, prayer, and ill intention; and their family's politics and membership in the Basij.

The Breakfast Sofreh: *Bread and Blessing*

Fed by the national media and "correct eating guidelines," the significance of breakfast for overall wellness and spiritual health was catching on in Fars-Abad in 2010. Dissimilar to the Euro-American call for a nutritious breakfast of whole grains and fruits, however, the emphasis was on energy and power, and, relatedly, on breakfast as a means of constituting "spiritual zeal" (*gheirat*). Breakfast, my hosts said, was the first step to readiness—not only for work and school, but also for daily prayer and control of "inner passions" (*nafs*) throughout the day.

Nushin often talked about her struggle to enlighten the rest of her family on the virtues of breakfast. She warned her children almost daily of the ill effects of not eating a substantial breakfast and argued that they would be sick and lackluster without it. In particular, she worried that without good food in the morning, her sons, Reza and Ali, would be more likely to get caught up in bad activities such as flirting with girls or smoking the hookah, or, the ultimate worry, might become opium addicts. But her remonstrations were to little avail. Two of her three teenage children barely touched food in the morning, drinking only hot black tea with a copious amount of sugar cubes.

In Fars-Abad, as well as elsewhere in Iran, breakfast is the least ornate meal of the day, especially when there are no guests or events. The immediate family eats breakfast quickly and quietly after they wake from sleep, singly or in groups of twos or threes. The first person awake in the family—usually the mother/wife—spreads the *sofreh*, either on the kitchen table or the living room floor. She has likely already read her predawn prayers and has tidied the house. Breakfast, however, differs from other meals because she rarely needs to cook or otherwise serve dishes to her family.[13] Even if she prepares more elaborate breakfast foods, the entire family need not be present, and food is largely obtained via self-service.

The key ingredient of breakfast, and often dinner, is fresh bread from a local bakery. This bread is brought home either the previous evening or hot and fresh the same morning by the father, a brother, or the mother. For Muslims, including Shi'as in Iran, bread is called blessing (*barakat*). It is God's gift and bounty. To honor God, my hosts told me, bread should be torn off by hand and not carved with a knife. They informed me that the Prophet said: "Do not cut bread with a knife, but give it due honor by breaking it with the hands, for Allah has honored it."

Above all, my hosts valued bread for its purity and simplicity and associated it with Imam 'Ali, the successor to the Prophet and his son-in-law, a key source of Shi'i emulation. "His Holiness 'Ali was a bread and salt eater," Nushin explained on one occasion. "We have a feeling of religiosity when we eat bread and salt. It is not that His Holiness 'Ali was poor and could not afford anything else. Rather, he wanted to build his character by eating simple foods. This was the type of person he was."[14] Nushin, her family, and their extended kin prized bread because they saw it as God's blessing and because it was "a simple food." On her part and on the part of other state supporters I met in Fars-Abad, this valuing of simplicity was not accidental. It was also a revolutionary quality, associated with the moral strength, character, and purity of Imam 'Ali.

This connection between bread and good character was also tied to Fars-Abad's recent history. Nushin's mother, Goli-Mehrebun, for instance, likened having good character to being complete (*kāmel*) or cooked (*pokhteh*). In contrast, she and others described a person whose character was not yet fully formed as dough (*khāmir*) or uncooked (*khām*). Their evaluations were intimately tied to the 1979 Revolution. Before the Revolution, they said, bread was a more important staple of their cuisine than rice. Hajj Bibi, the eighty-year-old mother of Ahmad, recalled: "We had to bring wheat from the fields to the flour mill up the hill. I used to spend five hours making home-made bread for my family every fourth morning." In Fars-Abad, few still carry out this process, although more do so in a neighboring Basseri nomad settlement. But Hajj Bibi vividly remembered other details. She described how she and the other women in the then still-walled town mixed flour, water, and salt to make the dough by hand, pressing it with their fists. They then used a giant metal pan or basin (*lagan*) to mix and roll the dough, a stick (*tir*) to thin and shape it, and another concave metal pan (*toheh*) to heat the bread over a fire or gas flame.[15] The process was arduous and time consuming, but it was also described as "character building." Hajj Bibi told me that when she made bread this way, she was helping to imbue her family with blessing.

Today, most Fars-Abadis, like people elsewhere in Iran, purchase bread in local bakeries. The main breads used for breakfast are a local variety of round flat bread known as "Fars-Abadi bread"; a rectangular, nationally available flat white bread known as *barbari*; and another rectangular, whole wheat bread baked on a bed of stones, called *sangak*. And although bread is now readily available, it remains central to the *sofreh*, its blessing, and embodied values of purity and simplicity. For this reason, my hosts take great care where they buy their bread. They much prefer to purchase bread from the bakeries they trust and, in the privacy of their homes, they discuss the personal and pious qualities of local bakers and their life histories, as well as the qualities of each bakery's staff and facility. For instance, during my time in her home, Nushin often asked her sons and husband when they returned from shopping for bread: "Where did you buy this food? Who handled it?" Often, the bread buyer—usually a teenage son—was met with criticism: "Why did you buy from there?" Nushin and her family eventually agreed to purchase bread from one particular bakery, which happened to be farther away from some others, not only because the owner was an acquaintance but also because the owner had fought in the Iran-Iraq War and was known as a pious Muslim. As Ahmad explained, he was a "good person" (*ādam-e khub*). By visibly waiting in this baker's breadline, the family was showing the surrounding community that their household supported this baker and his values.[16] These intersecting themes of personal and national histories, support for the Islamic Republic, and religious foodways also shape daily lunch preparations.

The Lunch Sofreh*: Intimacy and Protection*

> The effort (*zahmat*) involved in the lunch meal is of fundamental importance to the wellness and the spirit (*ruh*) of the family.
>
> —Sami, Fars-Abad, June 15, 2010

In Fars-Abad, parents and children, occasionally accompanied by grandparents, return from their outside jobs, school, or farming to have lunch at home. Lunch is the most intimate meal of the day. The preparation of the lunch *sofreh*, made from the freshest ingredients and with the most laborious work, is a daily project for women, consuming much of their time and effort (up to four hours every morning). As Ahmad's nephew's wife, Elaheh, exclaimed, reflecting on her daily routine: "All we [Iranian women] do is cook, eat, and sleep! That is what life is."[17]

The lunch *sofreh*, however, is also a means of demarcating and shaping the immediate family who share blessing; as a result, it is shared with others only on special occasions. During my time in Fars-Abad, as an intriguing American visitor, I received hundreds of polite invitations for lunch and other meals.[18] At first I refused these offers because I was too involved in helping to prepare, cut, or wash foods for my host family's lunch meal or had dinner plans in the family household. There was no reason for me to leave the house and accept an invitation elsewhere when I was already a part of the everyday cooking process. I quickly realized that family members almost never shared their lunch *sofreh* with others—whether in the homes of their acquaintances or even with their "degree one" relatives. In Fars-Abad, lone children never ate lunch at another person's house without their parents. Although teenage boys sometimes bought fast-food sandwiches from shops on Imam Boulevard, Fars-Abad's main street, they either ate these sandwiches in public places or brought them home.

Furthermore, while young women sometimes invited their female study partners to the house during lunch, I never saw these invitees eat with the rest of the family at the *sofreh* even though they were always invited to do so. Rather, they would take snacks upstairs or to a separate room. This apartness was the correct moral action for such a visitor, who should not come into contact with her friend's brothers at the family *sofreh*.

There were only three exceptions to this implicit family-only lunch meal during the entire duration of my fieldwork. On one occasion Ahmad ate with Nushin's brother (his brother-in-law) and wife after their son had died of a drug overdose. On another occasion, we all (myself, Nushin, her son, her daughter, and her husband) went as a family to the house of another aunt to eat lunch. And finally, the entire family visited Ahmad's old friend from the war, also a member of the Basij, on the occasion of his son's imminent wedding in a neighboring small town. In almost all of these cases, the entire family was invited to lunch or there was some sort of special occasion: the Iranian New Year, a wedding, or some other event. As for myself, and despite the vast number of lunch invitations I received, I only ate lunch at another person's house on a few occasions, and in one of these instances I had little choice. A nice older couple whom I had interviewed trapped me in their home with their polite hospitality and refused to take me home! When one of my hosts came to pick me up, Nushin and Ahmad asked me to list everything I had eaten and asked why I hadn't called sooner to be picked up.

There are multiple reasons for this implicit, but obvious, emphasis on eating lunch together as a family at home and not elsewhere. The first is the effort that goes into hosting in Iranian hospitality. Convention dictates that guests must be provided with huge piles of fresh fruit and vegetables, tea, and a two- or three-dish meal, which is an unspoken imposition on even the most eager host. This is a burden that people do not normally want to place on others and one that involves a reciprocal responsibility. Relatedly, sharing food is a sign of alliance and relationship, whether egalitarian or hierarchical, and visits involving food sharing, when they occur, are purposeful and/or ceremonial (e.g., an engagement, a wedding, a New Year's celebration).

As Basijis, my hosts accentuated the need to eat lunch together at home as a means of protecting and maintaining the purity and morality of their household. As I discussed in chapter 1, Ahmad and Nushin did not wish to create reciprocal visiting obligations with certain kin or others who might negatively influence their children by modeling unethical or impious behavior such as drug addiction or fighting. This concern extended to food, a substance they saw as a potential vehicle not only for intimacy and blessing, but also for corruption. Food consumed at the homes of those they did not trust might be impure, unlawful, or otherwise suspect. Indeed, my hosts believed in the possibility that others with ill intent might engage in prayer-taking over food or tea, which could spiritually and physically harm the family. When Nushin and Ahmad did have to visit with such ill-intentioned kin, they made a great effort to refuse food and drink or only consume a bare minimum, unfortunately often alerting the host of their suspicions. Indeed, the complexities of visiting and sharing food with others were so great that Nushin was constantly anxious about who the family should visit, how they should visit, or who planned to visit her home.

In contrast to the moral ambiguities produced by sharing meals with others, sharing the lunch *sofreh* with members of the "small family" at home was a means of protecting and distinguishing an inner and trusted circle of kin relations. At home the food could be vetted, and meals served by the mother at the lunch *sofreh* were the product of careful moral evaluation and, very often, weeks or months of preparatory labor. The moral quality of food cooked and shared within the household was known and ensured by the family. The husband, wife, and children had chosen the ingredients, and the wife/mother had cooked the food in coordination with her daily prayers and with pure intentions. The work of selecting, discerning, and making good-quality food for the (lunch) *sofreh* was critical to shaping and protecting a pure and halal family.

Sacrifice for Family Protection

The process of gathering ingredients for the daily lunch meal often begins weeks in advance with the selection of a lamb or goat for slaughter and sacrifice for the benefit of the family. The father takes a son or cousin to a nearby seminomadic village to find an appropriate animal. He chooses a herder with whom he has an acquaintance and whom he trusts and brings the sheep back to the home in the truck of the same or yet another extended kinsman. Generally, the family will coordinate the day of sacrifice with some special day on the calendar, such as the "Day of Sacrifice" (Eid-e Qorbān), or with a family member's return from a pilgrimage. It is also common to sacrifice a lamb when a baby is born. In Fars-Abad, family members bring the animal into the courtyard or into the parking garage of the home, where the mother puts henna on its forehead to bless it. The halal sacrifice takes place just outside the home, and a skilled and pious layman/member of the family usually performs this task: he first cuts the animal's throat to bleed it correctly, then he utters, "In the Name of God, the Merciful and the Compassionate." After the sacrifice, the wife or husband cleans and cuts up the meat. It is also the wife's responsibility to divide the meat and give a portion to the poor, particularly to the families who are "descendants of the Prophet" (*sayyed*s) or to close family members in other houses (a grandmother, an uncle, a sister). The people of Fars-Abad carry out this distribution with great attention to fairness, as unequal portions are a sign of differential treatment and can provoke family arguments. The general philosophy is that both the givers and the receivers of such food charity are filled with blessing.

Such a sacrifice is also a way of protecting the family from harm. When my host family bought their first car (a Samand, the national car of Iran), they cracked four fresh eggs under its wheels to dispel the evil eye, and they sacrificed a lamb. Ahmad and his son, Ali, smeared the blood of the lamb on each of the vehicle's four wheels, saying, "In the Name of God, the Merciful and the Compassionate." This sacrificial blood, they said, increased the blessing and the "security" of the car. Nushin explained: "The blood of the lamb is given so that the car's occupants [the family] will not spill their own blood."[19] The process of obtaining and preparing meat for the *sofreh* is thus deeply interconnected to the work of blessing and protecting the family.

Discerning Halal, Local, and Processed Fare

But how are other food ingredients vetted before they become a part of household meals? For my hosts, key areas of inquiry include whether the outside fare is halal, local, trustworthy, or processed/factory-made. For instance, whenever her husband, son, or daughter brought food home from the market, Nushin began asking the same kind of questions she asked about local bakeries: "Where did you buy that and for how much? Who was the store owner? Who are they related to? Why didn't you buy it at such and such location?" This line of questioning occurred on a daily basis and was largely used to determine whether the food was halal; if the origin of the food was trusted or not; and whether the food was local, fresh, and homemade or processed and packaged.

HALAL FOODS

Since the founding of the Islamic Republic and the inception of the 1979 Constitution (Mir-Hosseini 2010), Islamic laws concerning halal food, drink, and culinary etiquette have been emphasized and enforced by state policy makers. Most obviously, these dietary laws prohibit the export, import, and production and consumption of "unlawful" substances—such as pork and alcohol—within and across Iran's territorial borders.[20] (Other forbidden items include animals that are improperly slaughtered, other intoxicants, carnivorous animals, birds of prey, and any food contaminated with any of these products.)

My hosts were very mindful about halal food and often talked about the significance of Muslim dietary laws. They made careful distinctions between recommended, halal, suspected, and forbidden foods, often talking about how to characterize one food or another. In the context of Fars-Abad, however, they were not so much concerned that food was forbidden because it contained pork or alcohol, as these substances were not generally available. Instead, they were concerned that food be justly purchased and not stolen (e.g., from a neighbor's garden) or that it be correctly slaughtered, and so on. They emphasized and discussed the halal practices of *procuring* food: for instance, ensuring that lambs were correctly slaughtered or considering whether vegetables, fruit, bread, or restaurant fare had been purchased from a trusted vendor who did not steal. A point of evaluation was the pious character of the seller or outside cook. Had the person ensured that the food was halal? Indeed, both restaurant food and other items were purchased based on the perceived purity and accountability of the seller. "I like to buy [meat] from Hammed," Ahmad explained, "*ādam ast*," meaning he is a complete, cultured, and pious person.[21] This perception of accountability, moreover, was linked to the seller's personal history. Had he fought in the Iran-Iraq War? Was he a member of the Basij? Did he participate in Friday prayer?

Notably, their attention to the halalness of food was also linked to the broader meaning of halal in Islam, a subject I address in more detail in chapter 4. Muslims classify an entire range of acts as either halal or *harām* (unlawful). These include not only diet but also sexual relations, daily habits and customs, marriage and divorce, family relations, public morality, occupation, income, and types of entertainment. Eating halal foods, my hosts argued, is key to making and maintaining halal family relations.

LOCAL FOODS

In Fars-Abad, the localness of food to be incorporated into the lunch *sofreh* was a further matter of careful attention. One morning Nushin, her younger son Reza, and I sat at the *sofreh* discussing a locally made sheep's milk butter. Nushin had mixed it with honey and was attempting to offer it to us. She told us that the butter was from a herd owned by nearby nomads and that it was potent and strengthening. When her son leaned over to smell the concoction and subsequently made a face, Nushin was surprised: "We buy this wonderful butter for you and you don't eat it." She turned to me and, in an effort to convince him, explained that the butter was natural and local, and that it was more powerful and beneficial than the processed and packaged varieties. Although she admitted that doctors had told her that she should only eat small amounts of this type of fat due to its high cholesterol, she maintained that this particular type of butter was very healthy. She added that the purchased jam we ate at the same *sofreh* was not nearly as good as her homemade jam. Similarly, she compared the packaged yogurt drink that was in the fridge to the much preferable homemade, traditional variety available from settled nomads.[22]

Nushin was not alone in this positive assessment of local foods. Many people I spoke with valued food grown or made in the local town or its surrounding villages more highly than foods produced in other provinces of Iran or outside of the Islamic Republic. One reason for this, they said, is that local food is more "compatible." It comes from the same nearby "water and air" (*āb o havā*) as "us." As I mentioned in the introduction, small-scale farming, gardening, and animal husbandry are central to Fars-Abad's local economy. Agricultural land surrounds the town and is irrigated by wells drilled into underground water tables as well as by a few key rivers that cross the dry desert landscape. Farmers raise a diversity of crops: wheat, barley, corn, sunflowers, green cucumbers, tomatoes, peas, beans, lentils, beets, eggplants, and potatoes. In addition, orchard products are a regional mainstay. These include apples, plums, black plums, yellow plums, dark red peaches, apricots, quinces, grapes, walnuts, and almonds. Currently, people in Fars-Abad mostly prepare and cook whole fruits and greens bought from trucks or markets linked to local and regional farms.

Another reason for this preference for local food is its freshness. Fruits and vegetables, in particular, are valued for their seasonal availability, and many families own their own gardens. In addition, although some industrial-style meat is increasingly available in parts of Iran, most people in Fars-Abad do not buy (or cannot afford) the nationally available brands of meat. Rather, they purchase an entire lamb or goat from nearby herders, which they ritually sacrifice and carefully chop up, separating the meat into plastic freezer bags for future consumption. Every part is used, including the brain, the stomach, and the tongue. However, there is more at play than compatibility or freshness in assessments of local food. Fars-Abadis also value local, home-made foods because of their purity and trustworthiness.

"THE FACTORY-MADE STUFF IS WORTHLESS."

Nushin has been making "quince lime syrup" (*beh-limu*) and "pomegranate sauce" (*rob*-e *anār*) every summer for her entire life. Despite the easy availability of store-bought varieties, her husband and sons spend hours in the hot summer sun gathering fuzzy yellow quinces from nearby trees. During my stay, they brought them into their home in large sacks full to the brim. Nushin carefully scraped the fuzz off and quartered each fruit. She boiled the fruit until it was soft and pressed it through a type of colander to separate the liquid from the pulp. Finally, she boiled the quince juice with sugar until it thickened into syrup before adding large quantities of homemade lime and lemon juice. The quantities for this undertaking were so large that they required a fifty kilogram vat heated by a gas flame in the parking garage. While she worked, Nushin discussed the famous long-lasting qualities and medicinal value of quince: "A quince hung out in the fall will last until spring" she remarked at one point. "Its seeds are good

Figure 6. Pomegranate statue, Fars Province, Iran

for colds."[23] Nushin told me that one cold remedy is to boil the quince and drink the water. This is because it is a rare "warm" fruit, especially when cooked. She said that she also mixes the quince lime syrup that she makes with ice water and serves it to family and guests in the summer.

Pomegranate sauce involves similar effort. When the pomegranates ripen, Nushin and Ahmad make a yearly trip to a local town famous for its pomegranates (about an hour's drive away). They inspect and choose the fruit, arriving home with burlap sacks filled to the brim with hundreds of pomegranates. In 2010, Nushin and Ahmad, the neighbors, and I worked together to separate each seed from the rind by hand into a giant four

Figure 7. Nushin and Ahmad making pomegranate sauce, Fars-Abad, Iran

gallon bucket. Ahmad later took the fruit to a juicer, who used a machine to separate the seeds from the juice. Nushin then boiled the product and added sugar, making a thick sauce that is good for making walnut pomegranate stew or cool summer drinks.

For Nushin and Ahmad, the process of making pomegranate sauce is an act of spirituality and pure intention for the family. The pomegranate is mentioned in the Qur'an as a heavenly fruit. According to Nushin, "The way that the pieces of the pomegranate fit together, their shape . . . [she points to the pockets of juxtaposed ruby seeds] is a sign of God. The fruit needs to be respected. Every piece needs to be eaten." On another occasion we were talking with a neighbor when the woman said that if you manage to eat every jewel of the pomegranate without a single one dropping to the ground or being lost, especially on Thursday night, it has religious merit. It is as though you have eaten a jewel from heaven. "Pomegranate," Nushin added, "is full of special qualities." It makes the blood even (*sāf*) and ordered (*radif*). "It is a blood builder" (*khun sāz*).[24]

I asked Nushin why she devotes so much effort to making quince lime syrup and pomegranate sauce, when they are easily available for purchase in nearby stores. She explained: "Compared to the factory-made stuff, the taste is so much better. We know that the factory-made stuff is worthless. The quince syrup doesn't even have quince in it! Making quince lime syrup or pomegranate sauce at home takes a lot of time and energy, but the product is delicious and the quality is so much better."[25]

In a similar manner, Nushin consistently placed a hot dish of Iranian saffron rice at the center of the meal spread, a food combination that she believed critical to the daily physical and spiritual sustenance of her family. She and her husband preferred rice from the nearby region of Kamfiruz—sixty kilometers from Fars-Abad in Marvdasht—over other regional and international varieties. This rice, often purchased in bulk quantities, is valued not because it is clean (indeed, it comes full of little stones that must be sorted out) or cheap (its cost is midrange), but because it is from a nearby location and a known farmer and therefore is pure and trusted. Indeed, as I mentioned previously, "inside," local rice from nearby farms is of the utmost value and is the most powerful, nutritional, and tasty, even if it does come with lots of stones that must be removed. If local rice is unattainable in the region, they settle for rice grown in Iran. However, there is a hierarchy of rice grown outside the Islamic Republic: Pakistani rice is "okay" because Pakistan is a Muslim country; Chinese rice is terrible. Here, the positive evaluation of local Iranian rice, grown in nearby fields, is based not only on taste but on purity and the ability to positively nourish the family.

For people in Fars-Abad, "local food" not only designates fresh food; it can also refer to processed canned goods produced in local town factories, particularly the main town industry, a canning and pickling factory, which I call "the Factory."[26] Fars-Abad's town website lauds the Factory as a major "pole" of the regional economy: "[Our factory] has worldwide fame and produces a number of goods that, in addition to being available inside [the nation] (*dākheli*) are also sold in world markets" (my translation). The products of this factory include lemon syrup, tomato paste, pickles, eggplant caviar, jam, conserves, and pickled goods. Locals value products from the Factory because of their national and international repute as well as their quality. My hosts, their friends, and their neighbors often described Factory products as unusually pure and trustworthy—for factory food. The company's website explicitly advertises the extra-nutritional quality of its products: "Our honey is strengthening... [and] our rose water is healthy for body and soul."

Indeed, many of those I spoke with throughout the town said that it was better to buy or eat the local company's products than foreign or even other regional products. They explained that the Factory's products were an acceptable basis for a home-cooked meal or could be used as a convenient yet pure form of quick meals for a light dinner (particularly the beans and eggplant caviar, most often eaten with fresh bread). Importantly, most of the halal foods manufactured at the Factory are ingredients for "Iranian" or "traditional" cuisine rather than foreign or fast food.

The halalness and localness of ingredients used at the Factory were not the only reasons for eating Factory foodstuffs. My hosts also evaluated the spiritual and pious character of the factory managers and workers. They said that they trusted the Factory's products because they were "certain" about the people who made them. The jobs of Factory employees were at least partially dependent on their self-presentations of religiosity. When his sons gained temporary employment at the Factory, for instance, Ahmad advised them to show their piety by regularly praying and performing ablutions with fellow employees while they were at work. "You must be aware of this (*havās-et-o jam' kon*)," he warned them on several occasions. Later, he told me that factory leadership expected employees to dress in a halal manner (e.g., long-sleeved shirts, long pants) even when employees were not at work. Factory leadership also expected females, whether they were employees or the family members of employees, to dress in the full chador (a sign of Islam and nation). When I interviewed neighbors and the extended kin of my hosts, I learned that there were cases in which Factory employees had been fired because they had been caught engaging in *harām* conduct outside of work (e.g., wearing a T-shirt, drinking alcohol). In other words, there were very real personal and socioeconomic consequences for not following a code of visible halal conduct and piety. Public comportment, expressed religiosity, and employment opportunities were multiply entangled.

Notably, not everyone agreed with these policies, and many were vociferous about the control the Factory has over local employment opportunities. My hosts' sons were no exception. "How can I pray at work if it is superficial or forced?" Reza asked his father. He confessed, "I can't make myself pray." Ahmad, perhaps surprisingly, was empathetic. He trusted that his son believed in God and was a good Muslim, despite his difficulty with this public display. Especially when it came to his own family, he most often praised their pure intentions and inner goodness rather than their outward self-presentation.

Nevertheless, throughout my stay in Fars-Abad, and with the important exceptions of bread from a trusted local baker and a few items made by the Factory, very few store-bought, factory-made products met Nushin's standards for the "right" foods at *sofreh*. She only very reluctantly accepted jars of jam, boxed milk, butter, and cheese, and she frequently criticized these products, both for their lack of taste and nutrition and for their lack of power and purity. Whenever homemade, local varieties were available, she strategically placed them on the *sofreh* for her family's nourishment (e.g., local walnuts or almonds picked from the family gardens, local fruit such as grapes, or milk products from the nearby settled nomads). According to Nushin and her Tehrani sister-in-law, Parvin, as well as many other members of their extended family, these kinds of food were better for their children's spiritual health than store-bought, packaged products. Yet despite their mothers' efforts, their teenage children sometimes eagerly ate sandwiches, ice cream, and treats, a subject I return to later.

Preparing "Right," Balanced Foods with Pure Intention

The most critical requirement for the *sofreh*, however, is that a pure and pious wife or mother cooks it at home with pure intention for her family.[27] Food affects kin not only because of its ingredients, but also because of the way it has been prepared, cooked, and served. A war veteran friend of Ahmad explained: "We prefer home-cooked foods to fast foods such as pizza or sandwiches. Fast foods are foreign style, and they are not healthy. But most important is that they are not cooked in the right way with pure intention at home."[28]

In Iran, "pure intention" (*kholus-e niyyat*) is the will or resolve to act with mindfulness of God from the pure internal core (*bāten* or *del*). It is through intention that the inner core may be brought out or corrupted, for instance, through certain kinds of intentional cooking and feeding. Ahmad's friend Mr. Hosseini had explained the significance of pure intention to us on his visit to the family home: "Religion must be profound (*'amiq*). It must be innate (*fetri*) and internal (*darun*)." Most importantly, however, "It must be goal driven and have intention." When I asked him what this meant, he replied, "If you simply say or do something, it means nothing. But if you do something because you love Allah, this is intention. Religion is the path that Allah has spoken."

Similarly, my hosts, their neighbors, their relatives, and their friends often spoke of this direct correspondence between intention and the embodiment of spiritual purity and religiosity. Acts as diverse as praying, fasting, ablutions, or cooking, they said, mean nothing without intention that incorporates love and assent to the will of Allah. One cool night during Ramadan, Goli-Mehrebun, Nushin's mother, who had lived her whole life in Fars-Abad, explained this concept by reiterating a proverb passed down to her through generations: "Don't be entangled in evening prayers, and don't put water in milk" (*Na namāz-e shab gir kon, na āb tu-ye shir kon*). In other words, prayer and fasting are useless without sincerity. We should not cheat ourselves or others by watering down milk. She added, "We have to change our behavior toward others."

Here, pure intention should be firmly located in the inner self: "the heart, the soul, and the stomach" (Torab 1996, 244). Those of pure intention speak from within (e.g., "he spoke from his inside"). Moreover, the verb "to intend" (*niyyat kardan*) may be more accurately translated as "to specify one's intention in one's heart." As many pious women I spoke with in Fars-Abad insisted: "If you truly pray to Allah from your interior self, your prayer will be received." This contrasts explicitly with both acts that are unintended (e.g., accidental good deeds or acts completed without awareness of Allah) and those that are ill intended (e.g., sins such as gossiping or purposefully trying to inflict harm on another), both of which stem from the more corruptible "outer self" (*zāher*). In contrast, pure and moral acts stem from deep within a person, from the inside, a heart and soul that is above all else in tune with love of and for Allah.

My hosts saw the combination of pure intention and action, despite its virtue, as a rare phenomenon, occurring at its deepest level only occasionally in a regular person's life. Only a select few had overcome this difficulty in all acts of daily life. Ahmad, for instance, cited famous poets such as Hafez or Rumi as people who had acted with pure intention in their lives and writings. He also cited the late Ayatollah Khomeini, "the father of the Revolution," as the epitome of pure intent and action.

Pure intention is thus also critical to food preparation, cooking, and eating and is central to creating and spreading blessing in the home. These (pure) intentions are linked to the mother's piety and mindfulness of God, and they have the power to shape the family. As Nushin's cousin explained, they "have a positive effect" on kin, imbuing the family with "shared blessing and contentment."

Notably, the emphasis placed on home cooking and pure intention is not limited to Fars-Abad and its surrounding towns, nor is it limited to members of the Basij or other supporters of the state.[29] As a pious grandmother informed me when I visited her home in Qazvin, Iran, a city north of Tehran: "If a person's cooking is not good, they are not good. A person whose cooking is really good, they say that they are very good." She continued, highlighting the relationship between the quality of the cook and the food: "Food is worthless if it is not made with love and pure intention."[30] However, what was unique about my hosts was the way they explicitly linked the pure intention of the mother and her cooking not only to the welfare of the family but also to the need to protect the family—and particularly their teenage children—against outside societal corruption, a theme that is consistently promoted by the state and by the Basij organization itself (Golkar 2015).

There are myriad ways in which Nushin and other women I met in Fars-Abad imbued the *sofreh* with their pure intentions for their families. Perhaps the most obvious method was cooking "with mindfulness of God and the family of the Prophet": for example, coordinating cooking with obligatory (and purifying) daily prayers when possible and avoiding gossip while cooking. Here, acts such as washing, dicing, stirring, heating, and cooling—as acts that alter food—were performed with the intention of creating blessings for the family, as well as health and wellness. These acts transformed not only the texture, shape, and taste of food, but also its physio-sacred quality.

Another way of caring for family was by ensuring that food at the *sofreh* was of excellent quality and consistency, a matter that had an impact not only on the tastiness of food but also on its virtue. At the *sofreh*, food items—such as soup, rice, or fruit drinks—were most positively evaluated when the wife/mother had "prepared them to the appropriate thickness/good quality" or *be qavām āmadan* (Khajeh and Ho-Abdullah 2012, 79). However, the evaluation of whether something had attained an appropriate state of thickness and good quality was not merely a physical concern. In both Persian and Arabic, *qavām* also implies rightness and virtue. Indeed, for Nushin and many others I spoke with in Fars-Abad, rightly cooked food and the formation of moral or spiritual virtue were linked, a manifestation of a mother's pure intention. Cooking that could best shape kin was that which had reached an "ideal form" (*nemuneh*). This was evaluated both by the perceived qualities of thickness, order, and consistency of the final product and by its effect on consumers.

This meant, for instance, that the rice should be perfectly puffed and separated; that the soup should be perfectly mixed together and neither too underdone or overdone; and that sugar and fruit syrup—measured in just the right amounts—should be fully dissolved into the cool summer-day beverage. When such food had reached this state, it was described as beautiful and tasty. The wife was praised for her "skilled hand at cooking" (*dast-e pokht-ash āli ast*). People said that such food "sticks better" to the body and that it positively affects the "mental/spiritual state of a person" (*hāl mideh*). In Persian, the term *hāl* conveys a sense of natural condition or predisposition of the body. For example, someone might say "my health is not good" (*hāl-am khub nist*). *Hāl* also conveys a more generalized state or condition—that is, the state of a family situation, politics, or economics. It can also refer to the body's humoral health or balance.

HUMORAL BALANCE

Many of the women I met in Fars-Abad and Tehran emphasized the need to instill in family members the appropriate balance of "coldness and hotness" (*sardi/garmi*), a system of humoral balance that has its origins in

Galen and was later developed by the Persian polymath Avicenna, among others. This balance of "hot" and "cold" food corresponds with and is constitutive of a person's natural predisposition or temperament (*tab'*) (Loeffler 2008). For Nushin and Parvin, however, the balance of hot and cold foods was more than a humoral issue of balance and temperament; it was a moral concern. Certain foods, they said, may bring contentment and happiness, while others may lead people to general upset, depression, or fighting, which is highly undesirable and sinful, especially if the fighting is occurring between parents and children. For example, whereas people said that saffron is good for the inner disposition, thought process, or nerves and brings happiness, food that is pickled or spicy is thought to make a person easily upset or to literally "make them boil." Other foods, however, are considered "cool," neither "hot" nor "cold."

This is important because the notion of a person in Iran is dynamically associated with three states of being—gas, liquid, and matter—whose combinations and mixing are greatly affected by having either "hot" or "cold" temperament (Shahshahani 2008). People are actively influenced by the consumption of either "hot or cold" or "wet or dry" foods (Loeffler 2008).[31] As such, certain people are known to have a particular temperamental disposition: one can be "cold" or "hot" in general, but one can also be "hot" in accordance to the life cycle. During pregnancy, women are "hot," but in old age they are "cold." Here, temperament is also a trait of a family as a whole. One might say that a certain family tends to be warm or that another family tends to be "cold." For the more elaborate lunch meal, in particular, it is the mother's responsibility to balance "hot and cold" ingredients as appropriate for her family.

Indeed, it was a key part of Nushin's daily practice to ensure that everyday meals were a balance of "hot and cold" fare. For instance, if lunch was composed of something "cold" such as cabbage and rice, Nushin would tell us not to worry because she had added pepper to balance it. If the lunch meal included a lot of "cold" potatoes, she might recommend countering it with "hot" crystalline sugar and tea afterward. Part of her "food work" (Carrington 2012) was thus the labor of considering and balancing the temperaments of her family against the cuisine she served, a task she carried out both in the kitchen and with reminders at the *sofreh* to her children about how much to eat of a given item and what to eat next.

Finally, preparing the right food at the *sofreh* with pure intention means ensuring its beauty and symmetry. When Nushin set the *sofreh*, for instance, she always attended to the symmetry and color of the dishes laid out for consumption, particularly the centrally featured silver tray of white or saffron rice. Moreover, she followed orderly arrangements of table setting so that each person had a personal plate, spoon, and fork, and she set a platter of food/meat/stew at convenient intervals along the dining spread. Here, the *sofreh* reflected and preserved halal and pure family relations.

At a typical meal, those who are family (e.g., brothers, sisters, fathers, and mothers) sit comfortably but hierarchically: the father/husband usually takes the place of honor farthest from the door, the mother sits closer to the kitchen for easy access, and the brothers and sisters sit so that the youngest brother can easily get up to answer the doorbell or phone. (In Iran, generally, people of high status "move" much less than those of lower status; Beeman 1986, 78–79.) The manner of leg placement while sitting further reflects these hierarchies and the accompanying emphasis on interfamily respect, an Islamic virtue. For more traditional families, those sitting at the *sofreh* kneel rather than sit cross-legged on the floor before respected male elders.[32]

To conclude, the *sofreh* represents a mother's power to constitute and protect her family on a daily basis. The *sofreh* is linked to blessing, to intimacy, and is the heart of the family. For my hosts, moreover, as a cohort that supports the Islamic Republic, the making of the *sofreh* is ethical, moral, and religious work, not unconnected to local politics and revolutionary values. Marked by its relative exclusivity, the lunch *sofreh* is characterized by the symmetry of its layout and the humoral balance of ingredients, the rightness of cooked fare, and the pure intention of the mother/wife. It is also consciously blessed: meat is sacrificed, and prayers to Allah are interwoven with eating and preparation. Similarly, products bought from outside the home are carefully evaluated for their lawfulness and purity as well as for the intentions, faith, and motivations of their sellers. While home-cooked, local, and religiously permissible foods are pure and trusted, foods cooked at restaurants, "foreign" foods, and foods made with religiously impermissible ingredients have the potential to corrupt the family's bodies and souls. Therefore, vigilance is imperative in all aspects of food procurement, preparation, and feeding, and a significant moral concern surrounds the ability and intention of the cook (most often the mother) to feed spiritually nourishing fare to family members. Here, for the most part, the *sofreh* is the mother's or wife's work, which includes a tedious and careful process of selecting, heating, stirring, dicing, and mixing foods. The lunch *sofreh*, in particular, (re)constitutes the pure inner core of the household on a daily basis and distinguishes who is counted as moral kin. It is a complex orchestration of pure-intentioned cooking and feeding and a powerful means of infusing the bodies and souls of family members with blessing and developing pure and halal kinship.

A Counterpoint: Strangers in the Home

The idea that relationships can be constructed or destroyed through feeding is paradoxically also apparent in the nuanced back and forth by which strangers or acquaintances are invited into the home to share "salt," a metonym for food. For example, it is customary to practice politeness when a stranger or distant acquaintance passes by and invite the person into the home. The usual invitation is: "Please, come in and have lunch with us." It is then customary for the invitee to decline: "Thank you, but I am on my way." However, if the host sincerely wishes the other person to enter the home, he or she may insist: "Come in, really, our salt won't get you!" (*namak gir nemishi*). This expression is built on the convention that the sharing of food (salt) is an act of mutual trust that creates a bond between persons. As one middle-aged neighbor explained, the expression means: "Don't be afraid. We have eaten salt together before, and we can do so again" (*natars, qablan namak khordim bā ham*). Again, the invitee politely declines with the following ritualized expression: "No, we have (already) been nourished by your kindness" (*nah, mā namak parvardeh hastim*). As a neighbor interpreted: "When you say this, it means that we didn't have anything and you nourished us. It means that if we have good breeding or civility, it is because of your existence. It is because you gave us salt." This kind of polite self-lowering in Iranian speech interaction has been carefully addressed (see Beeman 2001). It is a means of navigating status and hierarchy. But it also reveals the implicit emphasis many Iranians place on mutual trust and commensality.

For my hosts in Fars-Abad, when two parties are willing to share salt, they signify a willingness to either begin or to continue a friendship. Such a relationship is positively referred to in the expression "You have become stuck in our salt" (*namak gir shodi*). In other words, "You have eaten with us and can no longer betray us." Sharing of food, they said, establishes a bond of mutual trust and commitment almost equal to that among immediate family members. Yet even a "salt friendship" is fragile. If the same visitor enters the home and creates a problem or betrays the hosts, one might exclaim: "But we had eaten bread and salt with you!" (*mā bā shomā nun o namak khordeh budim!*) or "You ate salt, but you broke the salt shaker!" (*namak khordi, namak dun ro shekasti!*). Both exclamations signify a betrayal of a relationship previously established and maintained through commensality. Such a betrayal is a most grievous sin and is directly associated with immoral character.

Although the idea of the "salt friendship" is not explicitly about understandings of family, it reveals how commensality, trust, and intimacy interrelate.[33] Sharing food in everyday contexts creates a moral and sacred bond of trust and friendship. I now explore fasting as a means of protecting and maintaining the right kind of pure and halal family ties.

FASTING AND FAMILY PROTECTION

During my fieldwork, the holy month of Ramadan occurred in August. It was a difficult time for the fast. The days were long and hot, and the nights were short. The household routine shifted dramatically. Nushin woke up before dawn every morning to pray and cook a full, fresh meal. She woke Maryam and me from our slumber and ushered us downstairs to sit at the *sofreh*. We sat quietly, waiting for Ahmad to finish his predawn prayers. He prayed again before eating, as was his custom: "In the Name of God, Most Gracious, Most Merciful." I remember the smell of stewed lamb and lentil rice at 4:30 a.m. This was the time to eat. There would be little to no cooking or food in the house until after dark.

In Fars-Abad, fasting (*sawm* in Arabic or *ruzeh* in Persian), especially fasting during Ramadan, inverts the daily pattern by which the family is spiritually and physically nourished. Fasting entails abstinence from food, drink, sexual intercourse, and smoking from sunrise to after sunset. As such, much of regular home life, and in particular processes of cooking and feeding, are reversed. The central lunch meal is made invisible and is shifted to the darkness of the predawn meal.

Our sleeping patterns shifted dramatically, too. We remained awake late into the night, often picnicking as late as 10:00 p.m. in the town park, and those of us who were not tending the wheat fields (like Ahmad) or attending school (like Reza and Ali) slept much of the day. There was also more ritual activity. For instance, thousands of Fars-Abadis attended the commemorative Night of Power (Shab-e Qadr in Persian or Laylat Al-Qadr in Arabic), the night when the first verses of the Qur'an were revealed to the Prophet by the Angel Gabriel, in the town *hosaynieh*, an event I explore in more detail in chapter 4. We found out later that it was on the Night of Power that Ehsan had died. In our mourning, we did not celebrate the Eid al-Fitr, or the "Festival of the Breaking of the Fast," on the last night of the holy month. Somehow, though, Ahmad, his daughter Maryam, and his son Ali had all vigilantly kept the fast. They had done so despite Ehsan's passing and despite the heat.[34]

Against this backdrop, and the constant reminder of Ehsan's death, my hosts and other Basijis I interviewed in Iran saw fasting as a form not only of spiritual refinement, as it is most often described, but also as a form of family protection. In chapter 4 I explore how fasting is also a matter of public morality in the wider context of the Islamic Republic.

Fasting, Ramadan, and Islam

Fasting is a major part of both Sunni and Shi'i jurisprudence and is mentioned several times in the Qur'an. It can alternately provide a means of supplication to the will of God, worship of divinity, purification, or penitence for transgressions against particular Qur'anic codes. Fasting is also a way to mourn the deceased, and it is obligatory for all Muslims during the month of Ramadan (Qur'an S:183 and S:187).

For (Shi'i) Muslims, the significance of Ramadan derives from its link to the Qur'an and the Prophet. The first revelations came to the Prophet via the Angel Gabriel on the specific night(s) known as the Nights of Power (see the Qur'an verse "al-Qadr" [S:97]). Fasting during Ramadan, and prayer during the Nights of Power, are thought to allow exceptional proximity to God and God's blessings, and therefore pious Iranians variously call the month the "blessed month," the "month of compassion," the "month of Allah," and "month of worship." While those who are able to fast are lucky and blessed, fasting is completely forbidden for people who are sick and women who are menstruating, breastfeeding, or experiencing postpartum bleeding. Abstinence from food, drink, sex, and smoking is paralleled by abstinence from making false statements to Allah, the Prophet, and the Imams and from other sinful behavior such as backbiting or slander.

According to the late Khomeini (2003, 22), moreover, whose sentiments were often expressed by my hosts, "the meaning of fasting is not merely refraining from eating and drinking; one must keep oneself from sin. In this noble month, in which you have been invited to the divine banquet, if you do not gain insight about God the Almighty nor insight into yourself, it means that you have not properly participated in the feast of Allah." Here, fasting means not only refraining from food and drink but also replacing such worldly appetites with "God's divine banquet": a spiritual banquet that, if properly "consumed," should lead to self-refinement and proximity to God. Spiritual foods replace tangible food substances, and fasting brings spiritual insight to the fore, sublimating the body and its passions (*nafs, tahzib-e nafs*) (Torab 2007, 226). When I asked two Basiji Tehrani seminar students to explain this concept, they argued that the objective of fasting is twofold: holding back from sin and bodily desires or appetites and lifting up toward the divine spirit. Similarly, in Fars-Abad, our neighbor explained: "By holding back the inner passions, self-perception deepens and the spirit awakens." The focus of fasting extends beyond the subjugation of the bodily passions to the "refinement of the soul" (*takziyeh-ye ruh*).

In addition, those keeping the fast are prohibited from being in a state of "major ritual impurity" (*janābah* in Arabic and *jenābat* in Persian) during the hours of fasting. According to Ahmad, for instance, even unintentionally being in such a state during Ramadan invalidates the fast (see also Khomeini 2003, 282). Polite conventions also surround fasting. In particular, it is incumbent upon nonfasters to refrain from eating in the presence of those who are observing the fast. Anyone who does so is derisively called a *ruzeh khor*, a term that disparages the impolite person who eats in front of someone keeping the fast.

In the home of my hosts this meant that food consumption and activity was surreptitious and restricted to the kitchen area during daylight hours. It also meant that people attended more closely to idle chitchat, reminding fasters and nonfasters alike not to gossip or curse. In addition, people took even greater care to avoid loud voices, anger, or other tensions between family members. Ramadan intensified the will to maintain and create a harmonious and pure household.

Scholars of the Middle East and Islam have explored Ramadan as a site for understanding how socially prescribed forms of behavior, such as fasting, constitute the conditions for the emergence of the self (whether as pious, modest, or some other) (Mahmood 2005; Schielke 2009). Schielke (2009), who conducted a study of young Muslim men in northern Egypt, describes the month as a time of "exceptional morality" but criticizes the idea that acts such as fasting should be understood as a perfectionist project of self-discipline. Rather, he explores the contradictory views and experiences of Muslim youth during the fast. Schielke further notes that the exceptional moralism of Ramadan—when religious obligations and prayers "must be fulfilled"—necessarily contrasts implicitly with what he describes as the more flexible nature of norms and ethics for the rest of the year (2009, 28).[35]

Fasting in Fars-Abad is, to some degree, a project of self-discipline, but it is also complex and contradictory in the manner described by Schielke. Not all of my Basiji hosts, neighbors, or friends were able to fast, and not all who were able to did so for the right reasons. As Nushin's brother explained, "Most people [here in Fars-Abad] fast because they fear hell and because it is written in the Qur'an. But some people, a very few, fast because they want to be close to God." He said that he valued this second reason more.

But even when fasting did occur for the right reasons, its object was not limited to self-refinement or "gaining proximity and connection to God" (*qorbat va rābeteh bā khodā*). Rather, acts of fasting, praying, cooking, and alms paying associated with Ramadan were also directed, in some manner, toward blessing, purifying, and protecting the immediate family who live together and its relationships. Fasting was a means of accruing religious merit and blessing, not only for the self but also for the household and family.[36]

Fasting and Family

The two meals that surround the fast during Ramadan, the predawn meal (*sahari*), and the evening meal that "opens" the fast (*eftāri*), are a marked time for imbuing the family with blessing. The pre-fast breakfast is for close family members, specifically those who are an active part of the daily household. Often it consists of a large breakfast, including a possible leftover meal, flat bread, feta cheese, eggs, or bread and jam served with tea. Dates are always served and are a source of blessing. The *sahari* meal on the first day of 2010 Ramadan in Fars-Abad was a lamb and lentil stew served with rice. The family rose, bleary eyed, at four in the morning. By the time I arose, Nushin had laid out the *sofreh*, and I helped her bring cutlery and dishes from the kitchen. When everything was ready, we waited for Ahmad to finish his predawn prayer and join us. Even those in the family who were not fasting participated in this ritual rising.

Similarly, on most days of Ramadan all immediate family and often extended family, too, share the Iftar meal, which breaks the fast. As Nushin's sister-in-law told me as we walked around the park one Ramadan evening: "Even if you are sick and do not have the luck of fasting during the month of God, you still can't help but be drawn to the *sofreh* of Iftar. All of the family 'gathers around' (*dor-e ham*) the *sofreh* and with a short prayer of Iftar, with a few dates and a sip of hot water, those that have fasted sit and feast." Typical Iftar foods include tea, bread, cheese, fresh herbs from the garden, dates, *halvā*, and specialty sweets. Another common Iftar food is *zulbiā* and *bāmieh*, a sweet made of starch, yogurt, sugar, oil, and rosewater that is purchased from confectionary stores. At the family *sofreh*, hot water, dates, fresh bread, and cheese were served before a more proper meal but not before the fast was "opened" through prayer.

Many pious Muslims such as Ahmad begin meals, irrespective of fasting, with the first line of the Qur'an: "In the name of God, the Merciful and the Compassionate." During the month of Ramadan, this phrase of devotion takes on special significance as a device for breaking the fast and is the precursor to prayers said before the meal. Indeed, people in Fars-Abad say that those who fast with pure intention will be granted three prayers at the moment of Iftar. For Ahmad these prayers were always for the protection and care of his family. On the first day of Ramadan, he broke the fast and said the following prayer: "Oh God, forgive our sins and help us" (*khodā-yā, gonahān-e mā bebakhsh va be mā komak kon*). Although many who sat around the *sofreh* had not fasted with him, he employed the "we" pronoun, quietly listing the names of his family members: "Help Maryam, help Reza, help Ali, help Nushin." In Tehran, several Basiji seminary students confirmed the family orientation of Ramadan prayers. One woman explained, "I do it for my children." She and others described a variety of prayers to mark the breaking of the fast, such as the reading of Qur'anic verse, the Surah Al-Qadr, which speaks of the revealing of the Qur'an on the Night of Power. Another devotional prayer (in Arabic), recommended by Imam Sadeq and entitled "al-homa rab-e al-nur al-azim," is frequently read during Ramadan. They said that for those who say this prayer, God "forgives them their sins," "takes away sadness," and helps the supplicant "arrive at his destination." Yet regardless of the prayer spoken at Iftar, the self is not the only subject of potential transformation or spiritual protection; prayers are frequently turned outward to family members.

The giving of *fetriyeh* (also called *zakat al-fitr* in Arabic) makes this concept visible. *Fetriyeh* denotes alms (*zakat*) given specifically at the Festival of Fetr (*eid-e fetr*) at the end of Ramadan. According to my hosts, the Islamic Republic high school textbooks, laymen, and ulama all agree that what they call the "bread-provider" (*nun-āvar*) or head of household must give alms "for each person who eats food in the house." These people are called the "bread-eaters." The rule thus has the secondary effect of distinguishing all who live in the house from all who do not live in the house. For example, as Nushin's daughter explained, Ahmad would give a *fetriyeh* for me this year as I was a "bread-eater" in his house, which he did. She elaborated: "My father gives *fetriyeh* for us. He does not have to give it for himself." The person, the "bread-provider," who gives the alms of *fetr* "must be near God." In contrast, Ahmad did not give one for his eldest daughter Fati, who lived just down the street, "because she eats with her husband." The money is collected at the Festival of Fetriyeh and is given to the poor.

The giving of *fetriyeh* reveals the implicit structure of the household and maps who eats together, those who provide food (per the distinction between bread-providers and bread-eaters), and those who are not active members of the household. In doing so, it reveals the spiritual connection among the family members who live together and sit side by side at the *sofreh*. The principle guides the "bread-provider" (*nun-āvar*) to ensure the spiritual well-being of the family as a whole, again drawing a clear association between "those who eat together" and the family who share kindred spirit.[37]

There are thus key convergences between fasting in Iran and the creation of kindred spirit in the household. Not only do the ceremonial meals of *eftār*, *sahar*, and the *eid-e fetr* demarcate a ceremonial *sofreh* shared by family and intimates, but fasting is frequently conducted for the spiritual well-being of other family members.

"COOKING VOTIVE SOUP IS AN ACT OF PRAYER": BLESSING THE FAMILY THROUGH VOW MAKING AND FOOD CHARITY

Parvin often prayed for her family. She prayed that her daughter would find an appropriate fiancé. She prayed that her eldest son's business would be successful and that she would be able to find the money for her youngest son's university degree. She prayed that she could move to a bigger house that would better accommodate her children. And she prayed for the health of her husband, a taxi driver who was suffering from the lingering effects of mustard gas and nerve agents from his service during the Iran-Iraq War.

All of these prayers were coordinated with the distribution of blessed votive foods, foods that are cooked and shared as part of the fulfillment of a vow to one of the twelve Shi'i Imams. She provided votive soup or *āsh* to neighbors weekly on Saturday, as she believed it was auspicious.[38] She distributed votive candies whenever she visited her mother's and father's grave in Tehran. And she paid the equivalent of over $200 for the breakfast of other women at a prayer gathering in her community "so that her daughter would find an *appropriate* fiancé." This latter affair was particularly important. Her daughter's suitor needed to come from a "good" and "moral" family, a family that would meet her standards. And Parvin was proactive. At one point, she arranged to give the votive soup directly to the mother of a prospective groom! A strong sign of interest. When I asked about this, she laughed and explained, "I myself cook votive food (make vows) for the health of my children. Food is full of blessing. On the night of

Imam Husayn, I cook 'saffron sweet rice pudding' (*sholeh zard*). I believe in this very strongly."

Women's votive offerings for family prosperity, health, purity, and blessing were a constant part of social life in Fars-Abad and among my hosts' relatives in Shiraz and Tehran. Carefully coordinated with life-cycle events (weddings, funerals etc.), the Islamic calendar (the birth days and death days of the Twelve Imams), and pilgrimages to the shrines of Shi'i saints, these offerings were significant for creating, shaping, or otherwise protecting kin. In Iran, food that has been blessed by those who cook it, eat it, stir it, or come into contact with it is more nourishing both to body and soul than any other type of food. Indeed, a whole category of religious prayer in Iran centers on the creation and distribution of votive food to create blessing and fulfill personal vows to God or the Shi'i Imams. It is called "vow making" (*nazr kardan*).

While the first part of this chapter described everyday *sofreh*s at home and processes of fasting, I now turn to the subject of marked ritual vow making, in which blessed foods are distributed outward for the benefit of both the family and those receiving the blessed fare. As Sered has written in her analysis of Middle Eastern Jewish women's charitable deeds, "a major aim of such ritual is to involve God in networks of interpersonal and interdependent relationships" (1988, 131). In Iran, women similarly attest both to the proximity to God gained through votive feeding and to the effectiveness of such feeding for the welfare of their families. They see their acts of ritual feeding as reciprocal: votive food is provided to others to care for all human beings, and critically, it is provided so that God will grant favors for their own kin.

I here briefly relate three diverse examples of votive offerings that are strategically employed to protect family members from childhood to beyond death. In these contexts, family members, usually women, distribute blessing by providing a votive *sofreh* in their homes or by performing the labor of cooking ritual foods such as *halvā* (a sweet wheat paste), labor that they see as a sacrifice of their effort and wealth. Each votive offering described here highlights the "relationship oriented religiosity" of Iranian women: namely, the centrality of interpersonal relationships in their vow making (Sered 1988, 131). In the examples provided, women perform and sacralize feeding work to provide an immediate means of protecting kin from physical or spiritual injury/pain, to ensure and initiate a happy and prosperous marriage, or for healing family discord and strife, both of which are immoral. These efforts crosscut many other ritual acts of caring for kin, including prayer and pilgrimage.

The Votive Sofreh

The most obvious example of votive feeding is the votive *sofreh*. This type of meal preparation is often the consequence of having made a vow to an Imam or a descendant of an Imam to intercede with God for a favor. In return, the supplicant cooks a "votive offering" (*nazri*) that has been specified in advance (Torab 2007, 118). For example, a vow maker might sponsor three meals, two of which must be held before the fulfillment of the vow, while the last is held in abeyance until after the request is granted (Torab 2007, 120). While such votive *sofreh*s are normally carried out and participated in by women, men often help sponsor them and ask their wives or sisters to make a votive offering to a saint on their behalf. *Sofreh*s are often offered to female Shiʿi saints, who are felt to be particularly receptive. These include Bibi Seshambe, who was born and died on a Tuesday, and Bibi Nur and Bibi Hur, who are said to be two of the Prophet's daughters. Another common *sofreh* is held for Abu'l Faz'l, son of Imam Hassan and one of the martyrs at the Battle of Karbala. In addition, it is often said that adult males cannot attend the votive *sofreh* ceremony or partake of the food because misfortune will befall them (Shirazi 2005; Jamzadeh and Mills 1986).[39]

Votive *sofreh*s are cooked for key moments in the life cycle, like birth and death, and common ingredients, such as rosewater and saffron, are associated with regeneration. Another common offering, a germinating wheat dish called *samanu*, indexes the craving of Fatemeh, the Prophet's daughter, during pregnancy, and the swelling of the pregnant womb more generally. Notably, votive *sofreh*s are controversial. They are tolerated by religious authorities but are often seen as "superstition" rather than "true religion." This was not a concern for the Basiji women I met in Fars-Abad or Tehran. They saw the *sofreh* as a means of incorporating blessing into the body and of transformation. Reasons for giving votive *sofreh*s included fertility, moving to a bigger house where the children will be more comfortable, ensuring the successful surgery of a sick daughter, getting accepted into university, and helping a daughter find a husband. In most, but not all, of these examples, *sofreh*s were "thrown" for the physio-sacred health of kin.

Votive Soup for Teething

In Fars-Abad, when a child begins to teethe, his or her mother cooks a large vat of *āsh*, a soup made of vegetables, beans, and wheat noodles and elaborately decorated with mint, fried onions, and *kashk*, which is similar to sour cream.[40] Hamideh, the wife of one of Ahmad's nephews and the daughter of a Basseri nomad, for example, cooked *āsh* for her eight-month-old baby, Arezou, who had recently gotten her first tooth. She explained that the soup was a prayer for her daughter's other teeth

Figure 8. Women praying and stirring votive soup for teething children, Fars-Abad, Iran

Figure 9. Women sharing votive soup, Fars-Abad, Iran

to come in easily. Members of her husband's family, who lived next door and shared a courtyard with her, helped her cook the soup in a large pot in the courtyard over a gas flame. She began by adding the water with the greens, then the beans, and finally, a special kind of noodle called *reshteh*. When the soup had cooked, she evenly poured it into small plastic containers to give to neighbors and extended kin. Once portioned, she decorated it with a traditional Iranian cheese, fried onions, and fried mint leaves. I walked with her as she distributed the soup to everyone in her family's alley as well as to neighbors and relatives of her husband living around the corner. Only after making a round of the neighborhood did we eat some of the soup ourselves. Hamideh explained that she did not expect anything in return from her neighbors. It was charity (*kheyrāt*), she said. She did, however, hope that her prayers would be answered.

Fati, Nushin and Ahmad's eldest daughter, also performed this ceremony when her baby first showed signs of teething. She, her mother, and her matrilateral aunts cooked the votive soup in the garden across from Nushin and Ahmad's home over an open fire. They invited some forty women, along with a handful of husbands and children. Invitees were extended kin: grandparents, aunts, uncles, cousins, in-laws, and so on. The women stirred the forty-liter pot of soup clockwise, reading prayers.

As they cooked, I helped my hosts by spreading the *sofreh* on the ground under a walnut tree so that people could eat comfortably. Unlike at traditional votive *sofreh*s, men are allowed to take part in these gatherings. The men and women sat about fifteen feet apart on two adjacent patches on the grass. I also videotaped the event, at Fati's request. Younger women such as Fati's sister helped distribute the food, bowls, and spoons to the guests, standing barefoot on the spread *sofreh* while the baby slept in one corner. Nushin's mother, the family matriarch, sat cross-legged on one corner of the *sofreh* in a flowered chador and adamantly saw to it that everyone received a full serving of soup.

For Fati, the votive tooth soup had a clear purpose: to protect her baby from the pain of teething and from other future spiritual and physical calamity or illness. It was a bulwark against the negative effects of the evil eye and ill-intentioned harm from those outside her immediate kin whom she did not trust. In addition, it was an effort to create a protective relationship between her family and God by making a vow to one of the Twelve Imams or their descendants (Betteridge 1985). Fati believed in this very strongly. But the event had another, less explicit purpose as well. It gave her extended kin and neighbors the impression that she was taking care of her daughter and that she had supportive family members helping her. This appearance protected not only her daughter but also her standing as a good mother in the community (Wellman 2017a).

Other Food Practices

Teething soup, however, is only one type of votive fare cooked and distributed for the benefit of the family. Women cooked *āsh* in many other contexts to spread blessing or give thanks to God. For example Sepideh, the wife of Nushin's brother, made *āsh* on one occasion to thank God for protecting her son, who had survived a near fatal car accident relatively unscathed. She explained: "God took mercy on him" (*khodā rahm kard behesh*).[41] As Nasrin, Nushin's sister, and I helped her combine the ingredients in the walled garage, Sepideh explained: "We stir the *āsh* clockwise not because it will cook better, but because it is a prayer."

In Fars-Abad, moreover, women often bring votive food to the town's graveyard every Thursday. They arrive at dusk with their immediate families to pay their respects to the dead and begin distributing little candies, sweets, or pastries to other visitors. This practice is called *pāksh kardan* and extends beyond kin to acquaintances, extended kin, and strangers visiting the graveyard. The intention is that those who receive a sweet will reciprocate by reading the first verse of the Qur'an, Al-Fātihah, for the soul of the sweet-giver's deceased relative and share condolences, saying, "May God have mercy on him/her." On almost every weekly visit to the graveyard, I would join Nushin's daughter, Maryam, or one of her sons in this practice, giving sweets away around the cemetery. The teenage children carefully attended to the graves of their grandparents, tapping the stone surface of the tombs and reading Al-Fātihah so that, as one of Ahmad's nieces told me, "their soul will come up, and they will understand that we came." Such prayers, they say, will help the kinsman enter heaven when the Day of Judgment arrives. In addition to buying pastries and candies from local shops, many people cook and distribute *halvā* (a sweet wheat paste made from browned flour and butter, rose water, sugar, and saffron). As one mother explained in an interview, "We cook it because of the dead, because it has a scent—the scent of flower water and saffron. We bring it outside to the graveyard so that the dead (our ancestors) become happy. It is also strong. This is because it is wheat flour, and also because it has oil."

Finally, the "Aqiqeh Prayer" provides a clear example of votive offering for the blessing of the family. This well-known prayer, which is specifically "for the blessing of children" (*be hājat-e farzand*), is prescribed in the key Shi'i text, the Mafatih, and was described to me by interlocutors both in Tehran and Fars-Abad. In Tehran, Basiji Islamic law student acquaintances described the prayer as "divine insurance for the baby" and explained that most people kill a male sheep for a boy and a female sheep for a girl on the seventh day after birth. One woman related: "We ask Allah to accept the blood of the sheep in order to protect our child. The blood of the sheep protects the bones and the meat of the sheep protects the flesh of the child." They said that they then invite relations, guests, and/or the poor to share the meat. In Tehran, some also provide meat to the doctor who oversaw the child's birth or pay an organization to sacrifice a sheep on their behalf. In contrast, people in Fars-Abad said that the sheep's gender is not important. They emphasize the slaughter of an *unblemished* and *pure* lamb in front of the house. There, they wash the sheep and its meat completely, cutting it into small pieces. They then make a "meat soup" (*āb-gusht*), which they distribute to extended family, neighbors, or the poor. Importantly, they said, the parents should not consume even one drop of the soup. At the same time, they hold that no part of the animal or soup can be wasted. When the main ceremony is complete, the parents bury the bones of the lamb in the backyard, a blessing for the continual protection and health of children. The ritual is accompanied by protective supplications collectively decided upon as effective in preventing misfortune by the women participants.

In sum, the women who take part in votive rituals and food charities are very often seeking to protect, bless, and otherwise help their family members. They take part in this work in the context of their worries for their children's future and in the context of a society that they say is increasingly corrupt. Food piety is a bulwark against harm. It is a means of blessing and protecting family.

In contrast to these pure-intentioned food practices, ill-wishers and those with the right knowledge of Qur'anic number symbology (an esoteric way of reading the Qur'an that attends to its hidden, inner meanings) can engage in prayer-taking (*do'ā gereftan*) over food, often tea, to harm others. Here, the prayer "takers" share the detrimental food with those whom they wish to afflict, usually because of jealousy. The most dangerous foods are those made by people who know how to do this themselves or who have access to a seer, a kind of expert in mystical knowledge.

Notably, in the contemporary Islamic Republic, belief in prayer-taking is often classified with belief in sorcery and/or divination, which are regularly denounced by state media as anti-modern and antithetical to the project of creating a republic based on Islam (Doostdar 2018, 42). My hosts, as Basijis, recognized that their views on these matters were not always in direct alignment with this statist discourse and kept their beliefs private. However, they were not dissuaded. Ahmad, for instance, sometimes cited his support of certain ayatollahs and religious leaders who believed in mystical phenomena and had knowledge of the unseen. He often spoke, for instance, about Ayatollah Mohammad Taghi (Taqi) Bahjat Foumani (1913–2009), an Iranian Twelver Shi'a Marja', known for his work on ethics and mysticism. "When he [Ayatollah Bahjat] looked at a cemetery, he would see everything, including jins and spirits. He had a relationship with the Imam Mahdi (final Imam). He was humble and simple and taught at the religious school in Qom. He never put aside the *ziārat-e 'āshura'*." On another occasion Ahmad continued, "Ayatollah Bahjat saw present, past, and future. He loved prostrating to God as a child loves the skirt of his mother.... And, he was so pure and his teachings were so pure that those [who] followed him have fastened their lips and spoken very little of what he taught."[42]

Despite statist concern with "superstitious" popular religious beliefs, religious scholars in Iran have themselves often debated the precise boundaries of "true religion" (Doostdar 2018). Ayatollah Bahjat was a student of the famous mystic Sayed Ali Qadhi Tabatabaei, and many of his students, such as Ayatollah Mutahhari, were formative in the creation of the Islamic Republic. In his early years, too, Ayatollah Khomeini had argued for simultaneously upholding the possibility of miracles while rejecting certain ideas as unreasonable or superstitious (Doostdar 2018, 44). He claimed that although they might eventually believe in a miracle, true religious scholars would be the last to do so (i.e., would need the most evidence and rational basis for acceptance of a miracle). Khomeini's logic would become a key basis for the Islamic Republic. My hosts, for their part, not only had differing ideas within their family about what solutions in prayer or action were acceptable, but were also aware of how their more metaphysical beliefs might be negatively viewed by others.

RETURNING TO THE BEGINNING: WHY THE *ZIĀRAT-E 'ĀSHURA'* "SAVED US"

I began with Ali's desire to rid his house of evil and purify his family from such ill-intentioned prayer with a *ziārat-e 'āshura'* prayer and the sharing of blessed saffron pudding. Very possibly, my hosts said, one or more of us had drunk tea or consumed food that had been prayed over for ill by a jealous aunt or neighbor. This had caused infighting, and the household needed to be purified.

Approximately one hundred women came to the house on the day of the prayer: maternal and paternal female family members. No female family member was excluded from the invitation; even some of those whom the family suspected of being the main cause of harm to the household were invited. The *ziārat-e 'āshura'*, my interlocutors explained, is "for cleansing sins," not only those of the host but also "the souls of others."

The prayer began with the strong voice of the female prayer reciter. She sang the prayer's verses melodically through her microphone: a declaration of allegiance to the compassionate Imam Husayn, peace be upon him, and a rejection of his "hostile" enemies, those who took his life at the Battle of Karbala. The guests, cloaked in black chadors, sobbed in solidarity with Imam Husayn's plight. Yet the power of the *ziārat-e 'āshura'* lay not only in its message of love and support for Imam Husayn and simultaneous rejection of his enemies. Rather, the ritual's ability to bless and purify occurred to a large extent through the parallel preparation and distribution of votive, blessed food.

The night before the *ziārat-e 'āshura'*, we stayed up late preparing. We tied one hundred packets of nuts and candies with red ribbons, symbolizing the spilled blood of Imam Husayn on the fields of Karbala. In addition, we washed and prepared several large crates of fruit. In the morning we began to cook the main part of our votive food offering: a huge vat of saffron sweet rice. As the rice pudding cooked, several of the women who were helping—a maternal aunt and some others—took turns stirring it clockwise while reciting prayers and verses of the Qur'an under their breath. They debated the ingredients as they stirred. Had we included enough saffron? Enough sugar? Sometimes we tasted the pudding straight from the ladle, assessing its readiness. As the guests arrived and during the prayer, the large vat of saffron rice stood steaming in the next room.

After the women's *ziārat-e 'āshura'*, the family agreed that the votive meal and prayer gathering had been successful. We had spread forgiveness of the sins of those suspected of ill intentions and had reconstituted our bodies—as well as the inner spaces of the house—with prayer and pure, blessed food. The aunt's attempt to cause discord had been averted, and her prayer-taking—the "dangerous" combination of food and prayer that was believed to be the source of our current household's difficulties—had been nullified. "The *ziārat-e 'āshura'* saved us," they said. At least temporarily, relationships between family members had been healed.

Sharing the "Right Food"

For those I interviewed in Fars-Abad and beyond, kinship is reckoned not only through bodily substances such as blood but also through the channeling of vital immaterial and sacred qualities between the bodies and souls of kin. It is thus both material and spiritual. It is configured, moreover, through ongoing pious and ritual acts such as food sharing. Here, kinship expands or contracts not only according to evaluations of shared blessing, trust, and rightness, but also through the *creation* and *maintenance* of these qualities in the bodies and souls of kin.

Food is a key means of this physio-sacred transformation, not only of the self but also of the family. Sharing and consuming the "right" food is central to the ongoing work of cultivating the "physio-sacred" family, its kindred spirit (*ruh*), and of delineating those who are closest to its intimate and trusted core. Food, together with prayer, (re)constitutes and demarcates (and can also destroy) the family as a whole. The inner space of the household and its thresholds are permeable and susceptible to outside harm (such as the evil eye).

For my Basiji hosts, the family and household are also susceptible to the failing morals of post-Revolution, postwar society and to Western "cultural invasion." In the context of dangers such as drug addiction, family fighting, and moral decay, food (and prayer) become vital ways of maintaining Islamic purity and harmonious and halal family relationships. After all, food can be wielded to incorporate the "right" qualities of purity and morality into kin, but it can also be a means of channeling harm, illness, and strife into the pure inner moral core of the family, embodied by the *sofreh*. In the following chapter I turn to the commemoration of martyrs in Iran to explore the literal flow of these kinship-related substances and pious acts between the intimate spaces of the home and the nation.

3 Regenerating the Islamic Republic

COMMEMORATING MARTYRS IN PROVINCIAL IRAN

The martyr is "the heart of history and the blood of each martyr is like a bell which awakens the thousands."

—Ayatollah Khomeini, *Iran Times* (Tehran),
November 16, 1982

It was only a week after the burial of the two unknown martyrs (*shahid*) from the Iran-Iraq border on top of the dusty hill in Fars-Abad when I asked my host brother, Reza, to escort me up the steep path to the park where they were interred. In minutes we had walked up the dirt path that started just outside our front door, and we entered the park that locals called the "water reservoir," or *āb-anbār-u*.[1] Reza, usually quick to joke and smile, was serious as we entered the almost empty, manicured space where two women dressed in black chadors were walking around a man-made pond, the park's distinguishing feature. We followed the path taken by the commemorative procession we had attended a few days before, up the hill and to the right, ending at a rounded gravel circle on an outcrop that overlooked the town. This was the site of the unknown martyrs' burial, the fresh earth still visible.

A simple tent structure formed a canopy over the deceased: a banner of red, white, and green, the colors of the Iranian flag. Nearby, a few flowers that had been strewn on the earth lay wilted amid the lingering scent of rose water. "What memories I have in this place!" Reza exclaimed as we approached the gravesite. He took out his smartphone and showed me a pixelated video of a fire and some shadowy figures. "Last year, before you came," he continued, "we made a bonfire on this very spot for the Iranian New Year celebration of Chahār Shambeh Suri [Wednesday Light]. There was music and dancing. It was unbelievable."[2] But he also recognized that a substantial change had occurred at this site. "These martyrs sacrificed their lives for God and for Iran." He continued, "They are truly honorable. They are great, greater than you or I. This is now a place of respect."[3] Still standing next to the graves, Reza talked about his own desire to do important things and be taken seriously in the world. As we left, we said a prayer for the dead, for the young unknown war heroes and their sacrifice.

Before the arrival of the unknown martyrs from the border of Iran and Iraq, the town park on the hill had been unambiguously a site of festivity, picnics, and even small rebellions of hookah smoking and gossip. Sometimes a little shop sold tickets for a ride on a plastic swan, which could be steered and paddled about the shallow water. Nearby, a bright orange, metal playground and exercise unit, reminiscent of hundreds of such sets in Iran's parks, drew the attention of children, teenagers, and exercisers. On summer nights, the entire family, including uncles, aunts, and cousins, had often hiked up the same short, steep path or around on the vehicle route to sit on raised squares of cement or in the irrigated grass with picnic accoutrements: tea, sugar, sweets, blankets, and fresh bread. Young men, as many as two or three aboard, regularly rode by motorcycle around the pond, Persian pop and hip-hop music blasting from their phones.

The interment of the martyrs' bodies had marked a new chapter in the history of the town. The Foundation for the Preservation of Heritage and the Distribution of Sacred Defense had delivered new overseers to town life: two unknown martyrs. Their very anonymity as brothers, fathers, and sacred defenders of Iran made them accessible as imagined or real relatives. For many Fars-Abadis I spoke with, the fresh gravesite on the dusty hill constituted a great honor. It exemplified not only the influence and connections of the local imam and other town officials but also the piety of the townspeople. The arrival of the martyrs, their sacred corpses, together with the associated official posters depicting spilled blood and wounded soldiers, had transformed the town park into a place of commemoration, memory, and mourning, conspicuously sacralizing the landscape. According to the Friday Imam, the town's religious leader, the burial site would now be a place of healing and pilgrimage, a place for resolving family difficulties through prayer. And although certain persons I spoke with sometimes criticized the increasing religiosity of the town—such as the recent addition of a men's Islamic seminary—these individuals were mostly silent on the subject of the martyrs; they seemed to understand that having the martyrs interred in the park might mean more government benefits and subsidies for the town, such as new roads, parks, and schools. They also knew that any criticism of the interment of martyrs would be interpreted locally as a critique of the Revolution or the Supreme Leader, Ayatollah Khamenei, a position rarely taken by locals due to the town's ever-present and watchful religious hierarchy, the Friday Imam(s).

Setting the Stage

The commemoration of war heroes and martyrs has long been a part of Iranian Shi'ism. The martyrdom of Imam Husayn, the grandson of the Prophet, at the Battle of Karbala in 680 CE is commemorated every year in the rites of Muharram and in vivid reenactments of his death and suffering called *ta'ziyeh* (Chelkowski 1979). Imam Husayn died on the tenth of Muharram on the sun-scorched plains of Karbala in present-day Iraq. According to Shi'i doctrine, he is "the king of martyrs," who sacrificed himself in the cause of faith for justice and truth. As a living history and one that is continuously reembodied and remembered, Husayn's sacrifice continues to provide a model of and for "true" (Shi'i) Islam (Al-e Ahmad [1962] 1997; Shari'ati 1981; Flaskerud 2012). His sacrifice is indicative not only of a discrete historical event but also of an ongoing sacred battle between good (the pure Husayn) and evil (Yazid) (Deeb 2009, 247; Beeman 2005, 71).

Leading up to Iran's 1979 Revolution, a powerful cohort of religious scholars and citizens explicitly drew on Muharram commemorations of Imam Husayn's sacrifice to help galvanize opposition to the "spiritually vacuous" policies of the Western-led shah and the ever-present threat of "Western cultural invasion" (*tahājom-e farhangi*) (e.g., globalization and imperialism). During the Iran-Iraq War, moreover, Ayatollah Khomeini argued that fighting in the war meant protecting the values of Imam Husayn in the Battle of Karbala. And today, the events of Karbala continue to remain a pivotal reference point for Iranian identity, a model of and for national, religious life.

This chapter examines the ongoing cultural salience of martyrs' blood and bodies for nation-making in postrevolutionary Iran. Fashioned through the pure-intentioned "act" ('*amal*) of martyrdom, the blood and bodies of martyrs are considered purifying, healing, and spiritually nourishing to the citizens, the land, and the territory of the Islamic Republic. On the one hand, martyrs' blood and bodies powerfully recall the martyrdom of Imam Husayn at the Battle of Karbala, the 1979 Revolution, and the Iran-Iraq War (Torab 2007). On the other hand, martyrs' blood and bodies are multiply evocative of the vital substances of kinship: their blood resembles, typifies, and is literally spilled from the veins of the (mostly) male fighters, sons and brothers who fought for the nation. Their blood further recalls the shared divine substance of the family of the Prophet Muhammad and his prophetic lineage. In postwar, post-2009 Green Movement Iran, blood and bodies of martyrs have renewed significance as a source of purification, blessing, and legitimization. They are being wielded by state officials, as well as by state supporters, to help constitute and naturalize relationships among citizens and among those same citizens, the land of Iran, and God.

The first part of this chapter approaches the matter of martyrs' blood in Iran by drawing from ethnographic research of a martyrs' commemoration and burial in Fars-Abad. I explore the continuing practice of exhuming the bodies of martyrs from the Iran-Iraq War battlefield and reburying them with great fanfare at sites across the national landscape. In these commemorations, officials and laymen display caskets containing the bodies of martyrs to local townspeople and inter them at strategic locations, often an overlook or town park. For state elites and members of the Basij such as Reza, the burial of martyrs' bodies at these sites dramatically shifts the landscape, transforming specific provincial places into "sacred," "purifying," and "healing" space.[4]

In the second part of this chapter I focus on blood itself as a potent material and metaphor in the postrevolutionary landscape. Emerging anthropological scholarship has explored blood's special quality as a substance, material, and metaphor and has highlighted blood's powerful involvement in concepts of life, death, nurturance and violence, connection and exclusion, and kinship and sacrifice (Carsten 2013; Copeman

2013; Feeley-Harnik 1981). As Laqueur (1999) argues, blood is "relentlessly material" even as it is overburdened by meaning. Perhaps most interesting, however, is blood's unique capacity as a material substance to participate in and flow between domains that are often presumed to be distinct in scholarly analysis (such as between kinship and nation or kinship and politics) (Carsten 2013). I here analyze this flow of blood between domains of kinship and state in the context of postrevolutionary Iran. In so doing, I aim to highlight the granular, material, and microprocessual aspects of (religious) nation-making.

Finally, this chapter draws on my research in Basiji households and at local events in Fars-Abad to understand how and why Basijis, in particular, are participating in the Islamic Republic's ritual statecraft.

HISTORICAL CONTEXT: THE IRAN-IRAQ WAR

The commemoration of martyrs and war heroes has long been part of Iran's cultural landscape, both in Muharram ceremonies and in reenactments of the Battle of Karbala. These practices were intensified and increasingly politicized during and immediately after the Islamic Revolution and the Iran-Iraq War. On September 22, 1980, Iraq attacked Iran, leaving approximately 220,000 dead and 400,000 wounded (Ehsani 2017).[5] Among those fighting were several members of my extended host family, including my host father, Ahmad, and his younger brother Mahmud, a taxi driver now living in Tehran who suffered from a chemical warfare–related lung condition. Many of my hosts' cousins and in-laws, now living in both Fars-Abad and in Tehran, also fought in the war.

While historians and political scientists argue that geopolitical and territorial issues were the original causes of the war, particularly the boundaries of the Arvand River, the focus of the war for Iranians gradually shifted from a fight over territory to one of sacred defense (Donovan 2011; King 2007). A famous billboard quoting Khomeini, for example, proclaimed: "Our war is an ideological war which doesn't recognize any geographical or frontier limitations." Khomeini and other influential members of the Islamic regime argued that fighting in the war meant protecting the values (*arzesh-hā*) and beliefs (*bāvar-hā*) of Imam Husayn in the Battle of Karbala. They positioned the conflict as a struggle between the oppressed and outside, Western-led corrupt oppressors. In daily conversation, my interlocutors, particularly those who had fought as members of the Basij, referred to the Iran-Iraq War as the "Sacred Defense and Imposed War."[6]

Ahmad, my host and a member of the Basij, for instance, relates his spiritual and mystical experience of the war:

> The generals were worried. But the Imam [Khomeini] said "go!" And what a victory! I was in the war. There was an old man with me, one hundred and nine of us. Only five hundred meters over there [he pointed] was the other side. The younger ones were afraid. But the old man had a dream. He said don't have any fear. Another soldier said, "why not fear?" The old man responded, "I dreamed that this valley was full of soldiers ready for war. They came from the Imam-e Zaman [the Imam Mahdi, the final and hidden Imam]. They came to defend us. Because of this, Iran was always victorious in the war. The Hidden Imam sent us power."[7]

Here, Ahmad remembers how he and his surrounding unit overcame their fear and great numbers of opponents by attending to the mystical powers of the Hidden Imam, and therefore of God, in the name of Iran's sacred defense. For him, the call for war by Khomeini was utterly supported by high powers as a spiritual necessity. Indeed, he recalls another occasion during the fighting: "One time we were on the frontline behind a rock and the enemies came not ten feet away . . . [he paused]. They walked right past, Thanks to God. My comrades and I were not even seen."[8] Here, divine intervention is seen as proof of the rightness of the sacred defense and the sacrifice of the martyrs. Ahmad remembers friends who passed away as exalted martyrs and smiles at the memory.

The concept of the martyr and its symbolic force in contemporary Iranian politics developed in and through these political-historic events. In the 1960s and 1970s, in particular, several key intellectuals drew vivid parallels between Husayn's uprising at the Battle of Karbala and protest against the unjust rule of the shah (Flaskerud 2012, 25). Ayatollah Taleqani and Ayatollah Khomeini furthered this link during the buildup to the Revolution, framing their discontent with the shah in terms of events at Karbala. In 1979, they and others adapted the already strong cultural salience of the reenactments and mourning of Husayn's sacrifice during the month of Muharram to help mobilize revolutionary forces. 'Ashura', the tenth day of Muharram, occurred on December 11, 1978, and more than a million people responded to the call to participate in the demonstrations throughout the country (Flaskerud 2012, 25).

Khomeini encouraged women and children to march at the head of processions: "Our brave women, embrace their children and face the machine guns and tanks of the executioners of this regime.... Sisters and Brothers be resolute, do not show weakness and lack of courage. You are following the path of the Almighty and his prophets. Your blood is poured on the same road as that of the (martyred) prophets, Imams, and their followers. You join them. This is not an occasion to mourn but to rejoice" (Khomeini 1999, 510–12). Speaking to protestors against the regime, Khomeini here referred both to an Islamic brother- and sisterhood and to the courageous spilling of blood "on the same road as that of the Prophets, Imams, and their followers."[9] In so doing, he linked the act of spilling blood in protest against the shah to a prophetic lineage of religious Muslim belonging and to the martyrdom of Imam Husayn. During my research, this message was reinforced by people in Fars-Abad via the common slogan, "Everywhere is Karbala, every month is Muharram, and every day is 'Ashura'," a phrase first coined by the intellectual Ali Shari'ati and adopted later by Khomeini as a banner of the Revolution. The slogan is a reminder of Husayn's sacrifice, of the Revolution, of the Iran-Iraq War, and of the continual Islamic/nationalist fight against Western imperialism (Aghaie 2014).

Yet the association between spilled blood and the sacrifice of Imam Husayn is more than a mere analogy; it is a material and transformative act. According to the late Ayatollah Mutahhari, for instance, the blood of the martyr is never wasted. Rather, it "infuses fresh blood into the veins of society" (Dorraj 1997, 511). Spilled through the act of self-sacrifice, the efficacy of spilled blood is exponential: "Every drop [of blood] is turned into hundreds of thousands of drops." It is a transfusion for a society "suffering from anemia" (Mutahhari quoted in Taliqani et al. 1986, 136). These statements make a direct link between the blood of the martyrs and the regeneration of (Islamic) society. They imagine the Islamic nation of Iran as a single body, wounded or sick and in need of a transfusion.

But what are the particular traits of martyrs? Ayatollah Taleqani (1911–79) argued that, as a witness (*shahid*), the martyr sacrifices his life with full consciousness. Similarly, the late Ayatollah Mutahhari (1920–79) defined the martyr as the individual who sacrifices himself/herself consciously for a cause. Indeed, in Islam more broadly, martyrdom is a free pass straight to heaven.[10] The act of the martyr's sacrifice is so noble that the corpse requires no ritual bath.

In Fars-Abad, Basiji veterans and family members emphasized that martyrdom was selfless. Death was not a reason for mourning. Rather, it was a progression toward "proximity and connection to God" (*qorbat bā khodā*). Ahmad and some of his war comrades related that to be a martyr was precisely to turn away from all corruption (and ultimately hell) and attain a direct link with the divine. It was to have ultimate pure intentions in this life for the more important and much more extensive next life. They emphasized that martyrdom was not a matter of choice, but of divine selection. Finally, they underscored that the volunteer soldiers who had become martyrs had fought with their souls and exalted spirit; as one Iran-Iraq War veteran told me, the martyrs "charge the air with courage and zeal, reviving the spirit of valor among those who have lost it."[11]

Sitting in her Ekbatan apartment in Tehran in March 2010, just before I left for Fars-Abad, Parvin, the mother of five children and wife of Ahmad's brother, Mahmud, an injured war veteran, told me:

> We are indebted to the martyrs. If they had not existed, we would not be. When America occupied Afghanistan and Iraq, if there had not been any martyrs, they would have occupied us. They went [to fight] because of the nation and because of Islam. They chose to be martyrs themselves. It is not a problem. In other words, I don't become sad. Families don't become sad that they gave martyrs. They say that it is because of Islam. They say that it is because of our religion. They say that religion needs martyrs to protect it. War is because of Islam, because of religion, because of the Qur'an. For example, Imam Husayn became a martyr because of Islam.[12]

For Parvin, martyrdom is a choice and a sacrifice "for both the nation and Islam." Moreover, rather than a reason for mourning, the martyrdom of a loved one is necessary for the protection of Islam, in the same way as it had been for Imam Husayn. Here, the spilling of blood is an ongoing "defense of Islam" that has continued through the American occupation of Iraq and Afghanistan.

Notably for Parvin and her family members in Fars-Abad and Shiraz, the martyrs' selfless sacrifice and "rank near God" is sensorial and embodied. On a visit to Tehran's national cemetery, Zahra's Paradise, Parvin hurried me over to a grave where twenty or so women had gathered, some men standing behind them. She chanted, along with the others, "the smell of rosewater!" (*bu-ye golāb miyād!*), referring to the scent of rosewater that was wafting from the grave. They repeated this, crying, and bending over the grave to touch it and pray. When I asked why, Parvin explained that the martyr was giving off the scent from the grave. Indeed, she and others related that the bodies of martyrs do not putrefy in the same way as other bodies; instead they remain corporeally and spiritually whole.[13] As such, both physical and spiritual contact with them is possible.

For the members of the Basij and their families in Fars-Abad, then, the memory of the war and its martyrs was deeply connected to their service on the front lines of the border and to the mystical experiences they shared with their comrades. Those I spoke with, moreover, said that Iran's victory in the war was evidence of their fellow soldiers' tremendous spirit, valor, and purity. Here, although they distinguished themselves from the families of martyrs who received more "government benefits," they also saw themselves as akin to martyrs: fellow soldiers who had been willing to sacrifice their lives.

THE DRIVE TO EXHUME BURIED MARTYRS' BODIES

Iranian military institutions contend that more than fifty thousand bodies of soldiers remain in the former battlefields of Iraq and Iran. During the Iran-Iraq War, a section of the Army of the Guardians of the Islamic Revolution called the Martyrs' Evacuation Brigade was created to exhume and collect the bodies of the dead. Some soldiers had "dog tags" made of metal while others went to war, especially early on, without any specific form of identification.

The project of finding martyrs who had been left behind began in earnest in 1989 when Col. S. M. Mirbagherzadeh proposed the idea to the Supreme Leader of Iran, Ayatollah Khamenei. A committee was formed, the Committee for Finding the Missing Soldiers. On the first expedition, the committee found three hundred unknown martyrs, and a public funeral ceremony was held (Khosronejad 2012, 14). But the work of finding martyrs is also considered an uncanny and somewhat magical process. Khosronejad reports that the Revolutionary Guard's process of finding bodies is itself interwoven with the divine. It involves rituals, appeals and supplications, dreams, and other miracles. Regardless, the exhumation and reburial of new martyrs' bodies has been central to the making of a sacred (national) landscape.

Importantly, the politics of who gets to make and define martyrs is a sensitive subject for researchers who continue to work in Iran. Although many of the families of martyrs experienced shared bereavement for the eight consecutive years of warfare, government institutions and organizations endeavored to joyously celebrate rather than shed tears of bereavement for important martyrs, attacks, and victories. Kaur (2010), for instance, argues that since the Iran-Iraq War, the state has claimed the power to make martyrs out of corpses. He argues that it has done so in strategic ways, with state officials literally collecting the bodies of unknown martyrs in order to create saints to be venerated by a new generation of Iranian youth. Some reformists and liberals in Iran hold that state officials put the sacred bones of martyrs on the map through the creation of sacred gravesites for the purpose of destabilizing political uprisings in key centers. They argue that unknown martyrs' bodies have been positioned at sites in cities such as Tehran at universities and public squares, often where Green Movement uprisings have historically occurred, to curb protest and sacralize the landscape. Only secondarily have the bodies of martyrs been positioned at the periphery, in small towns and villages. I suggest that the placement of martyrs on ledges and overlooks provides a means of creating and sacralizing national space. For my Basiji hosts, these changes were welcome because they believed in the religious purity and power of martyrs' blood.

The Sacralizing Efficacy of Martyrs' Blood

A great fanfare had accompanied the war heroes' arrival on the anniversary of the martyrdom of the sixth Imam, Imam Sadeq (~702–65 CE), during the Week of the Sacred Defense that commemorates the Iran-Iraq War, a commemorative week created by Khomeini. News of the annual Week of the Sacred Defense had already reached people in Fars-Abad through specially convened gatherings in the local meeting hall for Shi'i commemoration ceremonies and through national commemorative Islamic Republic of Iran Broadcasting showing Iran-Iraq War footage: soldiers marching, guns, men in the dirt and trenches, young male soldiers in uniform leaving their mothers, the resounding call "God is Great," and fighting or wounded men, covered in blood. Biographies and images of the more famous martyrs also fill televised broadcasts: Seyyed Morteza Avini, for instance, known as "The Martyr of the Pen" (Shahid-e 'Aql-e Qalam), or Hossein Fahmideh, a thirteen-year-old boy who sacrificed his life before an Iraqi tank to defend Iran.

The same organization that buries martyrs in Tehran, the Foundation for the Preservation of Heritage and the Distribution of Sacred Defense, brought the two unknown martyrs to Fars-Abad.[14] As I mentioned briefly in this book's introduction, I joined my hosts and more than a thousand people filling the street at the outskirts of town to welcome the martyrs to their new burial site. It is impossible to know how many of these thousands were local and how many had been mobilized by the Basij or the IRGC. Nevertheless, a significant number of Revolutionary Guard and Fars Province soldiers were also present, including a government band, complete with brass instruments and percussion. The music droned to the rhythmic beating of a Yamaha bass drum. Next to the band stood a table covered in the bloodied black-and-white scarves (*chafiyeh*) worn by Revolutionary Guardsmen during the war.[15] Two framed portraits of the late Ayatollah Khomeini, or "the Imam," and the Supreme Leader, Ayatollah Khamenei, rested on the blood-stained cloth.

It was nearing dusk when the trailer carrying the bodies of the unknown martyrs finally arrived in the streets of Fars-Abad, heralded by the town loudspeaker. A cameraman filmed the caravan's arrival for a local news agency, and behind him dozens of young men snapped amateur photos and footage with digital cameras and phones. The trailer stopped briefly as some officials stepped out to greet the town leaders, one in a simple suit and one bearded soldier in military uniform. Each greeted and kissed the local Friday Imam and several other town officials.

When the trailer began to move again, its valued cargo became visible: two wooden caskets in succession on a long flat bed, one for each martyr.

Each casket was wrapped in Iranian flags of red, green, and white cloth. Each also had two uniformed soldiers standing on either side. Other Iranian flags and inscriptions made a canopy over the trailer, and banners on the sides of the vehicle read "Yā Sāheb Al-Zamān," a call to the Twelfth and Hidden Imam and an elegy for the dead.

As the casket-bearing procession passed the crowded streets, hundreds of men, and then women, followed behind the trailer on "Imam Boulevard," Fars-Abad's main street, which had recently been lined with flags and signs for the occasion. Soldiers and veterans riding on the trailer threw rosewater and petals into the crowd. Men and then women rushed in succession to the sides of the vehicle to touch the float or to have a garment or other object rubbed on the martyrs' caskets, thus imbuing their possessions with the power of the soldiers' blood and sacrifice. Periodically, the crowd chanted, "Peace be on Muhammad and the Family of Muhammad." The procession finally ended ten blocks away at the central Islamic meetinghouse. Soldiers unloaded the casket, and the Friday Imam addressed a now much smaller crowd. He declared, as he would so frequently during several different events for the same martyrs, "Because this martyr is unknown, we the people are his brother, his sister, his mother," a reference to a sense of common kinship with the anonymous heroes.

The next day, a Friday at noon, thousands of townspeople and people from other parts of the Fars Province and the city of Shiraz again came out of their homes in the hot sun to carry the martyrs to their final burial site. They streamed up the hill to the park's overlook and prepared graves. On the top of the hill, women moved to the right and men to the left, surrounding the already prepared, flag-covered canopy.

Under the canopy seven mothers sat with photos of their own martyred sons on plastic folding chairs next to approximately seven uniformed soldiers. Positioned as such, they drew the attention of hundreds of other mourners, their expressions making tangible the emotion of the loss of family—and in this case of the unknown martyrs—the sacrifice of (male) national family members.

A nearby brightly colored sign read across its ten foot girth: "The martyrs of the Islamic revolution protected the face/esteem/honor (*āberu*) of Islam and of the Qur'an with the price of their blood."

Figure 10. Mothers of martyrs sitting behind the graves of two unknown martyrs from the Iran-Iraq War, Fars-Abad, Iran

Another read, "The martyrs, on this day of nostalgia, rose in defense of the values of Islam." Still more proclaimed: "Peace be upon the martyrs' path of virtue and freedom," and "Behold! The blood shrouded tulips in the cradle of martyrs." Other signs depicted the martyrs themselves. In one, the entire sky was the color red, and soldiers smiled. Below them a dead martyr lay on the ground, divine light shining on his face. He wore a simple jacket.

After a brief introduction and acknowledgment to the people of Fars-Abad and the commemoration's organizers, the Friday Imam led a standing prayer for the dead, a prayer that included five repetitions of "God is Great." Speakers, including the local Friday Imam, thanked the crowd for waiting in the heat, for coming to pay their respects to the martyrs. He said: "The first drop of blood spilt from a martyr purifies sins. Because their blood is spilled, they are pure. They then go straight to heaven. If you

Figure 11. Event welcoming the martyrs to their final resting place in the town park, Fars-Abad, Iran

have a problem in your life, it is possible that your problem will be solved [by these martyrs], because of their purity and because they are near to God." His statement thus attested to the special position of these martyrs vis-à-vis God. They had conquered all corruption (both personal and societal) and had found union with the divine.

Scholars such as Halbwachs (1992) and Connerton (1989) have developed a theory of "collective" or "social" memory to explore how extraordinary events such as the Iran-Iraq War are collectively recalled. In particular, they explore how memories are valorized, memorialized, and/or incorporated into bodies through "incorporating practices," or patterns of body-use that become ingrained through our interactions with objects (Connerton 1989). Martyrs' bodies and blood in Iran are multiply evocative of this kind of collective memory. The commemorations, un-burials, and reburials of Iranian martyrs organize the bodies of subjects around

Figure 12. Sign created for the martyrs' commemoration, Fars-Abad, Iran

heroic martyrs while simultaneously de-emphasizing and "forgetting" other historical sites such as ancient Zoroastrian temples or more recent "Western-influenced" Pahlavi palaces. Interestingly, these scholars further suggest that the desire to memorialize is often precipitated by the fear or threat of "cultural amnesia." Indeed, for many supporters of the Islamic Republic, such as my hosts, acts of remembering and memorialization of the 1979 Revolution and of the Iran-Iraq War were both explicitly and implicitly a defense against such amnesia, particularly as it related to their own experiences of sacrifice.[16]

On a more practical level, the unknown martyrs' commemoration in Fars-Abad reveals the town's and the state's mutual investment in the reburial of martyrs from the Iran-Iraq border. It also reveals the local passion with which the two unknown martyrs were welcomed to their burial ground in Fars-Abad by both members of the Basij, such as my hosts, and the general populace. The sheer number of people who attended the ceremony—in the thousands—is itself informative of the existence of a powerful cohort of rural Iranians who support the regime.

Through these reburials, many of my Basiji hosts and friends aspired to encounter, touch, or at least find proximity to a martyr's body in the same way that they sought to make pilgrimage to the tombs of Shi'i saints. They participated in the commemorative events, they said, to ward off increasing societal corruption and its negative effects on their families: the evils of drug addiction (opium from Afghanistan), premarital sexual relations, and alcohol consumption by youth. Notably, however, other members of their extended family did not attend such events.

Although other scholars have reported on the similar exhumation of bodies from the border of the Iran-Iraq War and their not uncontested reburial in the key squares and universities in cities such as Tehran and Shiraz (Kaur 2010), this is the first account of a provincial martyrs' commemoration and interment in Iran. Unknown martyrs are also being buried in the smaller towns and counties of Iran. Indeed, during my travels throughout several small towns in Fars, I noted not only the existence of frequent "known" martyrs' cemeteries in neighboring towns, but also an increasing collection of "unknown" martyrs' tombs, many of which were also placed strategically on hills or overlooks. These provincial burials, which help produce political connections between local officials and state elites, are part of a broader directive to (1) tighten relationships between provincial and national governance, which benefit local mayors and Friday Imams, as well as town infrastructure projects; (2) regenerate town space as national/Islamic space; and (3) produce a kind of field of visibility, with martyrs as overseers of town life. These provincial burials also reveal the significance of the Basij as a source of citizen participation in state rituals. It seemed that many of those who attended and/or organized these gatherings were affiliated with the regional chapters of the Basij.

Finally, there is a prolific and conspicuous display of blood in contemporary Iranian religious nation-making. Martyrs are made meaningful not only by means of their historic relevance and sacralizing power but also in the multiple ways in which their material blood and bodies evoke kinship and relatedness.

INTERSECTIONS: THE SPILLED BLOOD OF MARTYRS AND THE BLOOD OF KINSHIP

New scholarship has explored blood's special quality as a substance, material, and metaphor and has underscored its frequent involvement in matters such as life and death, violence and sacrifice, and inclusion and exclusion (Carsten 2013). Part of blood's peculiarity, Kath Weston argues, is its "meta-materiality": the way it extends beyond metaphor and material even as it simultaneously relies on both the material and the metaphorical to generate further resonances and naturalizations (Weston 2001). This unique capacity of blood as a naturalizing material substance is visible in postrevolutionary Iran. It participates in and flows between kinship and nation and between kinship and politics. It is associated with the family, the family of the Prophet, the Prophetic lineage, and the making of a nation-state.

As I described in chapter 1, my hosts imagine the extended family in terms of a *qowm-o-khish*, an active group of relatives who claim a common origin and relation through patrilateral and/or matrilateral ties (Wellman 2017a; Hegland 2013). Generations are primarily interconnected through inherited blood, or what people refer to as "being of the same blood" (*ham khun*). They are further regarded as being of the same body, a notion that appears most visibly in the *panj tan*, a banner or sign in the shape of a hand used during commemorations to depict the family of the Prophet Muhammad. As it appears in Muharram processional performances, each finger of the hand represents the members of the Prophet Muhammad's family: the Prophet himself, his daughter Fatemeh, his cousin and son-in-law 'Ali, and his two grandsons, Hassan and Husayn. Importantly, in the Qur'an and hadiths, shared blood and body index a wide range of qualities, many of which extend beyond the concept of relationship, affinity, or genealogy to include nobility, origin, honor, unity of purpose, virginity, love, and personality (Khuri 2001).[17] Blood is thus, from the very beginning, more than mere substance.

Blood—both the blood of kin and that of martyrs—is also clearly gendered. Although Basiji interlocutors recognize both patrilateral and matrilateral relations as kin, male blood (agnatic blood) is often foregrounded. Not surprisingly, patrilineal blood is also the determining factor for legal

Iranian citizenship. Iranian civil law confers citizenship on those persons whose fathers are Iranian, regardless of birthplace. Until very recently children could not acquire citizenship from their mothers (as stipulated in article 976 of Iran's Civil Code). Accordingly, a designation of citizenship depends on what interlocutors described as a "natural" "blood relationship" that extends, for the most part, via patrilineal descent.

Yet the blood of citizen martyrs is even more potent for contemporary nation-making. Strikingly red and tactile, it is featured in commemorations of unburied war martyrs from the Iran-Iraq border, museum exhibits, and martyrs' graveyards. It appears again in the redness of ribbons, street signs, red tulips, photographs, and the written word. During the Iran-Iraq War in the 1980s, red-dyed water literally flowed in Iran's national graveyard, Zahra's Paradise, and many graveyards in Iran developed martyrs' sections, such as the Paradise of the Martyrs and the Martyrs' Flower Garden. Most known martyrs' graves are white marble and contain basic information about the deceased. In the martyrs' section of Zahra's Paradise, small window boxes contain personal effects of the deceased, left by family members.

Outside of these graveyards and museums, still more images of bloody martyrs bombard pedestrians in the form of murals on walls and street posters across Tehran and Shiraz (Gruber 2012; Chelkowski and Dabashi 1999). In the form of beautified faces, they appear in small towns and cities alike and are so common that many passersby hardly notice them. Basijis in Fars-Abad, in contrast, frequently commented on these posters and murals. In the car on the way to a visit to the doctor or to shop, they pointed out the faces of the martyrs and their pure expressions. In general, posters alternate between the heroic faces of martyrs and images of their wounded bodies. Often they are accompanied by tulips, also depicted on the Iranian flag as a symbol of the martyrs and their regenerative power. Indeed, where the blood of the martyrs falls, they say, tulips grow. For many, the blood of martyrs is literally thought to bring life. Bloody soil from the Iran-Iraq War border is collected by pilgrims and planted in gardens to nourish and purify the bodies and souls of their kin.

Anthropologist Azam Torab (2007, 157) highlights the masculinity of such martyrs' blood. She writes that "representations of martyrdom are an exaltation of masculine gender centered on the blood of the patriline and cosmically enshrined as the only gender that brings eternal hope."

The legitimacy of Shi'i leadership is based on blood descendants of the Prophet, so that blood descent needs to be forcibly renewed."

For Torab, martyrs' blood in Iran is the key not only to renewal but also to the renewal of society. This observation is apt in the sense that there is a clear male gendering of martyrs' blood and bodies in Iran, a gendered sacrifice that is set against the image of the pious and veiled mother, sister, or daughter. Notably, however, this gendering is not explicit. State-supporting Basijis in Fars-Abad did not themselves emphasize the maleness of martyrs, arguing instead that any person could become a martyr.

What is it about blood that turns it into such a powerful site for reawakening memories of sacred and political history? One answer to this question is that at the interstices of blood, kinship, and the sacred, blood's physical and material qualities have long been the object of vigorous cultural elaboration. The vivid redness of blood, for instance, is strongly associated with (divine) power and energy: a Sufi who radiates power is called "red-mantled" (*sorkh-push*), and a martyr is imaged wearing a blood-stained cloak. Traditional bridal dresses are sometimes blood red, too, denoting life and fertility. Whether the color red seen on signs, banners, or belongings derives from spilled blood itself or is mimetically reproduced through paint or dye, it is striking because of its iconicity and resemblance to blood that flows in the veins or spills from a wound. In its most powerful form, as spilled from the martyr, blood is known to run or flow through the veins and spill to the earth, cleaning the streets or the nation. Yet as a token of the same liquidity, it is further seen as shareable, whether among citizens of the nation, among members of the family, or both.

Female Martyrs: Commemorating the Martyrdom of Fatemeh Al-Zahra in Fars-Abad

Thus far we have seen that concepts of citizenship, fighting, and martyrdom are largely gendered male in Iran. While men give their lives and blood to protect Islam and nation, women sacrifice their loved ones (Aghaie 2004, 120). The same theme appears in early narratives and depictions of the Battle of Karbala: though men are the actual ones being martyred, women embody the tragedy by becoming mourners or spokespersons of the Imam Husayn's message (Aghaie 2004, 121).

During the 1979 Revolution, this paradigm was reenacted when "exemplary" women contributed to the cause by donning the black chador (Moallem 1992, 29) and, as I have shown, by willingly sacrificing their sons and husbands to the Iran-Iraq War effort. Indeed, a popular slogan from that era declaimed: "My sister your veil is more contentious than my blood" (quoted in Moallem 1992, 31). Here, although many women fought and practiced alongside the Revolutionary Guard or trained in military camps (Nashat 2004, 31; Reeves 1989, 132) during the Iran-Iraq War, blood did not come to symbolize the female contribution in the same way that it did for men. The pure and (re)generative blood of martyrs was instead associated with the image of the martyred son or husband citizen.

Despite the emphasis on male blood, female martyrs are increasingly important in contemporary Iran and cannot be entirely discounted. The most important female martyr in Shi'ism is Fatemeh Al-Zahra ("the radiant one"). Fatemeh Al-Zahra is the only daughter of the Prophet and the sole link between the Prophet and the Twelve Imams. As such, she is frequently called the "mother of the Imams," and both she and her descendants are said to be immaculate and sinless (*ma'sum*). She is also depicted in the famous five-fingered hand of "the family of the Prophet" (*ahl-e beyt*), known literally as the "five bodies" (*panj tan*), mentioned in chapter 1.

According to most Shi'i exegesis, Fatemeh's martyrdom occurred amid the struggle over the succession of the Prophet. Omar, angry because 'Ali had publicly refused to swear allegiance to him, pushed open the door to Fatemeh's home violently, pushing it into Fatemeh's side and breaking her ribs (Fischer [1980] 2003, 14). Fatemeh, who was pregnant, subsequently delivered a stillborn, a (martyred) son called Ehsan. She is thought to have died later of the injuries she had sustained and is recognized to have died of these injuries as a martyr. She spent her last days mourning the death of her father, the Prophet, and she is said to eternally weep for the death of her two sons, the Imams Husayn and Hassan.

In his influential revolutionary text, *Fatemeh Is Fatemeh*, published in the 1960s, intellectual Ali Shari'ati argued that Fatemeh is more than the link between the Prophet and Imam 'Ali and the inheritor of the mission that is passed down from Adam through the Imams. Rather, he argued that she was willing to take on the struggle of justice against oppression and corruption.[18] He called on Muslim woman to "return" to what he termed the revolutionary role model of Fatemeh (Shariati 1981, 16).

Actual practices of mourning Fatemeh's martyrdom in small town Iran resemble those for her son Imam Husayn and similarly emphasize her spilled blood. In Fars-Abad, for instance, on the anniversary of Fatemeh's martyrdom, Maryam and I met Nushin, Fatemeh, and her infant daughter at their aunt's house. Having spent the evening shopping, we walked together to the building called locally "the Qur'an," a religious educational center in the middle of town. The enclosed outdoor grounds in front of the main building and stage were packed, with nearly four hundred women and two hundred men in attendance. As we searched for seats, women walked around handing out candies, tea, and cupcakes as "votive foods" (*nazri*). Nushin gave me some recently purchased toffee to hand out with Maryam, which we distributed until our plastic bags were empty.

When Maryam and I finally sat down, a prayer leader began to lead constituents in lamentation, repeating the word mother (*mādar*) in reference to Fatemeh and to the large number of women in attendance. Behind him, "black parchments" (*siyāhpush*) were inscribed with verses of the Qur'an: "Yā Fatemeh" in blood red ink. These parchments framed the space as a site of mourning. The stage itself was designed to resemble Fatemeh's home: the place where Omar had intruded upon her, broken her rib, and slain her unborn child. Most strikingly, a wooden door at the center of the stage had been spattered with blood red paint. From the men's side of the courtyard, the prayer leader called sadly: "I saw him [Omar] come in the middle of night.... I saw what happened, the baby was killed, sent to his martyrdom. [Fatemeh] Zahra, how she suffered.... Zahra, poor Zahra, Zahra, my dear. " His expression, "I saw," is typical for these kinds of commemorations. They position the prayer leader as an onlooker of the (timeless) event, increasing its reenacted and viscerally remembered intensity. As he spoke, Nushin and others sitting beside me cried and rocked back and forth, tears in their eyes, some sobbing loudly. Along with the prayer leader, they repeated the *salavāt:* "Peace be upon Mohammad and his descendants." At the end of the ceremony, the men stood in a circle, beating their chests to the rhythm of the prayer leader.[19] The women also beat their chests but stayed seated.

Figure 13. Women attending a commemoration for Fatemeh Al-Zahra, Fars-Abad, Iran

After the commemoration, Nushin and her two daughters, Maryam and Fatemeh, began discussing female martyrs in Iran. They both emphasized the presence of female martyrs and wanted me to recognize that during the Iran-Iraq War many women had *also* joined the war effort, both as nurses and auxiliaries.

Female blood and sacrifice are emphasized in such commemorations. Decorations and parchments are marked with red paint, and people partake in the same exercises of rhythmic chest beating as they do during rituals of Muharram (although in general mourning ceremonies for Zahra are smaller, rarely involving street processions).

Indeed, attention to female martyrdom and female sacrificial blood more generally is increasing. In 2003, for instance, the World Islamic Head Quarters for Remembering Martyrs was founded. The organization is based on the heroic model of Palestinian women martyrs. In 2008, the

Iranian magazine *Zanān* published an article entitled "They Die in Order to Kill" (*koshteh mishavand tā bokoshand*), which resulted in the closure of the magazine. In the article, the female secretary general of the World Islamic Headquarters for Remembering Martyrs said that the number of the female martyrdom seekers in Iran is about one-third of the total martyrdom seekers in the country. She also asserted that "after the U.S. invasion of Najaf and Karbala and their mistreatment of the holy Shi'i sites, we decided to recruit and enroll (female) volunteers for martyrdom to show the discontent of the Iranian people against those who threaten material and spiritual sources of the Islamic world." The women associated with the organization proclaim their willingness to walk in the footsteps of Palestinian female martyrs such as Vafa Idris, one of the first and most famous Palestinian female suicide bombers (Fazaeli 2009).[20]

The gendering of martyrs' blood is thus dynamic and shifting in contemporary Iran. While it is certainly primarily masculine in tone, it no longer is solely male. Rather than being mere mourners or spokespersons of tragedy, pro-regime female martyrs have been—at least to some degree—legitimized by the state.

Martyrs as National Kin in Fars-Abad: Inclusions and Exclusions

"Because the martyr is unknown, we are his brother, his sister, his mother." Repeated again here, the words of the Friday Imam at the commemoration of unknown martyrs in Fars-Abad explicitly called on townspeople to relate to unknown martyrs as they would their own kin. Indeed, in his speech the local imam made repeated claims that the two martyrs to be buried were unknown. This classification was a political act; after all, as "unknown," the two martyrs would have unique potency for current and future town commemorations.[21] By means of their very unknown-ness, their bodies, blood, and sacrifices would be made available to all. Townspeople I spoke with said, "What if he were my son?" "What if he were my father?"—questions that were viscerally real to those who had actually lost kin and made imaginable to those who had not.

In Fars-Abad, most argued that kinship with a martyr is a blessing. Nushin, for instance, told me with pride that she had not prevented her husband, Ahmad, from going to war, although others had done so, an immoral act of selfishness. On one occasion, as we walked past the town mosque, then under construction, she told me how a local *sayyed*, or descendant of the Prophet Muhammad, had almost—but not quite—been prevented from becoming a martyr by his sister. "His sister didn't want him to go to war," Nushin said. "She [the sister] said, 'you will become a martyr. You don't yet have any kids.' But the *sayyed* went to the local mosque and while he was there, he saw Imam Mahdi (in occultation) who told him that he should go. He went and became a martyr." Nushin's tone was full of awe at the *sayyed's* encounter with Imam Mahdi, so near to her home and at the local mosque she had grown up attending. She said that she respected the self-sacrifice of the *sayyed*, explaining that he had overcome his sister's mundane desires and even her concern for his Prophetic progeny to sacrifice his life in defense of Islam.

Other women I spoke with from Basiji households in Fars-Abad contended that "right" and "faithful" mothers and sisters urged their male kin to take part in the defense of the sacred motherland. They cast those who did not want to part with their husbands or brothers or sons during the Iran-Iraq War as morally inferior. Very often, and especially during the Week of the Sacred Defense, the subject of the "pure" and "good" martyrs would come up in conversation, such as after prayer or during food preparation. Sometimes these iterations were evoked by something on the television. Sometimes they followed prayer or a particular birth or mourning day of an Imam. For my hosts, however, they were recalled more commonly by town places, such as the local mosque or a tombstone of a loved martyr we passed when we visited relatives or ran errands.

In contrast, drawing on fieldwork in Tehran, Saeidi found that many of her interlocutors were skeptical about state depictions and the "use" of their martyred kin as propaganda (Saeidi 2010, 116). Some of the women she interviewed had begun foundations to publicly memorialize martyrs in their own way, rather than employ the frame guided by the state. Her work makes visible how many perceive the dominant narrative of the war as an imposition that silences dissenting perspectives (see also Ehsani 2017, 8). Most female interviewees in Fars-Abad, however, did not outwardly exhibit this resentment or skepticism. Many embraced the moral regulations expected of martyrs' families to become exemplary citizens, made visible in acts such as always donning the black chador, wearing simple dress, giving to the poor, cooking votive meals for townspeople, and going on pilgrimage.

It is important to note that with concern to the subject of martyrdom, my Basiji hosts only guided me to interviews with select individuals. For instance, when one family member suggested that I meet a certain local mother of a martyr, my host father said with concern, "You don't want to speak with her; she will give you a wrong impression." He also carefully went over my questions concerning martyrs, finally approving them. Needless to say, I never interviewed that particular woman. This censorship limited what I was able to ask, but it is also revealing. It shows my host father's concern that I would put not only myself but his family in danger with the state if I asked certain questions of certain people. Yet this censorship points to the possibility of more cynical perspectives within Fars-Abad, which my research was unable to address.

During the multipart commemoration of the unknown soldiers in Fars-Abad described earlier, a rumor began. At first it seemed benign: Had one of the "unknown" martyrs actually been identified? A mother, people said, had claimed that one of the "unknown" martyrs was indeed her "known" son. There was some talk of DNA evidence. During the burial ceremony on top of the dusty hill referred to in the beginning of this chapter, the women I stood with pointed to a mother in the crowd. "She is here! The martyr's mother," they said. Afterward, some people said that the official had ignored the mother's claims in their efforts to keep the martyr's status "unknown." Others said that the identity of the martyr had not been proven. But why did officials attempt to maintain the martyrs' unknown status so diligently?

In *Imagined Communities*, Benedict Anderson highlights the peculiarity of the *unknown* tomb as an emblem of modern nationalism, saturated with "ghostly national imaginings," a signifier of "connectedness" and of "continuity" (Anderson 1983, 50). In Fars-Abad, the unknown martyrs' commemoration and burial similarly drew on aspirations for national continuity and connectedness. However, what the Friday Imam and others highlighted is a particular kind of familial connection that is frequently emphasized by the Islamic Republic: the naturalized connectedness of Muslim brother and sister citizens, and of these same citizens, the land/soil of Iran, and God (see also Wellman 2017a).

ALTERNATE DISCOURSES THROUGH BLOOD

> It's the month, the month of blood
> Sayyid Ali (Khamenei) will be toppled
>
> —slogan chanted in Qom during the funeral
> marches for Ayatollah Hossein Ali Montazeri,
> December 21, 2009 (Fischer 2010)

Before concluding, it is important to note that concepts of blood, martyrdom, and sacrifice have had a long history of cultural salience, with differing interpretations over time. Indeed, it is not only the supporters of the Islamic Republic who have called on the spilled blood of martyrs and the Battle of Karbala. According to Dorraj, members of the leftist Mojahedin-e Khalq organization, some of whom were being executed by the shah's regime in their fight against the pre-Revolution monarchy, sang the song "From Our Blood, Carnations Will Grow" in the spirit of the myth of Siavash (Dorraj 1997).[22] Siavash, importantly, is a central figure in the Book of Kings, which was written by Ferdowsi between 977 and 1010 CE and tells the mythical and historical past of the Persian Empire from the creation of the world until the Islamic conquest of Persia in the seventh century. Innocent and chaste, Siavash was ultimately slain for purportedly making advances on his stepmother. It is said that when he wrongly died, three drops of blood fell on the ground, from which grew a red plant, an anemone. In Iran, this flower is often called "the blood of Siavash." The phrase, moreover, continues to stand for innocence and virtue betrayed. The epic resonates with the martyrdom of the innocent Imam Husayn and the corresponding efficacy of his regenerative blood (Dorraj 1997, 512). The Mojahedin saw the deaths of their group as a necessary drop in a flood that would ultimately cleanse the moral filth by washing away the shah's regime.[23]

More recently, others have wielded the symbolic power of martyrs' blood, explicitly evoking the martyrdom of Imam Husayn for reformist politics. The prolific images of the slain Neda Agha-Soltan, the innocent bystander killed during a Green Movement election protest in June 2009, provide one salient example. In the widely circulated photos and videos, her blood pours onto the street (Fathi 2009). Other examples include blood-covered protest T-shirts depicting former protestors and symbolic blood handprints on protesters' signs, digital and paper, indexing those who died in 2009 Green Movement protests.

Similarly, when Ayatollah Montazeri died on December 20, 2009, the third day of the month of Muharram, the seventh day of Montazeri's death fell suggestively on Sunday, on 'Ashura', the same day that Imam Husayn was killed at the Battle of Karbala. At his funeral, protesters drew on this sacred-historical layering and called Montazeri by Imam Husayn's title, "the wronged one, the oppressed one" (*mazlum*). The association with Imam Husayn, however, is complicated by Montazeri's own complex relationship with the Islamic Republic. He helped develop the idea of *velāyat-e faqih* and was a student in Khomeini's classes on gnostic ethics (Fischer 2010). However, he was also critical of the imprisonment and persecution of leftists. In a speech in 1997, he contended that the Supreme Leader of Iran, Khamenei, was not even a "guide for imitation." Following these comments, Montazeri was put under house arrest between 1997 and 2003 (Fischer 2010). To members of my Basiji host family, to provide some perspective, such comments about the Supreme Leader would have been blasphemous.

Such debates reveal conflicted opinions in Iran concerning the right path to closeness with God. Indeed, there is tremendous diversity among pious Shi'i Iranian Muslims in this regard. Yet despite their differences, many powerful groups in Iranian history have drawn in similar ways from the sacrificial power of martyrs' blood and the ongoing struggle against corruption epitomized by the Battle of Karbala.

NATURALIZING AND SACRALIZING THE IRANIAN LANDSCAPE

According to Katherine Verdery (1999, 25), "[Dead bodies] help us to see political transformation as something more than a technical process.... The 'something more' includes meanings, feelings, the sacred, ideas of morality, the nonrational—all ingredients of 'legitimacy' or 'regime consolidation' (that dry phrase), yet far broader than what analyses employing those terms usually provide." I agree. The blood and bodies of martyrs—together with their accompanying Islamic-national commemoration—have become integral to a carefully orchestrated effort to sacralize (and naturalize) the Iranian landscape and its citizens. The commemorations, exhumations, and reburials of martyrs are strategic religious practices that organize the bodies of Iranian citizens around key reference points (the Iran-Iraq War, the 1979 Revolution, and the martyrdom of Imam Husayn at the Battle of Karbala) while eliding other possible interpretations or critiques. Explicitly set against a spiritually vacuous, Western-powered exterior, the widespread mobilization of martyrs' remains in the Islamic Republic extends beyond mere nation-making in the traditional sense. Rather, the state and its supporters explicitly endeavor to make a *religious* (Islamic) nation, modeled on the family and oriented toward the divine. These efforts are not confined to state making but are tied to kinship and religion and to the "reordering of the meaningful universe" (Verdery 1999, 26). This reordering is all the more necessary when postwar Iran has often been characterized by "deep fragmentation" and "lack of consensus" (Ehsani 2017, 8).

The material blood and bodies of martyrs, as material substance and metaphor, are central to this effort. As bodily sensorial substances, they help ordinary people participate in an ideal sacred relationship, not only between citizens but also between citizens, the land/soil of Iran, and God. Here, bodily remains and substances are a powerful tool of memory in their ability to resemble and typify both the sacred history of religious prophets, heroes, and martyrs, and the bodies and blood of one's self and one's kin (Turner 1967). It is the associations of anonymous martyrs' bodies and blood both with the continuously reenacted religious past *and* with the vitality of kinship substance that make the exhumation of martyrs and their reburial such a potent force.

Importantly, however, commemorations of martyrs do not always fit the mold of the "official speak" of the Islamic Republic. Martyrs may be made and unmade at odds with the state, and the specific details of and claims to martyrs' bodies are often debated. Even further, for some of the Basiji families I interviewed, understandings of martyrs' blood and bodies as regenerative, purifying substances often have a sacred and tangible reality that at times extends beyond received discourses of modern war memorials, hero recognition, and remembrance.

More broadly, by exploring how Basijis in Fars-Abad participate in commemorations involving martyrs' bodies and blood, I have described a situation in which the substances and processes of kinship-making (e.g., agnatic blood) form a basis for nation-making. The patrilineal family (and its basis of agnatic blood) is mapped onto the model of Iranian citizenship. However, what is occurring in the Islamic Republic extends beyond mere nation-making in the traditional sense. Rather, the state and its (Basiji) supporters explicitly endeavor to make an Islamic nation, oriented toward the divine. Here, bodily substances such as blood evoke not only kinship but also God. Spilled martyrs' blood in particular has the power to sanctify national territory, persons, and communities by purifying them and connecting them with Allah. Specifically, the blood of martyrs helps purify an inner national core, with respect to both its citizens and its soil. Naturalized substances such as blood are combined with religious values and qualities to create sacred relationships between Muslim citizens and between citizens and the divine.

But blood is not the only aspect of Iranian kinship that infuses the grand rituals of state power. Kinship in Iran is physio-sacred, an object of ethical and religious work. Active networks of relations or circles of "coming and going" are transformed and altered through acts such as cooking, feeding, and prayer. This fuller spectrum of kin-making—in and beyond the blood of martyrs—also informs (religious) nation-making in Iran. There is a literal flow of kinship-related substances (e.g., blood) *and* the pious acts of kin-making between the intimate spaces of the home and nation.

In what follows, I focus on how this occurs through food and prayer. In the same way that food is a means of shaping, blessing, and protecting the family in Iran, it is also a site of nation-making. On the one hand, food policies, values, and aesthetics have been mobilized to create and contest the postrevolutionary state. On the other hand, state elites and supporters mobilize acts of food sharing and prayer in the rituals of state power to help constitute ideal citizens who embody familial piety, purity, and closeness to God.

4 Creating an Islamic Nation through Food

We leave for the Mausoleum of Ruhollah Khomeini, also referred to as the "holy shrine," at seven in the morning in Mahmud's green Tehran taxicab. Mahmud's wife, Parvin, sits next to me in the back seat as the taxi exits the suburban neighborhood of Ekbatan and merges into the traffic around Azadi Square, before turning south toward Qom on the Persian Gulf highway. As always, Mahmud pulls off the road just outside Tehran's city limits to get out of his car and radio his taxi company to confirm his itinerary. He sits back down in the driver's seat, coughing. This is our daily reminder of his mustard gas exposure during the Iran-Iraq War. Today, though, Mahmud is excited to visit the mausoleum and the graves of his family members in Zahra's Paradise, the adjacent cemetery. Parvin, too, feels "energized." She says that she "has belief" in what we are about to do. Adjusting her black chador smartly against her headscarf and clipping it under her chin with a tiny barrette, she explains that we are going to the tomb of "the Imam," the late Ayatollah Khomeini. "He was a good man," she says. "He didn't become a leader for money or power. He lived simply."

The spring air is warm as we pull into the twenty-thousand-car parking lot in front of the mausoleum. The enormous gold dome and four minarets, under construction, tower over Parvin and me as we bid farewell

Figure 14. Parvin, Mahmud, and their two sons in the parking lot of the Mausoleum of Ruhollah Khomeini, located south of Tehran in Zahra's Paradise

to Mahmud and his sons, who will enter the men's partition through a separate door.

Inside the women's partition, Khomeini's visage appears on billboards and posters. Parvin does not attend to these details, however. She immediately deposits one thousand toman (which was then about one dollar) into a blue donation box for the Imam Khomeini Relief Fund.[1] She then walks up to Khomeini's tomb and touches its metal grill, reciting the first verse of the Qur'an as she kneels on the floor. In a soft but clear voice, she prays for her daughter to find a good husband and be happy. She asks me, with a conspiratorial smile, to pray for her daughter as well, handing me a plastic bag full of sweets to give out to other women in the shrine. "It's a 'votive offering' (*nazri*)," she says. "Everyone does it." Before I can begin distributing the candies, several women come up to us and offer their own sweets. "Sister, please have some," one requests. Parvin responds for both of us, "May God have mercy upon your deceased."

The Mausoleum of Ruhollah Khomeini is both a monument and a shrine. While its golden minarets are modeled on those of the shrine of Imam Husayn, the grandson of the Prophet, the dome resembles that of Fatemeh Ma'sumeh's shrine in nearby Qom, the location of the 1978 uprisings that led to the Revolution (Rizvi 2003). The building houses the tombs of Ayatollah Khomeini, the founder of the Revolution, his wife, his second son, and several political figures, including former President Rafsanjani and Vice President Habibi, among others. It attracts both Iranians and foreigners, especially Shi'i Iraqis and Lebanese, and it is regularly visited by members of the Basij and other supporters of the regime. A placard hanging over the entrance asks visitors to protect the Revolution (and thus the Islamic Republic) from its enemies, with a quote from Khomeini: "Whether I am with you or without you," it reads, "I ask you not to allow the Revolution to die in the hands of the enemies."

Although officials describe the mausoleum as a "meetinghouse for Imam Husayn," many participants move through its spaces in the same way they would through a shrine of a Shi'i Imam and/or mosque.[2] They give votive offerings in the mausoleum. They pray and perform supplications. Indeed, for Parvin, Mahmud, and their children as well as for their Basiji relatives in Fars-Abad, a visit to the shrine and the larger complex of Zahra's Paradise is at once a ritual of mourning, a celebratory family outing, and a pilgrimage. They pray for their daughters, for their marriages, for their children's health, and for divine blessing, all in a specifically state-owned and -run center. Some Basijis take this even further, calling Khomeini "the Thirteenth Imam," thus positioning him alongside the Twelve Imams of Shi'i Islam and emphasizing his religious leadership vis-à-vis his *sayyed* status (genealogical descent from the Prophet).

After leaving the mausoleum, we meet up with Mahmud and his sons and continue our trip by visiting the adjacent Zahra's Paradise, the largest graveyard in Iran. The cemetery, which is named after Fatemeh Al-Zahra, the daughter of the Prophet and the so called "mother of the Imams," has both a regular graveyard, where Parvin's deceased kin are buried, and a renowned martyrs' section that houses and commemorates Iran-Iraq War martyrs. Displays and signs emphasize the spilled blood of national war heroes and the sacrifice of Iranian families whose sons, brothers, and husbands have fought or died. They organize the bodies of constituents around a sense of what I have called "kindred citizenship," citizenship that is shaped by a sense of familial piety (see chapter 3).

In addition to the evocations of blood, foregrounded in chapter 3, this "kinning" (Howell 2003) of citizens is induced at the mausoleum through the cooking and sharing of blessed food. Families at Zahra's Paradise stand on the pavement distributing *āsh*, a traditional votive soup made of stewed herbs, noodles, and vegetables, and *halvā*, a sweet wheat paste. They spread out a dining cloth or *sofreh* on the grave of a kinsperson and then share the food with their family members as well as with other visitors. On our visit to the martyrs' section, one family gives us warm milk in plastic cups from behind an official-looking kiosk. We thank them by saying prayers for their family and deceased. These are very much like the votive offerings shared at Fars-Abad's cemetery, but on a larger scale. The milk, Parvin says, is blessed.

The sign over the kiosk reads, "This is the fifth day that we are under siege [by the Iraqi Army]. Water has been rationed; thirst is killing everyone, everyone but the martyrs who are lying next to each other in the end of the canal. Oh Fatemeh's Son [Imam Husayn]! We would sacrifice ourselves for your thirsty lips!" This text, which is from the journal of an Iranian soldier, likens the soldiers' thirst in the desert to that of the family of the Imam Husayn killed during the Battle of Karbala. The family's choice of warm milk implicitly recalls the nourishing (and kin-making) efficacy of breast milk in Islam. When we receive our steaming cups, the men behind the kiosk call us "brother," "sister," "mother," or "father," depending on our age and gender (Wellman 2017a).

When I ask, Parvin's eldest son explains why they use these terms: "[It is] because they and I have Islam" he says. "We are like brothers. To someone who is older, I say 'father.' If there is an elderly lady, I say 'my mother.' She is my mother. Religion is important. It is very important in this manner" (Wellman 2017a). Religion and kinship here are inseparable. A few months later, when I am in Fars-Abad, Parvin and her daughter, Haleh, tell me over the phone that they have visited the mausoleum again, this time for the birthday of Khomeini. They send me pictures of thousands of people and plastic containers of kebab and fruit, food that they say is sponsored by the state.[3]

CREATING AN ISLAMIC NATION THROUGH FOOD 157

Figure 15. Kiosk serving hot milk in Zahra's Paradise

· · · · ·

While chapter 2 explored the relationship between the blessed food shared at the *sofreh* and the making of kin, this chapter expands outward to examine how state elites and Basijis are mobilizing food at the level of the public sphere and/or nation-state to create kinship among citizens and among those same citizens and God. For "ordinary," "inactive" Basijis like Parvin and her family in postrevolutionary Iran, participation in state religion is a regular part of everyday life. They frequently take part in national/ritual commemorations that involve both prayer for their kin and the public and pious sharing of votive soup, lemon drink, and other foods. This blessed food is distributed in graveyards, public parks, pilgrimage sites, and streets in both the provinces and the urban centers of Iran. It is featured in contexts as diverse as Islamic-national commemorations for martyrs, the birth and death days of the Twelve Imams and their descendants, and commemorations of political-religious figures such as Ayatollah Khomeini.

Giving and receiving food in these contexts is a means of participating in the divine and sharing blessing. At the same time, however, and for supporters of the Islamic Republic in particular, this outpouring of food also typifies the tremendous labor involved in protecting and blessing a pure and pious family. Indeed, like the family, the nation is organized by the imperative to create and contain inner purity within its borders. It depends on the continual regeneration of a pure, Islamic interior composed of the right kind of virtuous (*bā-taqvā*) citizenry composed of brothers and sisters of Islam, a bulwark against societal corruption.

When the state and its supporters share food on the broader scales of town, province, or nation, then, they draw from and inhabit these familial and religious resonances and typifications. In what follows, I explore how food as a biomoral, physio-sacred substance with strong ties, both to Shi'i Islam and to the substances of kinship, is being mobilized, not only as a source of symbolic nation-making but also as a means of shaping relations among citizens and among those same citizens, the land of Iran, and God. I begin by addressing how food and debates surrounding food are linked to citizenship as well as to the demarcation of Iranian national and religious boundaries (Bourdieu 1984; Douglas 1972).

FORGING A HALAL NATION-STATE: INNER PURITY AND OUTER CORRUPTION

Food has long been deeply entangled with Iranian nation-making (Mintz and Dubois 2002; Wilk 2006). Iranians have invented and valorized what is now a recognizable "national cuisine," with recipes that showcase delicious combinations of rice and meat, vegetables and nuts, as well as fruits such as plums, pomegranates, quinces, and prunes (Holtzman 2006; Allison 1991; Hobsbawm 1983; Appadurai 1988; see Batmanglij 1986).[4] Food has also been a key means of religious differentiation (Feeley-Harnik 1981).[5] The postrevolutionary Islamic Republic has sponsored the explicit Islamification of national foodways, including the standardization of halal (religiously permitted) foods and food certifications specific to Shi'i Islam (Attar, Lohi, and Lever 2016).

These food practices and policies are tied to changing notions of and imperatives for Iranian citizenship (Ohnuki-Tierney 1994; Farquhar 2002).[6] In her work on postsocialist China, Judith Farquhar (2002) documents how "appetites" for food (and sex) can shift in relation to larger societal changes, as well as in relation to power relations and structures of authority. Specifically, she documents the change from Maoist ideology—visible in what was then an emphasis on food simplicity, comradeship, and austerity—to 1990s postsocialist consumerism, evidenced by pleasure/banquet eating. In Iran, the last century has similarly brought dramatic changes to "appetites" in relation to state authority and directives. The reign of the Pahlavis (1925–79) had embodied a national aesthetic of modernization and Westernization that was made visible, in part, by the "civilizing" introduction of foreign cuisine, tables, chairs, ingredients, and utensils to homes and restaurants. In contrast, citizens in postrevolutionary Iran have witnessed a state-led backlash against such Western "appetites," which the state and its most ardent supporters associate with a "cultural invasion." The professed aim of Iran's current leaders is to limit the global incursion of unlawful (*harām*), foreign (*khāreji*), and fast foods, which are associated with the "West" and with incorrect, bad behavior and sinning, symptoms of national moral decay.

This pairing of "Western" food practices and moral decay can be found in the buildup to the Revolution in the work of the influential Iranian sociologist Jalal Al-e Ahmad. In *Gharbzadegi* (Westernstruckness) ([1962] 1997), Al-e Ahmad criticized the increasing moral fragmentation of prerevolutionary, 1960s Iranian society as one aspect of "Westernstruckness": a disease of the West evidenced by the influx of the machine, economic dependence on the West, rampant urbanization, and "empty" or "soulless" Western mimicry. He called for Iranians to gain control over the machine and become producers rather than consumers, as well as for a return to Islamic authenticity. In one passage, he wrote: "Such a chronically starved individual [meaning a Westernized Iranian], who's eaten bread and dugh [an Iranian yogurt drink] all his life in the village, once he's filled his stomach with a sandwich in the city, will go to the barber and the tailor, then for a shoe shine, and then to the whorehouse. . . .

Mosques and altars have been forgotten... an entire city can't be fed on donated American powdered milk or Australian wheat" (Al-e Ahmad [1962] 1997, 76). It is no coincidence that Al-e Ahmad brought up the Western-style sandwich "from the city" as one catalyst of Iranian moral decay. The *sāndevich-e kālbās*, in particular, an imported sandwich not unlike the American "sub" or "grinder," became a favored lunch for a whole generation of teenagers in the 1960s and continues to be popular today: an easy form of *fast food*, as they call it in conversational Persian. For the wry Al-e Ahmad, the consumption of such processed, Western sandwiches, made from Western-style, plastic-wrapped bread and processed meats, signaled the first stage of moral corruption and was a harbinger of the whorehouse (Wellman 2020).

Al-e Ahmad's negative assessment of Western hegemony (including Western foodways) and its disease-like qualities is representative of an entire generation of prerevolutionary nativist intellectuals who critiqued the economic power imbalance of East and West and sought an Islamic solution to Western-backed Mohammad Reza Pahlavi's "superficial" modernization programs in the 1960s and 1970s (Gheissari 1998). As a remedy for Western hegemony, Al-e Ahmad and other nativist scholars, such as Ali Shari'ati, Daryush Shayegan, and Ehsan Naraghi, argued for a return to purity and to the authentic (*esālat*) Shi'i Islamic spirituality that they saw as particular to Iran (see Boroujerdi 1996).[7] Many of these scholars further argued that this Iranian citizenry should specifically be modeled on the lives, relationships, and virtues of the family of the Prophet (Shariati 1981; see also Moallem 2005). Ayatollah Khomeini built on this framing of a pure Islamic self against a corrupt outside in his seminal text, *Islamic Government* (Khomeini [1970] 2005): "Let them go all the way to Mars or beyond the Milky Way; they will still be deprived of true happiness, moral virtues and spiritual advancement and be unable to solve their own social problems. For the solution of social problems and the relief of human misery require foundations in faith and morals; merely acquiring material power and wealth, conquering nature and space, have no effect in this regard" (Khomeini and Algar [1970] 2005).[8]

Khomeini joined other leading clerics and revolutionaries here and elsewhere in clearly distinguishing the spiritual and moral virtue of the Revolution—and later the Islamic Republic of Iran—from the perceived materialism and spiritual vacancy of "outside" imperialist countries, which he compared to the Westernized shah and ultimately to the evil Yazid in the Battle of Karbala. For many Basijis, including my hosts, Khomeini continues to embody the conceptual opposite of the self-aggrandizing shah. His message, they say, was one of Islamic purity, justice, and integrity.

During my research in Fars-Abad, this call to defend the moral integrity of the Islamic Republic was also visible in speeches by the local Friday Imam. His weekly sermons asked townspeople to fear hell even as they were to have faith in Allah's bounty. He also specifically asked congregants "to love the Imam 'Ali whose spiritual light will guide them," guidance he saw as a "defense of state and Islam." These sermons were connected to geopolitical events. In one June sermon, he criticized the actions of the Americans, French, English, and Israelis for shooting at the humanitarian ships near Gaza as well as for their efforts to control Iran through sanctions. "Many times over the last thirty years," he said, "this Islamic nation has shown willingness to defend the worth of the Revolution and army and to seek protection in the leader [the Supreme Leader of Iran, Ayatollah Khamenei] and in the blood of its martyrs. In so doing they have respected the great ones of their religion." He then asked prayer participants to help make Iran as independent from foreign powers as possible. In Fars-Abad, this and other Friday sermons were a call for townspeople to live in constant readiness to fight for their "independence" at the behest of their great religious leaders.

Now some forty years after the Revolution, debate continues to revolve around the imperative to purify the Islamic Republic, or what an ethnohistorian of Iran, Afsaneh Najmabadi, has termed "the moral purification of a corrupt society" (1987, 203). The public face of this imperative is manifest as a continual "reshaping of morals" (Khosravi 2008): a directive to "engineer goodness" by helping the country achieve an "inner purity" (*safā-ye bāten*). This endeavor requires the vigilant warding off of satanic, Western temptations and impurities of many types and forms (Khosravi 2008, 23). Food (and "appetites" for food) is a subject of these debates. A biomoral substance that can be produced and consumed, shared or contained, pure or impure, blessed or contaminated, food has been critical to the political-religious project of making ideal pure and kindred citizens.

Postrevolutionary Foodscapes

Following the 1979 Revolution, key policy changes dramatically shaped Iranian foodways. The newly formed state outlawed companies such as Kentucky Fried Chicken and McDonald's, replacing them with locally owned, more "Islamically" friendly versions such as "McMashallah" (Chehabi 2003). Iranian food corporations similarly took up a model of Islamification. The Islamic cola company Zamzam, for instance, became its own corporation after the Revolution. Zamzam takes its name from the sacred spring in Mecca and is marketed as an alternative to Pepsi or Coca-Cola.[9] In 2010, Zamzam held a nearly 50 percent market share of soft drinks in Iran, owning multiple beverage plants within the Islamic Republic. Interestingly, the Zamzam soft drink company is owned by the Foundation of the Oppressed and Disabled, one of Iran's largest philanthropic foundations, which sponsors Islamic/national martyrs' commemorations and charities across the country.[10]

Despite these changes, Western-style fast-food venues and restaurants remain prolific. In Tehran, upscale shopping malls and squares such as Golestan and Tajrish are dotted with pizza, pasta, fried chicken, and sandwich restaurants that are heavily patronized by fashion-conscious young people, mostly from the middle and upper classes. These venues, popular in part *because* of their association with the foreign, double as venues for self-presentation and as meeting places for unwed couples. In addition, a wide range of restaurants offer (halal) high-end Asian, Italian, French, and nouveau cuisine.

At the same time, other neighborhoods in Tehran have very different configurations and expectations for the correct movements of bodies in streets and alleys. In the south of Tehran, for example, there are fewer foreign-style restaurants and more "traditional restaurants" (*resturān-e sonnati*). These include "coffee houses" (*qahveh khuneh*), which serve drinks and other refreshments; kebab shops, which cater to male workers or travelers and serve simple Iranian-style beef and chicken kebab; and restaurants that specialize in certain dishes such as "brain soup" (*kaleh pācheh*) or "thick meat broth soup" (*dizi*).[11] Increasingly, there are also high-end "authentic" restaurants, popular with upper-class clientele. These latter combine rustic decor, "traditional" foods, and music.

Finally, most cities and small towns now have a variety of relatively inexpensive generic restaurants, which I term "Iranian." These restaurants, also present in provincial towns such as Fars-Abad, cater to family groups or travelers and serve a common, affordable, national menu on plastic plates and cutlery. The menus are composed of foods that can be found in Iranian cookbooks—for example, "sultan kebab" (*kabāb-e soltāni*) with saffron rice and roasted tomatoes, "parsely, cilantro, fenugreek stew with rice" (*qormez sabzi*), "barberry rice" (*zereshk polow*), and "lentil rice" (*adas polow*)—and combine sweet-sour and sweet-savory flavors (see also Harbottle 2000).[12]

This vast range of differing restaurants yields very different—and sometimes competing—forms of appropriate behavior, class, gendered comportment, politics, and piety. Many of these forms are explicit. For instance, in an editorial in a 2010 edition of the magazine *Green Family Cooking*, available at newsstands across Iran, contributor Sara Ebrahami jokingly describes how people assess marriage partners according to what they eat: "The same pizza that many young people like more than their own mother and father is so controversial that calling someone a 'pizza eater' (*pitza khor*) is a bad swear. When they [a mother of a bride] want to give their answer to a suitor, they say 'The boy is a pizza eater! He isn't even embarrassed.' . . . At the same time, if a suitor has not eaten pizza, it's likely that everyone will look at him as if he has horns on his back and a tail on his head! This is a bad thingggg!"[13] In this satirical column, being a "pizza eater" is a fraught position. It implies a certain amount of Western-struckness, the neglect of religious and family values, and even a poor upbringing. Yet as Ebrahami also notes, it is perhaps even more strange to court someone who has not eaten pizza. The very idea is almost unthinkable. The pizza noneater, she implies from her perspective in urban Tehran, would have to be secluded, unworldly, and/or entirely too pious.

Ebrahami's article on this subject was likely written for a specific class of educated elite Tehranis and expresses some of the competing values of this cohort, in particular, a sense that those who actively avoid foreign foods are probably "too pious" or "too secluded." Perhaps surprisingly, Mahmud's eldest son, a member of the Basij, agreed with this assessment to some degree. On the one hand, he argued, pizza is not a real food because it is not cooked at home for the *sofreh* by a wife/mother with pure intention. On the other hand, he said that his mother implicitly endeavored to find marriage partners for her children with a certain, albeit acceptable and appealing, amount of cosmopolitanism, whether in the form of knowledge of foreign films, a bit of English, or, yes, (fancy) pizza—from the right restaurant. Yet he and his four other Tehrani siblings were also limited by other constraints: for instance, lack of a sufficient budget to spend money on expensive food or the fact that attire such as his sister's chador might seem out of place in one venue but not another.

Interestingly, "pizza eater" has an important conceptual opposite in this and other conversations about food: the "soup eater" (*āsh khor*). "Soup eaters," several middle-class Tehrani university students explained to me with a glint of humor, are young and poor Iranian soldiers who are forced to eat "traditional" soup and other austere foods while in military service. The quintessential "soup eater" works as a uniformed guard or laborer, possibly carrying out his service in his barracks far from home.

These two categories, "pizza eater" and "soup eater," exemplify just a few of the potent interconnections between "appetites" for food and people's differing experiences of class, piety, and politics in Iran. As members of the Basij and the vanguards of the Revolution, my hosts—and particularly their young adult children—had a very particular position within these competing categories, but they were often more eager to inhabit a worldly and cosmopolitan form of Iranian (food) citizenship—under the right, halal conditions—than might be expected given the state's call for moral purification. I now provide some examples of how they navigated Iran's postrevolutionary foodscape.

RESTAURANT 1

In 2010, Haleh and I visit a Western-style fast-food restaurant in an upscale mall in the northern Tehran neighborhood of Tajrish. Haleh, then an unmarried twenty-six-year-old university graduate student and member of the Basij, suggests the location and venue. She wants to shop for Iranian New Year presents for her kin as well as for a long cotton coat (*māntou*) for me. (Such a coat, if it approximates knee length and is accompanied by a scarf, is acceptable as a form of hijab in most parts of Tehran.) Haleh has dressed for the outing in a colorful headscarf under her black chador, nice blue jeans, low shiny heels, and a hint of fancy perfume.

We travel to the shopping area by way of a public (and mixed gender) taxi (*savori*), packed subways, and finally a bus, reaching the bustling shopping square filled with women and men approximately an hour and a half later. Tired and hungry, we stop and eat. Haleh says she knows a good place, a small but busy multistory restaurant that serves fast-food. From an array of Western options such as pizza and burgers, displayed with photographs on a numbered menu over the counter, we both choose a meal of lasagna (served with packets of ketchup), Zamzam cola, and Iranian plain yogurt, which we pay for and carry upstairs to the dining area on red plastic trays. The colors of the establishment are bright blue and red solids, resembling fast-food restaurants and chains in the United States. The (male) employees behind the counter wear standardized uniforms and hats and serve our food cafeteria style. We eat on the restaurant's second floor, a small room with crowded tables and picnic-style benches, looking out a window that faces Tajrish square. The customers, for the most part, are young. They include married couples with small children, some young men, and even a few couples who seem to be courting. The customers speak loudly with each other, often laughing and talking or checking phone messages. Most of the women around us are wearing stylish clothes and designer shoes and jeans, as well as makeup, with their scarves and cotton coats. Haleh's chador is one of the few in sight.

RESTAURANT 2

About a week later I travel with Haleh and her family in Mahmud's green Tehran taxi to a very different kind of establishment, a restaurant called Sofreh House of the Garden of Ferdous, situated next to a mosque. This restaurant, Haleh explains, caters to "religious people." The restaurant is gated, and Mahmud has to show his Basij card to enter. Once inside, Haleh's father and oldest brother fetch beef and chicken kebabs, flat bread, Zamzam cola, and yogurt for the family, while her younger brother and mother accompany us to one of many cordoned-off family gazebo-like picnic areas in an outdoor, colorful but softly lit park. All of the female customers in this establishment are dressed in chadors. They wander in pairs among the small canals and gardens that surround the dining gazebos, before returning to the company of their families. When the steaming food arrives, it comes in individual portions on plastic serving dishes. On the way home, Haleh says, "I really like it there because it is easy to wear a chador there but other places make chador wearing difficult." She says that she also likes the overall religiosity of the place (it is proximate to a mosque and has strategically positioned religious placards). She likes the separate, family-sized unit. She doesn't have to interact with "potential marriage partners" (nā-mahram).

Indeed, and in contrast to the openness of a typical fast-food restaurant in Tehran, the Garden of Ferdous is configured through the motif of enclosure. There is walled separation between the religiously oriented, Basij-only dining space and the possibly corrupt outside. Each table has its own gazebo roof and picnic bench and is spaced out such that each family need not hear the other family's voices, see them, or otherwise interact. Within the restaurant and gazebo, there is enough room to wear a chador comfortably, another form of enclosure. In contrast, other restaurants, such as the fast-food places in the north of Tehran, make wearing a chador difficult in the close proximity required for ordering and seating.

My hosts' experience at these two restaurants reveal how food and eating can shape and be shaped by multiple, and often competing, "moral rubrics" for what is right or appropriate (Deeb and Harb 2013, 23).[14] This morality is inscribed into the spatial organization of the restaurants, the foods they serve, and people's expectations for social interaction within them (Deeb and Harb 2013). Restaurant 1 and Restaurant 2 differently shape the movements of people within and outside them, coding for specific forms of morality, citizenship, and ways of relating. The specifically Islamic, Iranian restaurants, such as the Sofreh House of the Garden of Ferdous, make "correct" relating with kin and strangers possible. They allow customers to foreground their families, their kinship, and their modesty. For a young pious, unmarried woman like Haleh, this is more desirable. At the same time, and in relation to her education and social networks outside of home (including her American anthropologist friend), she is cosmopolitan, within reason, and is open to a diversity of foreign-style venues and spaces, especially when these venues are combined with shopping trips to more upscale malls such as those found in the north of Tehran. Her cosmopolitanism, however, also reveals generational differences. Her mother and father would not go to Restaurant 1 and eat pizza or lasagna unless they had little option—not because the cuisine was unhealthy but because it was foreign. Which appetites are appropriate thus can depend not only on religious tenets, but also on social obligations, gender, generational differences, class, and political affiliations.

Halal Appetites

The other major feature of Iran's postrevolutionary foodscape is its Islamic laws concerning halal food and drink. With few exceptions, state policy makers prohibit the export, import, and production and consumption of "unlawful" substances, such as pork and alcohol, within and across Iran's territorial borders.[15] Today, although not all Iranian Muslims follow these rules and/or do so to varying degrees, the Islamic Republic is largely bound by halal imperatives; laws concerning halal foods are legally enforced (Chehabi 2007; Attar, Lohi, and Lever 2016).

One of the ways the state emphasizes halal foods and the standardization of what is halal is through the Halal World Institute (HWI). Based in Tehran, HWI works in cooperation with both the Islamic Chamber Research and Information Center and Iran's government to offer a halal certification, similar to a kosher label on food goods, for food vendors. HWI certification provides a way to standardize halal foods nationally.

Notably, however, jurists and laymen regularly debate the particularities of what is halal.[16] Religious leaders, for example, originally classified Caspian Sea caviar as impermissible to consume due to the apparent lack of scales on sturgeon. They further regarded the fish with suspicion because of its association with Western cuisine (Chehabi 2007). However, when scales were supposedly found near the sturgeon's tail several high-ranking clerics, including Ayatollah Khomeini, met with fishing experts and reversed the traditional ruling. Skeptics of this shift argued that these clerics simply saw that Caspian Sea caviar had become a superb moneymaking industry, an accusation that Khomeini himself vehemently denied. In the end, the sturgeon was declared halal.[17]

Yet, and as noted in chapter 2, the designation of halal has application far beyond the religious or legal sanctioning of particular foods. An entire range of acts may be classified as halal or its conceptual opposite, *harām* or unlawful. These include diet, sexual relations, daily habits and customs, marriage and divorce, family relations, public morality, occupation and income, and types of entertainment.[18] My Basiji hosts in both Tehran and Fars-Abad consistently associated halal acts—including but not limited to eating the right foods—with becoming right (*dorost*) and developing character (*shakhsiat*). They said that such acts were a means of becoming "complete" and of attaining "spiritual sustenance" (*ruzi*). "We become closer to God when we perform halal acts. This is what the Imam 'Ali told us," Maryam explained. In contrast, *harām* acts were to be avoided, not only for the sake of the corruption of the individual or even the family, but also for the protection of Iran as an Islamic Republic more broadly.

I here draw from the story of a shrine in Fars Province and its pollution to show how my interlocutors understood the intersections between appetites for halal food, halal behavior, and the protection and purity of society, more broadly.

"PRISTINE WATER ONCE FLOWED HERE"

On the birthday of the Eighth Imam, the Imam Reza (~765–818 CE), Nushin, her youngest son, and I traveled to "the shrine of Imamzadeh Hamza," a descendant of the Seventh Imam, Musa Al-Kazem, and his sister, known locally as Bibi Khatun (Madelung 2012). The shrine is located in the district of Bavanat, about fifty kilometers away from Fars-Abad (Madelung 2012). Nushin told me that she was "called" to the shrine. She had dreamed that we must come. Imam Musa Al-Kazem and Bibi Khatun were kin to Imam Reza, and it was Imam Reza's birthday. But at the threshold, she stopped us from entering, remembering something.

"Pristine water once flowed here," she said, pointing beyond the gate to the dry canals in front of the beautiful portal, court, and dome. "It flowed in the intricate channels around the shrine that houses the sacred tomb. This water was pure (*pāk*) and carried divine healing. It spread blessing to the pilgrims who consumed it." We walked a little further into the complex and stood in the shadow of one of several giant trees growing between the stone tiles of the courtyard. She continued, "But one night some male youth who were 'without proper nature/self-control' (*bij-anbeh*) gathered and partied overnight in the shrine complex. They consumed alcohol and engaged in other illicit activities. Their unlawful acts led to the drying up of the spring that had flowed for centuries. I learned this from other pilgrims the last time I was here. I believe it absolutely."

Figure 16. Nushin praying at the shrine of Imam Reza's descendant, Bavanat, Iran

Nushin's words, spoken in the liminal space of the shrine's threshold, were a warning and a declaration of belief. The *harām* actions of corrupt youth—their drinking and other illicit activities—had polluted the spiritual power of the shrine and its ability to benefit others. The life-giving capacity of the spring had been obstructed, creating a thirst, one that evoked the collective thirst of Imam Husayn and his family and their martyrdom during the Battle of Karbala. The youths' *harām* actions, moreover, had consequences for everyone; they had altered the integrity of the shrine itself and the capacity of all its pilgrims to receive its blessing.

In chapter 2 I discussed Nushin's concerns and prayers for her children, specifically her teenage sons. These concerns are also reflected in statist discourse, which describes the nation's youth population as a battleground in the fight against "Western cultural invasion" and as "the weak point of the *ummat*" (Khosravi 2008, 20). In particular, the state disapproves of the numbers of young people who consume alcoholic beverages, drugs, and other substances illicit in Islamic law. Nushin, her relatives, and friends in Fars-Abad talked about these youth often, lamenting the young people who go to gardens to smoke the hookah, dance, and drink or who drive around in their parents' cars, blasting Iranian pop or rap music. These are the precursors, they said, of other *harām* acts like premarital sex.

Nushin's story of the shrine and its pollution is a moral reflection on these youth. Those responsible are "deceived hedonists" (*bi-dard*), "free from family ties and norms" (*bi-gheid az band-hā-ye khānevādegi*) (Khosravi 2008, 24). They are the implicit opposite of ideal Iranian Muslim youth and citizens. These latter youth, as portrayed on television or in film—and very much in alignment with the stated aim of the Basij—are the zealous "guardians of values," both of family and state (Golkar 2015). They are conscious (*āgāh*) warriors (*mobārez*), who are willing to perform "self-sacrifice," like Imam Husayn (Khosravi 2008, 10). They are beholden to and enmeshed within family ties. These youth do not engage in unlawful activities such as consuming alcohol; and what is more, they prevent others from doing so. Their goal is "the promotion of virtue and the rejection of vice" (Khosravi 2008, 24).

According to Nushin and other pilgrims at the shrine of Imam Reza's descendants, the "appetites" of these (male) youth had had consequences, not only for the young people themselves but also for others. I now turn more explicitly to how gender shapes these appetites in more granular ways, informing what is appropriate, excusable, or modest, and thus shaping brother and sister citizens.

GENDERED APPETITES

Reza and his sister Maryam were sitting at home in Fars-Abad answering my questions about the concept of brothers and sisters of Islam when they veered off to the subject of eating outside (*birun*). Reza said, "We know it to be ugly/obscene (*zesht*) to eat [fresh bread from the bread lines] in front of strangers [in the street]. Some other things you can eat outside—ice cream or chips." Maryam agreed but added, "Eating sandwiches outside is also ugly/obscene." Her brother shook his head, "No, you can eat sandwiches. Especially, if I go so far away, if I am a traveler and I don't know anyone, it is okay. In Fars-Abad, it is obscene. People know who I am. . . . It is ugly."

According to Maryam and Reza, certain kinds of public eating are *zesht*, a word that is used to describe something "ugly," "obscene," or "unbecoming." While the consumption of potato chips or ice cream outside is tolerated, certain acts of public eating are very negatively regarded and are linked to bad manners, uncouth behavior, and public immodesty. Indeed, according to conventions of modesty (*ru-dar-bāyesti*) in Iran, it is not appropriate to eat in front of people you know because you should actually be offering the food before you eat it yourself. This includes eating bread in breadlines or eating meal-like foods in the street.

Yet while for Reza occasionally eating sandwiches in public is okay, Maryam knows that it is not the same for her as a young unmarried woman. This assessment is linked to Maryam's understanding of her ability as a female to move through the streets and alleys in Fars-Abad. As an unmarried young adult, eighteen-year-old Maryam rarely left her home alone. When out with others, including her brothers, parents, or me, she walked rigidly and seriously, avoiding eye contact with strangers.[19] In contrast, her brother Reza was more comfortable on the street. He could sit in relaxed postures, stop and chat, and move unfettered. He and his friends were much more likely than their sisters to eat snacks or even sandwiches outside of the home.[20] Such gendered understandings of public eating and modesty reflect the strong connection between halal aesthetics, "correct" comportment, and the maintenance of moral social relations.

The public consumption of votive food in the street, graveyard, or mosque, however, is evaluated very differently. As Maryam remarked in the same conversation: "In the graveyard, you read Al-Fātihah, you eat, it is not *zesht*." On such occasions, participants call each other "brothers and sisters of Islam," or use other epithets such as "mother," "grandfather," or "Hajji." They share food to gain religious merit, protecting themselves on the Day of Judgment, and to share blessing. In so doing, they are divinely sanctioned to share and eat food in public just as they would at home.

Attention to "appetites" and their link to public morality is intensified during Ramadan. On one occasion in Shiraz, I stood sipping a bottle of water on Imam Reza Boulevard. Cars honked at the busy intersection as pedestrians tried to cross. Many more walked on the sidewalk on their way to work: a man wearing a blue workman's jumper, two women ushering a child, several others in business attire. It was mid-Ramadan, and

I was anxious to renew my research visa. I was with Reza, Nushin and Ahmad's son. We had just begun crossing the busy street when someone on the other side yelled at me for drinking in public. I was startled; the stranger clearly had no idea whether we were traveling or not, a category of activity that exempts a person from the fast according to Islamic law. Why had he reacted so vehemently? Reza explained, "It's bad to eat when others are fasting. You don't want to make it harder for them. If you eat in public, even if you yourself are not fasting, you lose face."

After seeing the visa authorities, we were hungry, but Reza and I could find only one open sandwich shop in Shiraz, a fast-food establishment in a tourist district. This seemingly lone shop masked its business by placing large dark curtains on all windows, literally blocking out the sight of eating. Indeed, most restaurants and small sandwich shops were closed both in Fars-Abad and Shiraz during daylight hours, and normal offerings of tea and biscuits in workplaces and universities were suspended. In 2010, even drinking water publicly or chewing gum was highly derided during Ramadan. Uniformed officers patrolled parks and streets, questioning eating and drinking and watching for other unlawful activity.

As discussed in chapter 2, the act of depriving the body of food through fasting during Ramadan (and at other times) is a means of gaining control of bodily passions and of spiritual refinement, a means of governing the self and its "appetites" (*havā-ye nafs*). But fasting during Ramadan also has consequences for the larger society. For state elites and state supporters, there is a clear public dimension to the control of appetites, a drive to create and control public morality through fasting and feasting. Just as it is inappropriate to eat in front of fasting friends and relatives, it is inappropriate to eat in front of complete strangers during the holy month.

· · · · ·

In this section I have examined how food provides a technology of religious nation-making in postrevolutionary Iran. Since the 1979 Revolution, state policy makers have been critical of Western appetites for food and their perceived consequences for individual behavior, family life, and national integrity/independence. These policy makers have seen the global incursion of foreign (*khāreji*) or fast foods as a catalyst for incorrect, bad behavior and sinning: symptoms of national moral decay. They have employed food to explicitly and implicitly distinguish postrevolutionary Iran from the nation's "spiritually vacant" prerevolutionary era (e.g., as manifest in the shah's Western modernization programs).

Many of my Basiji interlocutors in Tehran and Fars-Abad share these views, but in complicated ways. They value certain foods and restaurant venues for attributes of religiosity and modesty and others for their cosmopolitanism. Indeed, the young, urban Basijis I met were flexibly engaged with Western-style fast foods. Being a "pizza eater" was not always bad; it was a sign of worldliness and balance, as long as the pizza was made of halal ingredients and eaten in an appropriate manner.[21] Even as they explored the urban foodscape, however, these Basij youth were attuned to how foods and food venues can shape behavior, purity, and morality, both on an individual and societal basis. My most ardent interviewees saw halal foods, halal behaviors, and the making of a halal nation, in particular, as deeply intertwined, and they were aware and reflective of how different restaurants, streets, parks, and graveyards—as well as their own maleness or femaleness—required them to differently inhabit space and relate to others.

Food and the cultivation of certain appetites for food are thus deeply connected to the shaping of citizens. In Iran, these appetites for food and food practices are gendered and are connected to the forging of the right kind of pure and halal brother and sister citizens. But while the Islamic Republic successfully cultivates appetites for halal food in the public sphere, it is less successful—at least in urban areas—at cultivating appetites for foods that strictly align with an Iranian national cuisine. Nevertheless, most people I spoke with (including my Basiji hosts) continued to view the sharing of (Iranian) fare at home with family members as foundational to family integrity, health, and purity. As I discuss in chapter 2, food shared in this manner was an agent of transformation and a means of channeling divine blessing (*ne'mat*) to the pure family core. This process of blessing and purification—as well as of kinning—is reproduced on town and national scales through votive food-sharing rituals.

CIRCULATING DIVINE BLESSING: SHARING FOOD ON A NATIONAL SCALE

Shi'i Iranian practices of devotion are multitudinous. They include actions such as the creation of votive wall hangings and mourning banners (Flaskerud 2010), symbolic self-flagellation during the rites of Muharram (Aghaie 2011), and the attendance at and participation in Shi'i passion plays (Beeman 2003; Chelkowski 1979). They also include local pilgrimage to the tombs of Shi'i saints (Betteridge 1992) and participation in devotional celebrations on the birthdays of Imams (Torab 2007; Kalinock 2003).

Pious food sharing is a central part of many of these public and pious rites. "Blessed food," or *tabarrok*, is served from giant vats in graveyards, shrines of Imams and their descendants, public squares, sidewalks, and mosques. Typical offerings include "thick noodle soup" (*āsh*), "saffron rice pudding" (*sholeh zard*), "sweet wheat paste" (*halvā*), and "split pea soup for Imam Husayn" (*qeimeh-ye Imam Husayn*), as well as "meat, lentil, wheat porridge" (*halim*), which is associated specifically with Muharram.

Indeed, this outpouring of food is especially prevalent during Muharram (a month of mourning for Imam Husayn and the events of the Battle of Karbala) and is often overlooked in scholarly analyses that favor the more famous street processions and self-flagellation that also mark the holy month. Sometimes the recipients of this blessed fare are neighbors and kin, but very often they are passersby of any variety: fellow townsmen, citizens, mourners, and pilgrims who are referred to as brothers and sisters of Islam. Nevertheless, it is impossible to overstate the simultaneous religious and political force of Muharram rituals for Iran as a whole. As Mary Hegland writes, such rituals "have been instrumental in Iran both in the preservation of the political status quo and in the complete overthrow of the political, economic, and social order" (1983b, 96).

In what follows, I examine the tremendous political and religious efficacy of pious food sharing in Iran on the scales of town and nation. This food sharing, I contend, helps create pure kindred citizens.

Hajji Hamed's Muharram Vow: Food Sharing in Town

> During Muharram, you can't find a single house [in Fars-Abad] that has not received votive food inside its walls. My brother has a 350 kilos vow of rice. On 'Ashura' more than 2,000 people come to eat vowed food [at his house] and go. Many do the same thing. Many have a "heavy vow" (*nazri-ye sangin*).
>
> —Nushin, Fars-Abad, October 31, 2010

In 2010 in Fars-Abad, Hajji Hamed, the brother of Nushin, distributed twenty vats of rice and stew to hundreds of townspeople. With the help of male kin, he cooked the rice in the courtyard of his home in large metal vats that read "Yā Husayn" in blood red Persian script.

The women worked in the kitchen, preparing plates of food for guests. Nushin told me that Hajji had made a vow several years before to provide 350 kilos of rice to all who wanted it during the month of Muharram. He didn't tell us why, but every year his courtyard would fill with men and women, separated by gender, sitting around a *sofreh* that ran from one length of the outdoor space to the other. Alternatively, recipients received takeaway votive dishes in plastic containers for their families.

Although the cooking and distribution of votive food is prevalent throughout the nationally recognized holy month of Muharram, it is especially emphasized on the ninth and tenth days of the month, the specific day when Imam Husayn was martyred at the Battle of Karbala. Ahmad explained, "Because Iran is an Islamic country and a Shi'i country, from the first of Muharram to the tenth on 'Ashura', many people give a *sofreh* every afternoon [during this time period]." Nushin and her husband estimated that Fars-Abadis collectively cook several tons of rice each year. Rather than a single event, such offerings often take place sequentially: yearly, on every 'Ashura', for example, or for ten days in a row, from the first of Muharram to the tenth. There are two ways to share votive meals publicly: from a temporary kiosk set up on the street or in the form of a *sofreh-ye nazri* (a votive meal) in the courtyard of the home, the garage, or front outdoor alley. The latter form was more common in Fars-Abad.

Figure 17. Hajji Hamed's Muharram vow, Fars-Abad, Iran

Locals gave various reasons for this outpouring of food: "to keep the name of Imam Husayn alive," "to gain religious merit of the afterlife," "to solve big problems," or "to receive a divine favor."

For my Basiji hosts, in particular, these votive offerings had multiple levels of meaning. As with all such votive meals, they revealed their family's piety and commitment to the welfare of the community. They did this by turning the family resources (money) and hard physical labor of cooking large quantities of food into blessing, cast both inward toward the family and outward to the community. At the same time, the outpouring of food, hospitality, and blessing at Muharram was also a means of demonstrating economic well-being and sociopolitical allegiances. One had to be well off and connected to host such a large event, and such events were often followed by a careful accounting in the form of animated conversations about who visited whom and for how long, the quality of the food, and so on. For my hosts, attending these events depended on whether the donor was kin and was a "good person."

At Hajji's votive meal, as well as at others I attended in Fars-Abad, recipients of such holy food were greeted with respect: madam (*khānom*) for women and sir (*āqā*) for men. Alternatively, people used terms such as "brother" or "sister," indexing the postrevolutionary usage of "brothers and sisters of Islam" (*barādar o khāhar-e islāmi*). I also heard otherwise unrelated people calling each other mother (*mādar*) and father (*pedar*). In addition to this kinship terminology, the logic of these votive offerings was the same as that of votive food prepared by women at home on a smaller scale to protect and bless the family: blessing derives from the food's dedication to a Shi'i Imam, a descendant of an Imam, or saint, who acts as an intercessor for requests or favors. Both the giver and the receiver of food are imbued with Islamic blessing by their respective acts of laboring over votive fare, work that includes buying or growing ingredients, selecting and sacrificing a lamb, stirring, cooking, heating, praying, and so on.

When I asked Nushin whether there was any exclusivity to this ritual distribution, she was adamant that it was open and equitable: "No, it is for everyone. Anyone who wants to can participate. It is not such that only 'extended kin' can come, for example, and others cannot." She added, "In Fars-Abad, we have Sunnis, Afghanis. They also come. I've seen them at the *sofreh* of my brother. They eat. It's not just for Shi'as or even just for Muslims. . . . Everyone [in Iran] respects Muharram."[22] Nushin's impression of inclusivity, however, although genuine, was not shared by everyone. Even as she and her family took care to treat the local Afghan workers they hired to do farm work or well digging with respect, many I spoke with held negative stereotypes about Afghan immigrants; the Arab population of Fars-Abad, who were mostly Sunni Muslims; and Sunni Muslims in general. They variously called these groups dirty, impure, and dangerous, although people reported that intermarriage between these groups and Fars-Abadis was increasing. Not surprisingly, in actual practice these categories of person were not often invited to share a votive meal.

In contrast to his wife, moreover, Ahmad argued that people give and receive votive food precisely *because* Iran is a "Shi'i country and a Muslim country." Thus in practice, while all may ostensibly be invited to such occasions, and although the doors of the family's courtyard were certainly more open during Muharram than at other times to such persons, those who frequented Hajji Hamed's *nazri*, and others like it, consisted mainly of what my host family considered the "core" Fars-Abad community. They were those who lived near Hajji Hamed's home in the center of town (not its outlying partitions, such as the Arab neighborhood or the settled nomad neighborhood) and those who attended Friday prayers in the same locale, with the notable exception of one or two Afghan workers who helped with farm work.

Like other larger scale votive *sofreh*s, Hajji Hamed's meal resonates with the orchestration of the household *sofreh* by engaging participants in the enactment of "correct" relationships. At Hajji Hamed's votive meal, for instance, food was administered in a courtyard segregated by gender, and visitors carefully practiced Persian civility (Beeman 2001). Such civility included deference according to hierarchies, such as those between patrons and clients, elders and youth, and men and women. At Hajji Hamed's *sofreh*, people carefully enacted this civility in the form of greetings and other verbal exchanges of reciprocity, as well as in bodily practices such as serving food in a certain order or sitting in a particular manner (formal and kneeling or cross-legged and relaxed).

In addition, such public meals are formed around a *sofreh*, and the food served is often the same as what is regularly served at home. Indeed, there is a literal expansion of the home to the street when food cooked in the kitchen is distributed outside in the courtyard or beyond. Finally, as with food sharing at home, the food blesses the donor family and the recipients while fashioning pure and halal relations.

Sharing Blessed Foods during Ramadan

Like Muharram, Ramadan is a time for public and pious food sharing, even as it is a time for fasting. In chapter 2, I described the Night of Power (Shab-e Qadr in Persian or Laylat Al-Qadr in Arabic), the night when the first verses of the Qur'an were revealed to the Prophet.[23] Muslims regard this as the most important event in history, and the Qur'an says that this night is better than a thousand months (97:3). On this night, people say, angels descend to the earth.

In Fars-Abad, the Night of Power is commemorated in the local meeting house for Imam Husayn on the nineteenth, the twenty-first, and the twenty-third of the month of Ramadan and is led by the local Friday Imam, a government-appointed religious leader. My hosts described it as the most auspicious time of the year. According to one neighbor, "The act of staying awake and praying on the Night of Power has such a deep effect that it shapes the person until the next year or even until the end of life. It penetrates all thought, ethics, deeds, and behavior. It fulfills spiritual need." Accordingly, the night is critical to the development of Islamic morality, goodness, and spiritual refinement. It is a key night for the accumulation of religious merit and for partaking in blessing, whether through prayer, nourishment, or both.

The commemoration in July 2010 began at midnight and ended before sunrise (around 4:00 a.m.). Approximately fifteen hundred women gathered in the women's partition of the great hall, while the men sat to the left, made invisible by a heavy curtain. Nushin, Maryam, and I arrived with Nushin's male kin and then entered the building through gender-segregated doors. We joined friends and extended family who had already arrived and were sitting kneeling or crossed-legged on the carpet in rows. Children played raucously around the perimeter, running between the black and flowered chadors. The night began with a speech that echoed (almost incoherently) out of loudspeakers about Imam 'Ali, the son-in-law of the Prophet. My counterparts remarked that it was difficult to hear the speaker or the prayers, although we did catch the requisite sing-song medley that ends every Friday prayer in Fars-Abad: "Down with England, Down with Israel, Down with America." Around me, some of the participants attempted to concentrate on the distorted voices. Others took the opportunity to relax and talk about their lives, catching up on gossip or news about courtships.

Throughout the commemoration, women distributed votive food. In total, I counted more than fifty young girls (ages six to fifteen) sharing food with scores of participants across the floor—tea, *halvā*, dishes of saffron rice, stuffed dates, wrapped candies, "problem-solving candy" (*moshkel goshā*), "Ramadan confectionery" (*zolbiā o bāmieh*), and pastries—until everyone had consumed multiple servings.[24] Following this first food distribution, adult women fulfilled "heavier," or more serious, vows by offering those gathered sandwiches of herbs and feta cheese. The sounds of Iranian polite offering echoed in the hall, further obscuring the sound of the loudspeaker. Nushin, her sisters, Maryam, and I ate everything that was presented, even putting some sandwiches in a purse for later because the food was blessed. For the final prayer of the night, all fifteen hundred women attempted to balance a copy of the Qur'an on their heads, "keeping our hands free to open to God," as Nushin's sister explained. By this she meant that, with her hands unencumbered, she would be able to receive God's essence/light/blessing more easily.

As with other blessings distributed in tandem with prayer, the votive foods thus shared were recounted in the narratives and stories told about the night. Nushin later said that she had been frustrated by the poor sound system and quality of the sermon. She spoke positively, however, about the other women and the food they had shared. She told me that while she had recognized many of those providing vows, most were fellow townspeople with whom she did not have a previous direct acquaintance. She and her oldest daughter analyzed the quality of the sandwiches, the dates, and the tea. Their foremost experience of the town's (state-facilitated) ritual was thus one of shared food and prayer.

Pilgrimage and Votive Food Distribution

In addition to Mecca and Medina—sites that are holy to all Muslims—Shi'i Muslims frequently participate in pilgrimages to the tombs and shrines of successive Imams and their offspring. These sites form a critical location for the distribution of votive offerings to Shi'i Iranian stranger citizens and make visible how the national Islamic practice of sharing food with a transcendent religious community of brother and sister citizens extends beyond town confines. While some of these sites are found within Iran (particularly in Mashhad and Qom), others are located in countries such as Syria and Iraq. As an anthropologist of Iranian pilgrimage, Anne Betteridge (1985), has noted, these shrines are referred to as thresholds (*āstān*) and are liminal places where the conventional relations of cause and effect are suspended. This means that as one crosses into the interior of a shrine, one literally enters an enclosed sacred place, ultimately identified with the tomb of the Saint.

Such a pilgrimage to the shrines of Shi'i Imams and their descendants, both within and outside of Iranian borders, is central to Shi'i/Iranian identity. In 2010, almost all of the adult members of my extended host family had visited most of the major Shi'i shrines both inside and outside Iran (e.g., Najaf, Iraq, where the First Imam, 'Ali is buried, and Karbala, where the Third Imam, Husayn, was martyred.). Although my own research to date has focused on local pilgrimage within contemporary Iranian borders, it is clear that many Shi'as, as a community of believers, differentiate themselves through these practices.

LOCAL PILGRIMAGE

Although the spring at the shrine of the descendant of Imam Musa Al-Kazem in Bavanat had dried up, the location was still a sacred place for pilgrims. They often stayed the entire night, alone or in family groups, in tents in the *harām*, hoping to receive healing and divine blessing. On our visit to the shrine on a late afternoon summer day, an unknown woman and several female relatives greeted Nushin, Reza, and me. She had just finished cooking votive soup (*āsh*) in a big vessel. These women were publicly celebrating the fulfillment of a favor apparently granted by Imam Hamza.[25] Although she had never seen us before, she gave us a white plastic container of her soup, decorated with "dried whey" (*kashk*). Nushin said that this was a good sign as we entered the shrine enclave itself, where Nushin pointed out a bowl of votive candies by the door. Nushin handed each of us one of the holy sweets and carefully stowed away in her purse additional pieces to bring home for each family member. We also took the soup home to the family.

I have described how the sharing of votive meals or candies is a means of ensuring the purity and blessing of the family (see chapter 2). It is also a critical aspect of local pilgrimage to the tombs of Imams and their descendants (*imām-zadeh*). Indeed, many shrines include not only a portico and a mosque but also a place for cooking votive offerings. The votive fare thus shared is similar to that which is shared from homes or street kiosks. It may be the product of a relatively "light vow" (*nazri-ye sabok*), such as a bag of chocolates or pastries purchased from a bakery, or a "heavier vow" (*nazri-ye sangin*), such as saffron rice or votive soup imbued with Qur'anic verse and prayer to the family of the Prophet.

Moreover, as with other vows, such votive food distribution at shrines either represents a pilgrim's desire to forge an alliance with an Imam or Imamzadeh (thus compelling a future favorable response) or celebrates the granting of a favor, such as the solving of a family problem.[26] Yet regardless of the type of vow made, food prepared in the sanctuary of an Imamzadeh is considered especially potent (*moqavvi*) because of its proximity to the Imamzadeh's body, a body that does not rot or putrefy and from which is manifest his or her spiritual presence. The very "air and water" (*āb-o havā*) of such shrines is said to have a special quality. According to one of Nushin's sisters, "By cooking and sharing food from such sacred locations, the blessing is multiplied."[27]

While the sharing of votive food at shrines is in no way a requirement of local pilgrimage, it is so prevalent that pilgrims can almost always expect to receive at least a small quantity of holy food during each journey. Sometimes they also receive spiritual food in dreams during overnight stays at the shrine. Nushin recounted:

> I once went to Shah Cheragh [the shrine of the brothers Ahmad and Muhammad, sons of the Seventh Imam, Musa Al-Kazem, and brothers of the Eighth Imam, Imam Reza, located in Shiraz] and spent the night there with my husband. While I was sleeping I had a dream. I dreamed that I asked His Holiness Musa Al-Kazem to ask Imam Reza to help me. I had previously gone to the doctor. He had diagnosed me with a kidney stone. The doctor said that I would need to have some painful and difficult procedures. But I had a dream when I was there. I dreamed that all of the workers at Shah Cheragh were gathered around a *sofreh*. One of them was an old lady. I came to the *sofreh* and asked if I could have something. The lady gave me a glass of sherbet [a drink made of fruit syrup mixed with water]. I drank it and woke up with a start. I knew immediately that I had been healed. Imam Reza had healed me. I was certain that I would not need to go to the doctor again for this problem.[28]

On any night at important pilgrimage destinations such as Shah Cheragh, one might see hundreds of families sleeping on carpets or in tents around the outskirts of the shrine. During research, I heard several similar stories of healing by means of ingesting holy food in dreams. Such food is a gift from the Imam and is a means for divine blessing to enter and heal the bodies of those with pure hearts and faith.

The blessing of such votive offerings—whether consumed in dreams or in waking—works in tandem with other acts of prayer and veneration to purify the spirit and body. As one enters through multiple layers of the outer walls, the sanctuary, and the tomb, the shrine's physical place, walls, floors, and objects denote increasing proximity to the Imam or descendant, who is thought to be a worldly manifestation of Allah's reflection.[29] At the point of entry, pilgrims kiss the door of the enclave and recite a prayer of supplication, specific to the entombed saint. Having entered their gender-partitioned section, pilgrims place their hands on the golden cage enclosing the tomb and circumambulate, pausing at the corners. They deposit monetary gifts and notes of family troubles and other life difficulties between the rungs of the metal cage surrounding the tomb. On one occasion, for example, I helped a cousin of my hosts angle to the front of the crowded tomb of Imamzadeh Musa al-Kazem in Shah Cheragh so that she could deposit a piece of paper with a wish for an auspicious marriage. On other occasions, I watched as pilgrims tied votive rags or cloths or kissed the golden cage, hoping for divine blessing, peace, and wish fulfillment. Inside the carpeted sanctuaries, sounds of mourning intermingled with the whispers of pilgrims as they read prayers from Shi'i prayer books or from the Qur'an. In the outer portions of the sanctuaries, women sat chatting and catching up, perhaps even making a phone call.[30] Women pilgrims I traveled with almost always came back from their visits to shrines with beaming smiles and said that they felt calm and content.

PILGRIMAGE TO MECCA AND ZAMZAM WATER:
A CASE OF PURIFICATION FROM OUTSIDE

The first time I heard of the Zamzam well, I was in Ekbatan, Tehran, sitting at the computer with Haleh. As we talked, her mother, Parvin, explained that the water she had brought back from the sacred Zamzam well near the Ka'ba from the "house of God" (*khāneh-ye khodā*) in Mecca, Saudi Arabia, never goes bad, that it is blessed (*tabarrok*), and that it takes away impurities and has curative power.

According to tradition, Zamzam water sprang up miraculously for Ismael, the son of Abraham, when he was thirsty as a small child. His mother, Hagar, went seeking water but could not find it, so she prayed to God, imploring for aid. God sent Gabriel, who carved out a place in the earth with his heel where water appeared. Although Muslim tradition makes multiple references to the purifying potential of water in general (e.g., ablution) and also to several known sacred springs, the water of Zamzam is particularly important because of its location in Mecca. Pilgrimage rites in Mecca culminate in the drinking of Zamzam water, and the pilgrims have historically carried it home to give it to the sick. This continues today. Like other Muslims, Shi'i pilgrims from Iran travel to Mecca with the specific intention of bringing the blessed water back for their friends and family.

The topic of Zamzam water came up several times during the course of my research as an important gift brought by pilgrims for relatives and friends at home. On one occasion I sat in an Islamic school in Tehran with Elham and Soraya, two Tehrani seminary students, discussing how food can be powerful, blessed, or curative. Soraya brought out a book and opened it on the floor. It was a text—translated into Persian—called *The Hidden Messages in Water* by Dr. Masaru Emoto. She explained, "This Japanese researcher has shown that water molecules are more perfect and regular in Mecca. The molecules of food and water change to a more perfect shape when people pray devoutly. The scientist who said this was not religious." On another occasion, Nushin described how the water she had brought from her pilgrimage to Mecca never spoiled in its plastic bottle. She said that they had poured the water that her mother had brought back from her last pilgrimage into the farming well. "The water was plentiful after that, seriously!" It had replenished the family's farm well water in Fars-Abad, allowing for their household and community to prosper. This purifying water is thus brought from Mecca to heal and protect not only the family but also the community.

STATE-SPONSORED BLESSED FOOD AND THE KITCHENS OF IMAMS

> When we go to Mashhad, when we go to the "house of Imam Reza" (*khuneh-ye Imam Reza*), we eat food.[31] They have a kitchen. It is for blessing. They say that if you eat a

little, the spirit of the Imam appears and it brings blessing to your house.

—Parvin, Tehran, March 30, 2010

In addition to food sharing carried out by locals in small towns and cities, state-sponsored food offerings are also a common feature of key Islamic national events and appear in locations such as martyrs' graveyards, the kitchens of Imams, or public squares. On the birthday of Ayatollah Khomeini in 2010, for instance, the state distributed a votive meal of kebab and cut fruit to crowds of thousands of "brothers and sisters of Islam" in the parking lot outside the Imam Khomeini Mausoleum. This food was offered in conjunction with prayers that imbued it with blessing.

Similarly, parastatal martyrs' foundations fund formal and informal kitchens named for one of the Twelve Imams, and these adjoin key shrines at sites across the Islamic Republic. Imam Reza's kitchen (*āshpaz khāneh*) is a particularly famous example. Located in a beautiful complex in Mashhad, Imam Reza's kitchen is adjacent to the Imam's shrine. Mashhad, an ancient hub on the Silk Road, constitutes the second largest city in Iran today, and Shi'i Muslims all over the world recognize it as a holy city.[32] The shrine of Imam Reza has also been an important site in Iranian politics. In 1935, the haram was the site of protest against the "modernizing" and "antireligious" policies of Reza Shah. Bazaaris and other protesters chanted slogans such as "The Shah is the New Yazid" (Bakhash 1984, 22), a slogan that references both the Battle of Karbala and the sacred site of the haram itself, where Imam Reza was martyred. Despite the upheaval, the Pahlavis were ultimately instrumental in restoring the shrine, which was further "perfected" after the Revolution. Today, approximately twenty million pilgrims journey there annually, and the Iranian government continues to provide both religious guardianship and monetary support to the complex (Shaery-Eisenlohr 2007, 20). The Iranian government provides the same guardianship and funding to other key national and transnational Shi'i pilgrimage destinations, such as the shrine of Imam Husayn in Iraq and the tombs of the daughters of Imam 'Ali in Damascus. This effort, according to Middle East expert Roschanack Shaery-Eisenlohr, is part of the Iranian religious elite's attempt to cultivate Shi'i Iranian authority and legitimacy, both in and outside the country. She notes, however, that at least for many Lebanese Shiʻi pilgrims and clerics, this effort has often met with resistance and criticism (2007, 20).[33]

The kitchen itself is a four-floor building with more than six hundred chairs. About five thousand people receive services at the holy kitchen of Imam Reza's shrine each day. Four tons of fresh vegetables, rice, and meat are consumed every single day. Thousands more come to the kitchen during the birthdays of Imam ʻAli and Imam Husayn as well as the breaking of the fast during Ramadan. The birthday of Imam Reza himself, however, is the grandest affair, with an estimated ten to thirteen thousand people attending both for a chance to eat the food of Imam Reza and to participate in "ritual sermons" (*rowzeh khāni*) recounting the tragedy of Karbala.[34] People say that this Iftar gathering is the largest dining spread or *sofreh* in the world. The food from the kitchen, especially the rice, is said to have special potency.

According to Sima, a Basiji Islamic seminary student in Tehran, the food of Imam Reza "is the holiest food in all of Iran." Those who eat "his" food consider themselves fortunate. The food, she and others explained, shares the "unique" taste of blessed foods cooked at home. Goli, a woman living in Fars-Abad, similarly described this special taste: "It tastes better and gets better [over time]." Haleh, Parvin's daughter, related, "Some people . . . keep it in their freezers, and anytime that they make their own rice, they pour a little rice from the kitchen. They say that it is blessed and that it heals, and really, it does." Yet while there are many occasions when sick pilgrims travel to the Guest House of Imam Reza to heal personal sickness, just as often they are seeking to help other family members vicariously. Further, for many the food substance itself has special, near magical qualities that mimic those of slain martyrs. Because of its divine origins and blessed qualities, it does not rot, bloat, or mold. It does not putrefy in any way. Notably, placards and signs in such kitchens refer to all participants as brothers and sisters of Islam.

Perhaps the second most famous kitchen in Iran is that of the shrine of Shah Abdol-Azim in Rey, Iran, just outside of Tehran.[35] It is easily accessible via metro from the city center. In 2008 I accompanied Elham, a Basiji seminary student, and another foreign anthropologist to the shrine, whose complex included an Islamic seminary school. We peeked into the old part of the kitchen. It was full of huge pots for cooking rice that were probably only used for the yearly Muharram ceremonies to commemorate the martyrdom of Imam Husayn. The newer kitchen and restaurant area, however, was ornately set up like a restaurant, with tables and chairs. Its stucco walls resembled the inside of a mosque, complete with columns and arches, and was divided by gender. We noted that the male chefs stood over large tubs of food as we walked in. We paid for the food that we consumed: a simple American-style fried chicken dish next to a small bowl of traditional "votive soup" (*āsh*). When I asked where our money would go, Elham said that it would feed the poor. Framed signs written in both Persian and Arabic on the wall reminded all pilgrims to pray before eating.

Later, we stopped by to visit Soraya, a friend of Elham's who worked in the women's seminary school near the shrine. "Why is the food holy?" I asked. "It is because of the place," Elham responded as Soraya nodded. "The kitchen belonged to the person in the tomb. The food comes from the money that is given to the tomb. This money is also given to needy people. It is by fortune that you can eat that food." She further explained that the type of food served doesn't matter. Rather, what matters are the prayers and blessings that accompany eating at the kitchen: "The food is holy because it is made in his kitchen. It is his gift to us. But we must pray for it. The type of food doesn't matter. Just that it is made there. It changes every day. And every day they choose several people to eat there for free." In Fars-Abad in 2010, I recounted this experience to Nushin. She grasped my hand and said, "They say that any person that goes before Abdol-Azim . . . it is as if they have made a pilgrimage to the tomb of Imam Husayn. It is that important."

But the kitchens at the shrines of Imams are also not all-inclusive. Elham said that she was only able to obtain tickets to the ceremony in Mashhad because she and her husband were Islamic seminary students. If one does not have this privilege, full service at the kitchen occurs by chance. In Fars-Abad, one pilgrim to Mashhad, our neighbor, further explained, "The manager of this restaurant gives tickets out by chance to passersby." She said that women who work in the kitchen choose from among the needy: "The ladies who work in haram have the ability to select a needy person." Internet blogs and the website on Imam Reza shrine in Mashhad are full of narratives of experiences surrounding the selection of visitors for the kitchen, both personal and hearsay. Recurring themes in these accounts include stories of needy, simple, and good Muslims being selected to receive fare; the generosity of ticket holders who give up their tickets for the needy; and mystical experiences of encountering saints/persons at the kitchen who offer or receive food and then mysteriously disappear. Bloggers emphasize and seek to emulate the generosity of the Prophet. Although many insist that they take part in such blessed food according to an ethic of egalitarianism, hierarchies of wealth, perceived morality, face, and status shape who is included.

Food, Paragovernmental Foundations, and the Islamic State

This book began with an instance in which food was employed in a martyrs' commemoration in Fars-Abad, a ritual of state power. After the main commemoration, at dusk on a Friday, the town's prayer leader, or Friday Imam, introduced a "prayer giver" who read the Supplication of Kumail, a prayer for "the protection against the evil of enemies and for the forgiveness of sins." After the prayer, uniformed male soldiers distributed cups of yogurt, juice boxes, and plates of "lentils and rice" (*adas polo*) from giant metal vats. The food, which each participant ate, was paid for by the Foundation for Preservation of the Heritage and Distribution of Sacred Defense, a parastatal group that had organized the commemoration.

Later, the group of women I sat with discussed the offerings. The lentil rice was simple, pure, traditional, and blessed, they said. They explained that the choice of food was motivated by the purity and simplicity of the Prophet's family. As we ate, the Friday Imam addressed the crowd, calling on participants to think of themselves as the kin of martyrs. "Because this martyr is unknown," he said, "we the people are his brother, his sister, his mother."

For the women sitting next to me, this event was about protecting those gathered from evil and forgiving their sins through the combination of praying, being near the martyrs' bodies and blood, and eating blessed food. The Friday Imam's invocation of the purifying capacity of martyrs' blood was also a call for national kinship with martyrs, a kinship that was enacted as the uniformed soldiers and ritual participants called one another mother, father, brother, or sister. But this was only one of many such events I attended during fieldwork.

The state-run martyr's graveyard in Zahra's Paradise features similar pious food sharing on a national scale. When state-supporting pilgrims take part in votive offerings (e.g., hot milk, tea, pastries, candies) in the sacralized martyrs' section of the graveyard, they are connecting in a very visceral way to the political Islam of the state. They are accepting the Islamic Republic's often-contested definition of who is a martyr and are performing their common faith and citizenship with other visitors, fellow "brothers and sisters of Islam." Even further, on occasions such as the birthday of Khomeini, which was attended by Parvin and Haleh, the sharing of blessed food is often sponsored by the state itself. Finally, the Islamic Republic sponsors large quantities of pious food sharing in the form of the formal and informal kitchens of the Imams described here.

In small towns throughout Fars Province, food sharing is prevalent. Government-sponsored food offerings are widespread in the multiple martyrs' cemeteries, universities, and street corners across Fars Province, and the sharing of this food follows the same pattern. This food distribution is mostly carried out and paid for by martyrs' foundations, explicitly combining Islamic blessing and the nation. The process of making, distributing, and eating this food is understood as an act of piety and as an act of citizenship.

Interestingly, during most official national commemorations, and especially those sponsored more directly by the state, it is men who cook and distribute the votive food to the public. This is a striking reversal that contrasts with home, where men are not normally allowed to cook in the kitchen. Rather than being the producers of blessings at these grand rituals of state power, then, women (and men) are the recipients. State elites have appropriated female nourishing, blessing, and ethical and caring labor at home for the purposes of nation-building. They are creating rituals on the national stage out of the substances and acts of kinship to connect the intimacies of home life to state power, a process that naturalizes the way things are: here, a specifically paternalistic state. In so doing, they create a link between the family and the nation contoured by a notion of dependence on the state's protection, guidance, and blessing.

FOOD, KINSHIP, CITIZENSHIP

In Iran, food thus helps imbue citizens with purity and blessing in much the same way as the blood of martyrs. At the same time, infused with prayers, words from the Qur'an, and other divine elements, food resembles and typifies the experience of kinship. It resonates with the highly emphasized and laborious work of sustaining and creating a pure and halal family. There are several ways this occurs.

For state elites and for Basijis in Fars-Abad, including my hosts, there is an explicit and strategic analogy between the categories of kinship and nation: they are both units composed of "brothers and sisters of Islam," and they are both organized by the same kinds of tensions between inner purity and outer corruption. They are, further, both framed by an intense striving to leave behind a society that is in the process of forgetting its revolutionary values and to achieve a harmonious kindred society linked to God.

Food is part of this intense striving. It is an object of contestation: evidence of the fight for freedom and independence from Western powers and the tensions between youth and parents, who have different ideas about what food practices are acceptable. It is a means of sharing blessing and thus protecting Iranians from moral decay and corruption. And it is a means of distinguishing who and what is inside the nation and who or what is without.

At the same time, food brought from home or associated with the home is a key element in the rituals of state power. Women and men prepare food at home and bring it into a public graveyard, street, or other venue: an extension of the work of feeding the family. Even more than blood, food is a way of encouraging active participation in state ritual, which includes the enactment of kinship roles and responsibility and figures recipients of blessed food as brothers and sisters of Islam and as dependents of the state. Indeed, the prevalence of food in state rituals may be seen as a strategic means of creating the paternalistic relationship of giver and receiver, enacting a familial piety and kindred citizenship through commensality.

While scholars have recognized how kinship informs nation-making through shared ideas of ancestry, origins, genealogy, procreation, and blood (Alonso 1994; Bear 2013; Bryant 2002), they have not yet examined how a fuller spectrum of kin-making—in and beyond blood and law—can naturalize (and sacralize) the nation. The Iranian case demonstrates that a fuller spectrum of kin-making—including the more granular acts, substances such as food, and other processes by which kin are discerned, protected, and shaped—can create convincing concordances between the intimacies of home life and the grand rituals of state power. These acts and substances, because they are associated with the family, have a naturalizing effect when performed in the national sphere, making configurations of citizenship seem convincing, inevitable, and God-given.

Epilogue

Nistdar and her husband, Reza, live in a district of Fars-Abad called the "valley of the river of the birds." It is the first day of mourning for the martyrdom of Fatemeh Al-Zahra, the daughter of the Prophet and "mother of the Imams," and when I arrive, they are watching the television, leaning next to each other on divan pillows against the wall and drinking tea. I sit with them for a while. The Islamic Republic of Iran Broadcasting is showing a play performed by young girls that laments the martyrdom of Fatemeh. Boys read poems in her honor. Then there are scenes of a "celebration of duty" or *jashn-e taklif*, a religious ceremony designed to instill Islamic values in girls when they reach the age of nine.[1] This is followed by a prayer and lamentation for Fatemeh. Nistdar, now in her sixties, tells me through her tears that Fatemeh's story is especially moving to her. "Her male enemies came into her home without her permission, the ultimate sin," she explains.

According to Nistdar, a distant relation of my hosts, this kind of sinful behavior and breach of trust is increasing in Fars-Abad today. She tells me that young women feel unsafe and that there are prostitutes. She worries about drug-addicted taxi drivers. With a wave of her hand she adds, "People are different from the past. They used to have closeness/intimacy (*samimi*). If someone cooked something, they would offer it to a neighbor and to others. If someone performed a sacrifice, they would give it to all of the neighbors.... The family ate out of the same tray. They would eat together. There was more honesty, loyalty, and sincerity." She took a sip of her tea and continued, "[Back then] we didn't even have spoons. We also didn't have electricity. Everyone sat around a light, which we called a *musheh*. We cooked everything at the fire at home. We sat together in the afternoons and made wool carpets."

For Nistdar and other Fars-Abadis of her generation (people in their fifties and sixties with young adult children), the time before the Revolution was more intimate, honest, and sincere. People trusted each other. The food tasted better. People ate together out of the same dish. Very often, they described these changes in terms of shifting food practices. When people of Nistdar's generation were young, people in her town would sit together at the *sofreh*. They did not have spoons or forks but ate with bread. They survived on the crops they had farmed and on God's will.[2] On one occasion, Nistdar emphasized this point by giving me her recipe for *āsh-e esfandi*, a kind of stew that is cooked with seven eggs and seven kinds of beans. "The number seven is important for farming," she said. "It is auspicious. The farmers ate *āsh* to ensure good crops." The image of the past that she paints is nostalgic: simple and pure, yet precarious.

Iran's 1979 Revolution brought dramatic changes to Fars-Abad, many of which I described in detail in the introduction. There was rapid urbanization after the war with Iraq and a rapid increase in adult literacy. Schools were organized. An electrical grid was installed. In addition, government resources were channeled into health programs (see also Keddie 2006, Olszewska 2015b, 19). In Iran as a whole, "from 1985 to 1997, maternal mortality rates dropped from 140 deaths per 100,000 live births to 37. Infant mortality rates were also slashed" (Keddie 2006, 287). Many of these more positive changes directly impacted people like Nistdar and her family. "After the Revolution," she said, "we gained literacy. People progressed. People began to get salaries. Slowly, they began to become independently wealthy. Before that we were simple." Nistdar, like my host Nushin, Nushin's mother Goli-Mehrebun, Hajj Bibi, and other such women I spoke with, often talked about these shifts. They wanted me to understand that people had changed, but that they had also gained independence and equity. I was often told that things might have been much worse if the Revolution had not happened at all.

For the most part, this book has focused on Iranians who are card-carrying members of the Basij and supporters of the state. But I have also portrayed a broader perspective of the concerns and aspirations of people living both within and outside of Iran's urban centers, many of whom generally support the Islamic Republic.

ENTANGLED WRITINGS

Postcolonial scholars, anthropologists, feminists, and others have long recognized that any study of "cultural particulars" cannot be accomplished apart from webs of power relations. As Edward Said (1978) elaborated in *Orientalism*, the imagining of others has always been tied to a self-making project; further, these imaginings have often been used to create and maintain boundaries that facilitate and justify various kinds of politics or oppression.

As a population, Iranian state supporters stand at complicated angles both to the media and to academic scholarship. Sensationalist headlines depict Basijis, in particular, as quintessential of an untrustworthy, "Mad Mullah"-ridden Iran (e.g., Fox News). They are a dwindling cohort and the keepers of "official speak," a kind of "road bump" (*dast-andāz*) or a strawman to a rising tide of educated and secular Iranians. They are perceived as monolithic (Bajoghli 2017). Indeed, few categories of person attract a more powerful and unmixed opprobrium in the Euro-American popular view, as well as in the view of many Iranians. And, I would add, since the issues implicated in this disapproval are freedom, human rights, and the tolerance of difference, few topics present the anthropologist with a more complex terrain of difficulties.

As we have seen, my interlocutors' vision for their society runs counter to what many in Euro-America think of as progress: the separation of the religious from the secular (Asad 1993) and of kinship from politics (McKinnon and Cannell 2013). They argue that living life meaningfully means living as good, kindred Muslims in an Islamic country with an Islamic leader. They are trying to solve their societal problems by achieving a harmonious society shaped by familial piety and closeness to God, what might be described as an "alternative religious modernity" or a "nonliberal" religious community (Mahmood 2005).

This alternative religious modernity, however, is not circumscribed by the state. Actual practices of intimacy in the home, including visiting, prayer, sharing food, and family problem solving, are not confined to statist dictums. Rather, labors of food and prayer both enfold and counter fragments of the Islamic Republic's discourse. My interlocutors were striving to create the "right" kind of halal family, as modeled on the family of the Prophet and as idealized by the Islamic Republic. But their notions of family were also shifting and emergent, rather than fixed in blood or law. "Family" included those people who sit around the *sofreh* and share blessing. "Family" was contoured by changing circles of trust and piety. It was also fraught and dangerous, necessitating careful blessings and countermeasures against the evil eye and other ill-intentioned prayers.

The liberal (Western) media sometimes seek to soften the harsher representations of Iran. They portray a landscape of Iranian entrepreneurs, activists, and supporters of "reform." The imagination of these journalists—and our own wistful imagination as academics—depicts a rising generation of America-friendly Iranians who are "like ourselves": they are secular, educated, economy-minded, constantly on the internet, and modern. These Iranians do exist. Ahmadinejad's election was dramatically contested in Iran in 2009 by Green Movement protests, which challenged the election results and sought increased freedoms and a reformed Islamic democracy. More recently, in 2018 protests again erupted across Iran. Many gathered in Tehran's Grand Bazaar to rally against rising prices and the country's sinking currency value, which was caused in part by President Donald Trump's withdrawal from the 2015 nuclear deal. More than twenty people were killed by the police and Revolutionary Guard. Some protestors demanded the removal of President Hassan Rouhani.

In yet a different set of protests in 2018, a young woman named Vida Movahed bravely stood on a utility box in Tehran, waving her white headscarf, a garment required by law, aloft on a branch. Other young women followed suit in what has been called the "Girls of Revolution Street Protest" (Wright 2018). They posted their photos on social media and generated hashtags in Persian. While the government did make arrests, some parts of the political system took notice in a different way. Rouhani's office, for instance, released a report, with data from three years earlier, showing that 49.8 percent of Iranians favor making the hijab an issue of choice (Wright 2018). This was an acknowledgment of the need for public debate on mandatory veiling.[3]

Similar accounts of resilience and bravery appear in the writings of many anthropologists. Pardis Mahdavi (2009, 3), for instance, shows how youth embody their resistance to "the fabric of morality woven by the regime" by engaging in activities such as meeting friends, dating, drinking, and having sex. Similarly, Roxanne Varzi (2006) describes a sexual revolution enacted against a "repressive regime" that imposes harsh punishment on women and youth and that tries to enforce mandatory social and moral comportment per Islamic laws. In my view, these accounts are critical because they make visible the coercion and violence that is both implicit and explicit in many of the regime's mandates (Khosravi 2008). They show how easily moral watchfulness for some can become moral torment for others (Robbins 2013). However, because they are focused on mostly secular and urban youth, they tell us little about the population of Iranians who are actively participating in state power. We know little of the large numbers of non-elite state supporters in Iran who believe in figures like Ayatollah Khomeini and in his vision of the postrevolutionary Islamic Republic. Understanding more about this population is critical to understanding Iran.

POINTS OF CONTACT: KINSHIP AND STATE POLITICS

This book began with a question: What can an analysis of home life and everyday piety tell us about nation-making? I have argued that answering this question would require an exploration of kinship and the intimacies of family life. It would also require an exploration of the way these (pious) intimacies connect to state power. And finally, it would require contesting the so-called end of kinship and religion, the "disenchantment" and the "de-kinning" of world politics.

I have here approached citizenship not just as a set of legal rights inhering in individual persons but as what Sian Lazar (2012) has termed a "political-ethical project" (334): one that can emphasize "a much more relational and embedded conceptualization of the person" (Lazar 2012, 336; see also Ellison 2018, 229). This approach offers room for shifting notions of citizenship and sociality as well as for a more nuanced understanding of state authority and legitimacy.

One answer to my question about what an analysis of home life and everyday piety can tell us about nation-making lies in the realm of metaphor and analogy. For state elites and Basijis in Iran, there is an explicit analogy between the categories of kinship and nation: they are both units composed of "brothers and sisters of Islam," and they are both organized by the same kinds of tensions between inner purity and outer corruption. They are further both framed by an intense striving to achieve a harmonious kindred society linked to God.

But the link between the intimacies of home life and the state is more than a mutual structuring and transformation of nested domains. As I have shown, state elites and state supporters wield the actual, constitutive substances of kinship in the grand rituals of state power. The blood of the martyred sons and brothers of the nation is a means of purifying citizens, connecting them to God, and linking them as brothers and sisters of Islam. This blood signifies the renewal of society and is transformative, indexing male sacrifice and patrilineality. Nushin, Parvin, Ahmad, and others participate in these rituals as if they were mourning their own kin. The blood is visceral and tangible, and acts of mourning for these sons of the nation resonate with mourning for their own kin, losses, and sacrifices.

Pious acts of food sharing have a similar efficacy. Food helps people conceptualize and differentiate themselves in relation to others, and it resonates with the ideal of the pure and halal family (Dodson and Gilkes 1995; Ohnuki-Tierney 1994). At home, the careful daily orchestration of food and prayer is the mediation of the boundaries of kinship and the forging of the "right" kind of interfamily relationships. The model of and for a halal and pure family, as a particular form of "correct" relationality, has been explicitly reproduced by state elites and by families who support the state in the rituals of state power.

As a Fars-Abadi friend of my hosts explained, "If I make food and I give it to someone else at a commemoration or something similar, that is a very emotional experience. For me it goes back to being fed as a kid."[4]

Giving food is an emotional act and an act of kinship. Food distributed at national/Islamic commemorations, in public graveyards, and as votive offerings imbues constituents with kindred qualities, emotions, divine blessing, and purification on a national scale. It is also inherently relational. Like blood, but perhaps even more so, acts of cooking, feeding, and praying are a tangible way of interacting with other citizens, the state, and God. Food, after all, is uniquely sharable, movable, and changeable. It can be imbued with blessing and internalized in the bodies of kin or fellow citizens. Food helps regenerate and make tangible the cross-connections between and among kinship, the sacred, and the nation.

This focus on a relation between kinship and nation-making provides a radically new perspective from which to view Iran. Although scholars of Iran—in history, politics, and anthropology—have written widely on the Revolution of 1979 (Fischer [1980] 2003; Keddie 2006), the shaping of the nation (Vaziri 1993; Ansari 2007), and the "paradox" of sustaining an Islamic republic (Zubaida 2004), they have rarely sought to understand how kinship and ideas of intimacy are linked to the nation, its politics, or religion.

Of Conservative State Politics

My argument here is that kinship and religion, rather than being subsidiary or secondary, are often central political structures and allegiances in the twenty-first century. This may occur through a mutual structuring and transformation of kinship, nation, and religion as interrelated social domains (Yanagisako and Collier 1987), and it may occur through the literal flow of kinship-related substances and acts between the intimate spaces of the home and the nation.

This state appropriation of not only the substances of kinship but also the acts and rituals of family piety in the rituals of state power is not limited to Iran. State elites strategically use notions of kinship, including gender, reproduction, and marriage, to naturalize dominant ideologies of patriarchal authority, race, class, and religion (Heng and Devan 1992). As Anne McClintock (1993) notes, "the family offers a 'natural' figure for sanctioning social *hierarchy* within a putative organic *unity* of interests" (83; emphasis in original). In the United States, for instance, the same cultural understandings that underlie the family—"natural substance" (blood) and "code for conduct" (law)—also underlie ideas of citizenship and nationhood (Schneider 1969). Part of the reason for this is the particular power of "natural symbols" like blood, reproduction, and the models of hierarchy, inclusion, and exclusion that kinship provides. These ideas configure ideas of citizenship, ethnicity, and race.

But what I have shown in this book is that the "acts of kinship" are as much a resource for the creation of legitimacy and power as are the more obvious "natural symbols" like blood or genes. Even when kinship is not precisely seen as "natural" in the Western sense, the immediacy, granularity, and tangibility of the substances, materials, emotions, and actions of relatedness often have import beyond the domestic space. A focus on these acts allows us to see not only the ways in which kinship and citizenship are linked, but also how the relational aspects and qualities of citizenship are developed and shaped.

Notes

INTRODUCTION

1. To protect my interlocutors' identities, I have used pseudonyms for all persons in this book as well as for the town where I conducted the majority of my research, "Fars-Abad." Interviews, emails, and other personal communications with these persons are cited in endnotes using the pseudonymous names of the person and town and the date; for example, Ahmad, Fars-Abad, 2/22/2010.

2. The chador is a long outer garment, hemmed from a large, half circle of cloth worn by certain Muslim women. The black chador became a symbol of the 1979 Revolution in Iran and is common dress for those who support the regime.

3. The vast majority of Iranians are Muslim, and the vast majority of these are Shi'i Muslim. Shi'as claim that the son-in-law of the Prophet, Imam 'Ali, is the divinely appointed successor to Muhammad, and he is known as the First Imam. They extend this "Imami" doctrine to the Prophet's family, called "the people of the house" (*ahl-e beyt*), and the Twelve Imams who possess special religious and political authority. "Yā Husayn" is an invocation of the Third Imam, Imam Husayn, a grandson of the Prophet, who was tragically martyred at the Battle of Karbala (680 CE). Iran also has a small percentage of officially recognized minority religions, including Christianity, Judaism, and Zoroastrianism.

4. On September 22, 1980, Iraq invaded Iran. The war ended on August 20, 1988, after years of bloodshed and is known by many Iranians as the "Imposed

War" and/or the "Sacred Defense." See chapter 3 for more on the war and its history.

5. The Foundation for the Preservation of Heritage and the Distribution of Sacred Defense is a parastatal organization that participates in the memorialization of unknown martyrs, the creation of martyr memorials and collective shrines, and programming of all aspects of battlefield pilgrimages. Like the more widely known Martyrs' Foundation, it is parastatal because it is neither wholly of the state nor wholly distinct from it (Maloney 2000).

6. Shi'as commemorate the martyrdom of the Prophet's grandson Imam Husayn at the Battle of Karbala every year in the rites of Muharram and in reenactments of his death and suffering called *ta'ziyeh* (Chelkowski 1979).

7. My hosts in Tehran never talked about their socioeconomic class position. However, there were signs that they were struggling. At one point they had moved to a smaller apartment for a time to offset costs, and Parvin told me she prayed for her children's future financial stability. In addition, because of economic sanctions imposed by the United States, they often could not find or afford crucial medications.

8. According to custom, Nushin, in consultation with her sister and sister-in-law, arranged the day of the move on an auspicious day in the Islamic calendar. On moving day, she stopped us at the door and asked that each of us say the *salavāt*, "may the praise and blessings of God be upon Mohammad and the progeny of Mohammad," five times for protection before crossing the threshold, an explication in remembrance of the family of the Prophet or *panj tan*: Prophet Mohammad, Fatemeh, Hassan, Hossein, and Ali. She hung an evil eye protective ornament near the door to protect those within.

9. The 1979 Revolution was a popular revolution against the government of Mohammad Reza Pahlavi. Participants in the Revolution came from diverse political backgrounds. These included liberals, leftists, Islamists, and Marxist-Islamists. Their aim was to end the American-backed monarchy of the Pahlavis and create a republic. Ayatollah Khomeini, who was at that time an exiled religious cleric, ultimately became the leader of the postrevolutionary nation.

10. Ahmadinejad was a populist politician who appealed to lower and lower middle-class Iranians, particularly those living in provincial and rural areas and the Basij. Indeed, he had reportedly visited Fars-Abad (before my arrival) and addressed local needs in his speeches.

11. Ahmad, Fars-Abad, 2/22/2010.

12. Many recruits for the IRGC came from the lower and lower-middle classes and were vetted according to their religiosity. For instance, each guard had to pass an exam on the Qur'an, the Peak of Eloquence (*Nahj Al Balāgheh*) by Imam 'Ali, and Islamic government (*Hukumat-e Islāmi*) by Ayatollah Khomeini (Bajoghli 2019, 30).

13. Some scholars in the United States dispute these numbers. In *Captive Society* (2015), for instance, political scientist Saeid Golkar contends that these statistics are exaggerated. Drawing from texts produced by the Basij, as well as research produced by the US Army and the Rand Corporation, he claims that there are approximately four to five million members of the Basij. At the same time, he argues that the Basij is more widespread and more effective than most people realize, with tens of thousands of bases and offices spread throughout the country (Golkar 2015, 53).

14. Most recently, the Basij has been classified into five groups: potential, regular, active, cadre, and special (Golkar 2015, 51).

15. These recruits then undergo at least a week of active training. Courses include "Basij Ethics and Etiquette," "Major Islamic Rules," and "Fluent Reading of the Guardianship of the Jurist" (Golkar 2015, 48). High school students who pass a defense readiness course are exempt from this training (Golkar 2015, 48).

16. My hosts made a distinction between the government (*dowlat*), which is made up of the president, the parliament, and the minister, and the aspirations of the regime (*nezām*), a term that does not have a negative connotation in Persian. While they sometimes (though rarely) criticized the government and its public officials, it was not acceptable to criticize the notion of guardianship of the jurist or the Supreme Leader (in their case, both the late Ayatollah Khomeini and the current Supreme Leader of Iran, Ayatollah Khamenei).

17. In a further twist of something approximating cultural relativism, he accepted an American into his home, unveiled (I wore the chador in public). While also believing wholeheartedly in guardianship of the jurist (*velāyat-e faqih*) and maintaining ties with local authorities, Ahmad taught his teenage children that every society has boundaries and that they must follow the boundaries of the local system. At the same time, throughout my time in his home Ahmad upheld a purposeful "defense of Islam" and adamantly insisted that he would sacrifice his own life to prevent the burning of a Qur'an.

18. Although I interrogate common understandings about what it means to be affiliated with the Basij in contemporary Iran, this book does not deny the atrocities committed by particular categories of Basij or affiliated groups within the Islamic Republic, particularly during the 2009 Green Movement protests.

19. Mir-Hosseini further argues that although Khatami and the reformists failed to bring tangible changes to the structure of power, they provoked a new notion of the sharia as an ideal. In so doing, they appealed to Islam's higher values and invoked concepts from within Islamic legal theory, notably the distinction between sharia as "divine law" and "jurisprudence" as the human understanding of the requirements of divine law (2010, 355).

20. Mehdi, Tehran, 3/2/2010.

21. Zahra, Tehran, 2/28/2010.

22. Although the vast majority of Iranians are Shi'i Muslims (92.5% as of 2011), and Shi'i Islam is the official state religion, Iran has a population of Sunni Muslims (6.8%) and smaller communities of Christians, Jews, and Zoroastrians, which are recognized in the 1979 Constitution as official minorities (Afary, Mostofi, and Avery 2020).

23. During and after the Constitutional Revolution in Iran (1905–11), the family had been conceived as the foundation of a nation (*mellat*) composed of daughter and son citizens who were to care for a mother homeland (*vatan*) (Kashani-Sabet 2014). According to Kashani-Sabet (5/18/16), the notion of brothers and sisters of Islam was a new configuration, drawing inspiration from a different set of religious and political values.

24. Such statements connected the bloody sacrifice and courage of 1979 Revolution protestors with the sacrifice of the family of the Prophet at the Battle of Karbala. They entreated citizens to sacrifice their lives for each other, Islam, and country.

25. The curious ways in which this vision of a Muslim brother- and sisterhood is both nationalistic and pan-Islamic is a subject for future research. See for instance the rhetoric surrounding the notion of an Islamic Awakening (e.g., Ayatollah Khamenei's speeches concerning the Arab Spring in 2011) or the seeming inclusion of Afghani Martyred Defenders of Holy Shrines of the Family of Prophet as brothers and sisters of Iranian citizens (http://english.khamenei.ir, accessed March 27, 2016).

26. In their most stereotypical form, these roles caricature the "warrior brother" who sacrifices his life for the nation by spilling his blood in the act of martyrdom and the "veiled sister" who wears the black chador, a garment that symbolizes not only her modest bodily comportment and virtue but also her active political participation (Moallem 1992, 2005).

27. 2006 Census of the Islamic Republic of Iran, conducted by the Statistical Center of Iran. See https://irandataportal.syr.edu/2006-census.

28. This idea that the Revolution was founded on a more equitable social justice agenda was common among my provincial state-supporting hosts. It is further visible in the preamble of the Iranian Constitution, which states that it is the government's responsibility to create "equal opportunities" and "work for all." Under article 3, the Constitution further declares that the duty of government is to plan for a "just economic system" that provides for the general welfare.

29. According to data from the Statistical Center of Iran (SCI 2015), the country's population grew from 33.7 million to 75.1 million between 1977 and 2012 (an average annual rate of 2.32%) (Alaedini and Ashrafzadeh 2016, 19). At the same time, Iran's urban centers swelled from 15.85 million to 53.65 million (Alaedini and Ashrafzadeh 2016, 19). (See the Statistical Center of Iran at www.amar.org.ir for updated figures.)

30. In contrast, in the 1970s, before the Revolution, state resources had been directed to more privileged, urban regions (Salehi-Isfahani 2019).

31. Notably, the Construction Jehad was one of three postrevolutionary organizations working to develop rural areas and shore up state support (Lob 2017). Other significant bodies included the Construction Basij or Basij-e Sāzandegi and the Association of Trench Builders (Lob 2017, 26). Much of how this occurred was decided by Iran's individual leaders and their respective economic policies. In the 1980s Iran was shaped by strong anti-market policies (partially a result of the Iran-Iraq War), for instance. In the 1990s, the government became more pro-market under the administration of President Ali Akbar Hashemi Rafsanjani (1989–97). President Mahmoud Ahmadinejad (2005–13) ran on anti-growth populist economic policies.

32. Nistdar, Fars-Abad, 4/28/2010.

CHAPTER 1. THE MAKING OF MORAL KIN

1. During the month of Ramadan in the Islamic calendar, Muslims fast to commemorate the first revelation of the Qur'an to the Prophet Muhammad. For Shi'as in Iran, the Night of Power (in Arabic, Laylat al-Qadr and in Persian, Shab-e Qadr) is the night when the first verses of the Qur'an were revealed to the Prophet. It is also the anniversary of the martyrdom of the Prophet's nephew, Imam 'Ali. In Fars-Abad, the Night of Power is commemorated in the local Shi'i gathering hall on the nineteenth, the twenty-first, and the twenty-third of the month of Ramadan. It is considered the most auspicious night of the year.

2. Illicit drug use is a serious public health concern in Iran. Some estimates suggest that the prevalence of it is around 2.4 percent (Nikfarjam et al. 2016) and is seemingly higher among men (especially those with lower socioeconomic status) and among individuals who are widowed or divorced (Zafarghandi et al. 2015). Although the use of heroin is increasing (Amin-Esmaeili et al. 2016), opium is the most prevalent drug (Nikfarjam et al. 2016).

3. These formal laws indicate who can inherit and how much. At the same time, Islamic law regulates interactions between those who are *mahram*, intimate and unmarriageable because of a close kinship relation, and those who are *nā-mahram* or potential marriage partners.

4. The term "physio-sacred" is my take on the particular convergence of the spiritual and material prevalent in Shi'a Iranian concepts of kinship. It is adapted from the term "physio-spiritual," put forth by Naomi Leite in her role as a discussant for my paper presented at the Wenner-Gren conference, The Sacred Social: Investigations of Spiritual Kinship among the Abrahamic Faiths, which took place in March 2014 at the University of Virginia.

5. See also selections of Mutahhari's writings on women in Mutahhari (2009).

6. This theory of the Islamic law of nature was first advanced by the renowned Shi'i philosopher Allamah Tabataba'i in his Qur'anic commentary, *al-Mirzan*. However, it was the late Ayatollah Morteza Mutahhari who developed these "natural laws" into a powerful and influential argument for the natural and Islamic organization of gender and family (Mir-Hosseini 2004, 6).

7. He is here actually contesting the thesis of more traditional Islamists of his time, who argued that women are created of and for men.

8. Interestingly, for these Islamic scholars, "nature" as an object of scientific study was not understood in opposition to the divine, but instead as the spatio-temporal creation of God, embodying God's design for men, women, and society (Mir-Hosseini 1998, 9).

9. It should be noted that Mutahhari did not seek to entirely bar women from civil society or employment, so long as they wore modest clothing and avoided close interaction with the male sex (Paidar 1995, 177).

10. Importantly, however, Iranian feminists and reformists have made powerful and differing interpretations and exegesis of key passages in the Qur'an and hadiths concerning hijab and notions of gender complementarity (Afary 2009).

11. Hamed, Tehran, 3/8/2010.

12. In these and other instances, it is difficult, if not impossible, to know exactly how much my hosts' views on subjects such as gender and family were impacted specifically by their membership in the Basij, although this membership does entail certain statist leanings. In 2010, for instance, Mutahhari's life and works were widely influential and were taught in schools across the Islamic Republic. In addition, and as noted in the introduction, I observed many differences among Basij from different generations, those who were "active" in the organization versus those who were not, and those who lived in urban versus rural settings. Other differences emerged from socioeconomic status, personal and family histories, education, and social networks, as well as internet and media consumption.

13. In Shi'i commemorations the *panj tan* is depicted as a palm and five fingers, portraying the Prophet, his nephew Ali, his daughter Fatemeh, and his grandsons Hassan and Husayn as the members of a shared "body." The *panj tan* stands for the "witnessing" of the Battle of Karbala and support of Imam Husayn as opposed to the people of Kufa, who had sided with the evil Yazid.

14. Coulson (1971), a scholar of Islamic law, thus argues that what sets Shi'i law apart "is its refusal to afford any special place or privileged position to agnate relatives as such" (108). This dictum is expressed by the Shi'i Imam, Ja'far al-Sadiq: "As for the *'asaba* [agnates], dust in their teeth" (Coulson 1971, 108).

15. Interestingly, in "Persian Beliefs and Customs," Henri Massé describes the Persian belief that nursing a Christian child might bring a woman harm. In contrast, nursing a *sayyed* is highly beneficial and ensures a woman's breasts will be spared the fires of hell, presumably because of her close contact with the *sayyed* (Massé and Messner 1954).

16. In this case, Islamic kinship is not determined by agnatic blood alone (see also Clarke 2009; Abu-Lughod 1989; Eickelman 1998). There is persistent recognition of matrilateral relations in Iran (and procreativity), whether through blood, DNA, or milk. Indeed, kinship is composed of shared blood: both patrilineal and matrilineal, marriage, and breast milk, as is set forth in Shi'i law (*sharia*) (Torab 2007).

17. According to Khuri (2001), in the Qur'an and the hadiths, blood stands for a wide range of qualities: nobility, origin, genealogy, honor, unity of purpose, affinity, virginity, love, and personality; even further, they were developable and mutable.

18. In contrast, menstrual blood, for instance, is impure and can be defiling. For this reason, female family members carefully avoid touching the Qur'an or visiting the inner sanctuaries of the Imams and their descendants when they are menstruating. Haleh, for instance, avoided the inner sanctuary at the shrine of Masumeh in Qom when she was menstruating. At home, she and others instructed me to use the end of a pencil to flip through the pages of the Qur'an and pray during my menstrual cycle to prevent defiling the holy book.

19. Nushin, Fars-Abad, 4/24/2010.

20. Many have particularly copious amounts of esteem (*āberu*), which they inherit. See the section "Saving Family 'Face'" in this chapter for more on *āberu*.

21. Nistdar, Fars-Abad, 7/6/2010.

22. For more details on the Shi'i Muslim understandings of the desecration of the sacred Islamic order and life at the Battle of Karbala, see Fischer ([1980] 2003).

23. Nushin, Fars-Abad, 11/10/2010.

24. Ahmad, Fars-Abad, 10/1/2010.

25. Atefeh, Fars-Abad, 5/22/2010.

26. Nushin, Fars-Abad, 5/10/2010.

27. Here, socially prescribed forms of embodied conduct are understood as potentialities through which the self is realized, not as external constraints (Mahmood 2005, 148). Foucault (2000, 263) argues that ethics are emergent from within given techniques of subjection and describes ethics as a "reflexive practice of freedom" or a technology of "self-transformation" (see also Faubion 2001, 12).

28. They have also rarely accounted for the complexities and ambivalences of moral action and its associated discourses in practice (Schielke and Orient 2010).

29. Halal is most often translated into English as "lawful" or "religiously permissible." An entire range of acts may be classified as halal or its conceptual opposite, *harām* or "unlawful." These include diet, sexual relations, daily habits and customs, marriage and divorce, family relations, public morality, occupation and income, and types of entertainment. According to Schacht (1966, 121), a scholar of Islamic legal theory, there are two categories that divide human acts and transactions. The first is a set of declaratory rules that refer to the validity or nullity of an act of transaction. The second represents five categories through which human acts are evaluated with reference to their spiritual effects (e.g., reward or punishment). In Arabic, these include (1) "obligatory acts which in their omission incur a divine punishment" (*wājeb*), (2) "recommended acts which earn reward" (*mandub*), (3) "neutral acts with neither sanction nor reward" (*mobāh*), (4) "disapproved acts that earn divine reward when omitted but are not punished," and (5) "forbidden acts which incur punishment" (*mahzur*).

30. Generational labels vary greatly. My hosts were here referring to generations of Basij as war volunteers. Ahmad and his war veteran friends described the first generation as those who fought in the war, such as himself; the second as those who came of age in the 1990s and were too young to serve in the war, such as Ehsan; and the third generation as those born when the war was coming to an end and under the full auspices of the Islamic Republic (see also Bajoghli 2019, 35–36). This, notably, is different from the way in which generations are more generally demarcated in Iran according to decades on the Iranian calendar, which correspond to the 1980s generation and the 1990s generation (e.g., *daheh-ye shast, daheh-ye haftād*) (Behrouzan 2016, 31). See anthropologist Orkideh Behrouzan's *Prozac Diaries* (2016) for more on the struggles of those who were children during the Revolution and came of age during the war. Notably this group is often called *nasl-e sukhteh*, meaning burned, barren, wasted, but also sacrificial (for more see Behrouzan 2016, 174).

31. My hosts said that the worst kind of fighting was that between parents and children. According to Nushin, "If parents and children cannot come to an agreement, your prayers don't mean anything. Nothing that you do means anything."

32. According to Goffman (1956), face is an image of self that is delineated according to approved social attributes, for example, when a person makes a good showing for his profession or religion. It can also be a matter of collective reputation (Meneley [1996] 2016, 46), whereby maintaining face requires teamwork.

33. Ahmad, Fars-Abad, 11/5/2010.

34. For instance, the unwanted removal of a woman's hijab is perceived by men as an attack on male honor (Torab 2007, 152). Interestingly, members of the Basij I spoke with who volunteered to fight on the front during the Iran-Iraq War sometimes explained their service in these terms. They said that by volunteering, they were helping to defend the honor (*nāmus*) of the nation as well as the ideals of the Revolution.

CHAPTER 2. FEEDING THE FAMILY

1. In Iran, the eyes "are the doors toward one's inner self and they are also the windows towards the outer world" (Shahshahani 2008, 74). This play between the inside and the outside of the person is partially what gives the evil eye its power. Those who possess the evil eye are often out of balance with regard to their inside and outside; in other words, their inside (*darun*) and outside (*birun*) are not the same. The "striker" may appear pious and pure, but inside he or she is bitter or envious, a situation of conceptual opposition to what is desired: for one's pure inside to conquer the corrupt, appetite-driven outside (Bateson 1979; Beeman 2005). Importantly, though, possessors of the evil eye, even some who may be pure-intentioned, may not know their own power.

2. Many Iranians, including members of Iran's religious elite, regard my (Basiji) hosts' attention to practices of prayer-taking as superstition and, in some cases, as counter to ideal forms of piety in the Islamic Republic (Doostdar 2018, 7). Nevertheless, Ahmad, Nushin, and their children saw the *ziārat-e 'āshura'* prayer as a state-sanctioned means of overcoming what they described as the "ill-intentioned" practices of the evil eye and of "prayer-taking" that had caused their family's recent troubles. I discuss this in further detail toward the end of the chapter.

3. Vows are made to Shi'i Imams and their descendants to intercede with God for a favor. The supplicant cooks a "votive offering" (*nazri*) that has been specified in advance (Torab 2007, 118).

4. In the popular Iranian book on pregnancy, *Pregnancy and Childbirth from the Perspective of Islam*, Marzieh Akbarzadeh and Nasrin Sharifi (2010) similarly write that the mother in particular must attend to lawful (halal) and spiritual (*ruhāni*) food during pregnancy for the creation of a halal fetus. A sin committed during pregnancy, they argue, will affect both the mother and the baby.

5. Chapter 4 extends this discussion to the nation-state, exploring how Basijis and state elites similarly use food, food rituals, and prayer to constitute an Islamic Republic composed of pure kindred citizens.

6. In chapter 1, I use the term "physio-sacred" to describe the interwoven physical and sacred aspects of Iranian kinship. I use it again in this chapter to understand how women, in particular, constitute the bio-moral, sacred family through transactions of cooking, feeding, and prayer.

7. There are three kinds of *sofreh*: the presentational, the votive, and the gratulatory. The most common forms of presentational *sofreh*s are those of New Year *haft sin* and the wedding *sofreh* (Jamzadeh and Mills 1986). The concern of the following section, however, is the *sofreh* eaten as an everyday food.

8. The Iranian New Year (Nowruz) is the day of the vernal equinox and marks the beginning of spring. Its origins are Persian and Zoroastrian, not Islamic. My hosts, though affiliated with the Basij, did not express concern

about the celebration being pre-Islamic, nor did they criticize any of the festivities we witnessed, including (gender-segregated) games, lute playing, and dancing. The singing, in particular, became somewhat rowdy as night fell. I recall one song about women and men exchanging "kebab." Yet while my hosts' teenage children laughed at these displays, their own participation was decidedly more reserved than that of many of their non-Basiji cousins, aunts, and uncles. Ali, my host "older brother," intermittently reminded me to watch from afar and refrain from joining in.

9. As mentioned in the previous chapter "degree one" kin extend beyond the small family to include first cousins, aunts, and uncles.

10. More than politeness, *ta'arof* is defined by Beeman as the "the active, ritualized realization of differential status in interaction" (1976, 312). As such, in the form of compliments, invitations, and offers, it is a means of discerning, expressing, and creating status in relationships.

11. At home and outside, tea is offered in copious amounts to guests along with fruit, sugar cubes, and sweets.

12. The first saying competes with a second that provides a sense of the ideal portions of daily meals: "Eat breakfast like a king, lunch like a prince, and dinner like a poor person." I first heard this latter phrase on an Islamic Republic of Iran Broadcasting television series that aired in the morning in the summer of 2010. Breakfast, the health-oriented commentators argued, should be the biggest meal of the day (fit for a king), while lunch should be princely, bountiful yet relatively less. Dinner, they said, should be simple and small, befitting the poor.

13. There are key exceptions: sometimes a mother will cook a "soup of hot milk thickened with flower and infused with rosewater" (*ferni*), boiled eggs, lentil soup, or sheep's brain (the heaviest and most powerful breakfast food).

14. Nushin, Fars-Abad, 8/31/2010.

15. In 2010, however, most of these implements could only be found in basement storage areas or in the rafters of courtyards. The bakery had supplanted the practice of making bread by hand at home (except in outlying villages). When I lived in Fars-Abad, five small bakeries—all of which were subsidized by the government—dotted the streets. People said that another shift in their breadways was at hand. "We won't be able to afford bread this way anymore," they said. "They are making factories for bread—there's one in Tehran." "Bread will come in packages, like it does in America." This process resembles the gradual mechanization of the corn tortilla in Mexico described by Jeffrey Pilcher (1998).

16. In part because of all the negotiations surrounding the act of buying bread, it is a despised chore, especially for Nushin's sons. They complain about the length of the lines and the meddling of those they meet there; and especially about the vastly complicated social etiquette required for standing in line with distant kin and acquaintances.

17. In Tehran, this is very different. With more people working, including young women, lunch is often ordered out for the office. Some Tehranis lament the change, but others call it more efficient.

18. These offers stemmed from widespread polite Iranian hospitality conventions, consisting of a polite offer to lunch followed by a polite refusal. However, in my case, offers were both more frequent and more genuine. People hoped to meet the only American in town in forty years and imagined that their normal strategies of sharing lunch did not apply to me in the same way as they would to an Iranian daughter.

19. Nushin, Fars-Abad, 8/9/2010.

20. Significantly, these rules, though they are legally sanctioned, are not followed by some people (Chehabi 2007). Alcohol, often smuggled in, can be purchased on the black market, and some people produce it illegally. In addition, non-Muslim minorities such as Armenians and Assyrians are allowed to produce alcoholic beverages for their consumptions and religious rites.

21. Ahmad, Fars-Abad, 7/12/2010.

22. It was common knowledge that the local dairy and meat items raised by nearby settled nomads were of the absolute best quality. Sheep and goat meat, milk, butter, and *kashk* are known specialties. *Kashk* is a dairy product made by draining yogurt or sour milk, rolling it into a ball, and letting it dry. Finally, Fars-Abadis, including my hosts, valued "natural" desert mountain herbs and plants such as juniper berries and wild dill for their spiritual and health benefits.

23. Nushin, Fars-Abad, 11/7/2010.

24. Nushin, Fars-Abad, 11/5/2010.

25. Nushin, Fars-Abad, 10/31/2010.

26. Here, the quality of local products is interwoven with understandings of local landownership and the character of landowners. In my travels throughout the Fars Province, I often heard both people from Fars-Abad and outside remark on the piety and civility of the town as well as on its Islamic-ness. "Oh, you're a lad from Fars-Abad," a taxi driver would say to my host brother. "Fars-Abad has good lads" (*bachehā-ye Fars-Abad khuband*). As such, the notion of being from the same city or *hamshahr* implies a certain degree of trust.

27. Notably, daughters rarely spearheaded cooking. They washed and chopped vegetables, set out the dining cloth, and made salad. But they did not add ingredients to stew or rice, and they did not decide when food was ready for consumption. Moreover, with the exception of kebab and the occasional side of eggs, husbands and sons did not cook.

28. Ahmad's friend, Fars-Abad, 7/26/2010.

29. Lynn Harbottle notes a similar positive valuing of home-cooked food among Iranian immigrants in Britain: "The kind of work that Iranian women

engage in, to ensure the regular (although not necessarily daily) consumption of Iranian cooked meals, involves an investment of time, energy and love. The food produced in this way appears to carry an affective potency that commercially prepared food and other meals consumed outside the home seem generally to lack" (Harbottle 2000, 6).

30. Mamanjun, Qazvin, 7/14/2008.

31. Everyone agreed, for example that because I have pale skin, I "become cold quickly." To remedy this, Nushin and others would tell me to stay away from fish and chicken and cold salads and would feed me "warm" or "spicy" foods such as dates, cinnamon, or crystallized sugar candy melted in hot tea.

32. Notably, the arrangement of the *sofreh* changes dramatically when there are guests. The food, already an object of intense work, is further beautified and is often doubled, both in kind and quantity. When guests or strangers are present, status differences are heightened, and women kneel or sit with their legs neatly tucked together under their chadors, though men adopt relatively relaxed postures. If seated near male strangers, women sit with enough composure so as to never touch or come within inches of the men; often this is ensured by having women sit on one end of the *sofreh* and men on the other, with married couples or siblings occupying the middle space.

33. Indeed, when hosts tell their guests, "Our salt won't get you," they are being told not to be afraid to share food. But why should they be fearful in the first place? One reason is that eating food in another person's home is dangerous and can cause spiritual illness. Correspondingly, when people do share home-cooked food in Fars-Abad, they are signifying that their trust is *almost* equivalent to the trust shared by the immediate family.

34. Nushin had not kept the fast; she had been unwell. Her youngest son, Reza, had tried to fast on and off, but he said that he could not focus on God. His father, Ahmad, did not scold him. Instead, he described how, when he was Reza's age, the fast had brought him closer to God and had filled his eyes with tears of devotion. Reza nodded seriously. He was conflicted. Fasting was hard. Everyone asked me what I would do. I tried for three days but failed on the third. I was too thirsty in the summer heat.

35. Although Ramadan in Fars-Abad was a time of greater attention to Islamic piety, my Basiji hosts did not contrast the holy month with a more flexible or normal "rest of the year" in the manner Schielke describes. Rather, Ramadan was a time for multiplied blessings and spiritual reward, and it was time to set in motion piety for the year to come.

36. Interlocutors used the term *savāb* (the Persian pronunciation of the Arabic *thawāb*) for all forms of merit, including both "religious merit" and the "right and good," as in the concept of a good deed.

37. The Iranian Islamic Broadcasting Network corroborates this view on a wider scale. In an extremely popular show called *The Chef* (Āshpazbāshi), such

home-cooked food made with love and pure intentions embodies the inner moral core of the family. In particular, in the show's final episode, a large, "traditional" meal of kebab prevents family fragmentation and divorce. It is for the immediate family.

38. The *Encyclopædia Iranica* notes several additional kinds of *āsh* prepared as votive offerings, often for family welfare. These include *āsh-e mash*, prepared on the tenth day after childbirth and served in the public bath; *āsh-e reshteh-ye posht-e pā*, prepared on the third or fifth day after the departure of a loved one and served to neighbors in hopes of shortening the duration of the journey (this type of *āsh* is placed on a tray with a Qur'an and a mirror and is not eaten by the traveler but is rather sprinkled upon him); and finally, *āsh-e sholeh qalamkār*, an *āsh* made with meat and legumes, prepared on one of the holy days for the survival of children in the family or as a thanksgiving for recovery from sickness (Eilers, Elāhī, and Boyce [1987] 2011).

39. Remarkable similarities in objects and foodstuffs placed on the Muslim and Zoroastrian *sofreh*s have been observed. Yet despite these convergences, the process and rules of participation differ significantly among these groups (Jamzadeh and Mills 1986).

40. *Āsh* may be formed from various combinations of vegetables, rice, pasta, grains, peas and beans, meat, fruits, spices, and tart flavorings such as lime juice, tamarind, sumac, yogurt, or vinegar. Interestingly, the word *āsh* forms a compound with several other Persian culinary terms, suggesting that it is and has been a fundamental component of Iranian/Persian understandings of cuisine (e.g., *āshpaz*, cook; *āshpazi or*, cooking; and *āshpaz-khāneh*, kitchen).

41. The word *rahem*, interestingly, also means "womb" in Persian. In addition, it translates as compassion, uterus, and pity.

42. Ahmad, Fars-Abad, 7/26/2010.

CHAPTER 3. REGENERATING THE ISLAMIC REPUBLIC

1. The pronunciation "*-u*" is a feature of the local Persian dialect, placed at the end of sentence objects and often laughingly disparaged by its own non-Tehrani dialect speakers.

2. Reza, Fars-Abad, 8/24/2010.

3. Reza, Fars-Abad, 10/10/2010.

4. Terms employed both by Reza and by the Friday Imam in Fars-Abad on 8/22/2010, during the martyrs' commemoration.

5. These war casualty figures are highly contested. The most common consensus is 220,000 killed and 400,000 injured (Ehsani 2017, 6). But other scholars cite very different numbers, counting 300,000 dead and 500,000 wounded (see Khosronejad 2012).

6. Importantly, some non-Shi'i Iranian minorities, including Christians and Zoroastrians, also participated in the war. Many of these individuals willingly offered their lives, not because of a Shi'i or other religious culture of sacrifice, but because of nationalism (Bolourchi 2018). At the same time, the narrative of the Iran-Iraq War as a "Sacred Defense" is contested. Many resent the war and the way it has been used to shore up state legitimacy (Ehsani 2017, 8).

7. Ahmad, Fars-Abad, 7/21/2010.

8. Ahmad, Fars-Abad, 7/21/2010.

9. Although this chapter focuses mainly on the cultural elaboration of male martyrs' blood in Iran, many women supported the Islamic Republic in the early days of the Revolution and during the Iran-Iraq War (Hegland 1998, 1983a; Nashat 1983). Significantly, women themselves joined the war effort, as both nurses and auxiliaries. As a result, many thousands fought alongside the Revolutionary Guard and trained in military camps, and many were martyred (see Nashat 2004, 31; Reeves 1989, 132). This massive participation of women during the Revolution, which included women from all walks of life, also served to consolidate the presence of women in the public arena as active citizens of the new Islamic Republic (Hoodfar 2001; Bahramitash 2003).

10. This language continues to appear in the commemorations of martyrs in Fars-Abad.

11. Mahmud, Tehran, 3/23/2010.

12. Parvin, Tehran, 3/23/2010.

13. Note that the actual bodies of martyrs were not displayed in the martyrs' commemorations described in this chapter; rather they were enclosed in coffins. However, Khosronejad has photographed remains of the bodies of martyrs displayed in similar commemorations in urban Tehran that appear remarkably preserved (Khosronejad 2013).

14. The Foundation for the Preservation of Heritage and the Distribution of Sacred Defense is a parastatal organization that participates in the memorialization of unknown martyrs, the creation of martyr memorials and collective shrines, and programming of all aspects of battlefield pilgrimages. Like the more widely known Martyrs' Foundation, it is not wholly of the state nor wholly distinct from it (see also Maloney 2000).

15. These scarves are not only associated with the 1979 Revolution and the Iran-Iraq War but are also believed to be similar to the headwear worn by the Arabs at the Battle of Karbala.

16. In 2010, when I conducted my fieldwork, this defense was all the more salient, occurring as it did only a year after the 2009 Green Movement protests, which had contested the election of President Mahmoud Ahmadinejad and legitimacy of the regime.

17. In contrast, menstrual blood is impure and can be defiling. For this reason, female family members carefully avoided touching the Qur'an or visiting

the inner sanctuaries of the Imams and their descendants when they were menstruating. Haleh, for instance, avoided the inner sanctuary at the shrine of Hazrat-e Ma'sumah in Qom during our pilgrimage there because she was menstruating. At home, she and others used the end of a pencil instead of their fingers to flip through the pages of the Qur'an, preventing any defiling of the holy book.

18. Shari'ati argued that Fatemeh, along with her daughter Zaynab, or the "Lioness of Karbala," are role models for everyone, especially women. Since the 1979 Revolution, Zaynab is revered not only for her simple living and piety in faith but also for her courage, generosity, and selflessness as well as her work as a scholar and educator (see also Aghaie 2011; Kashani-Sabet 2005).

19. A minor, one-person *ta'ziyeh* drama calls on similar themes. It depicts Fatemeh washing the clothes for her children, Hassan and Husayn. Taking each piece of clothing from the wash basin, Fatemeh laments that Husayn will one day be martyred. The audience weeps wholeheartedly for Fatemeh, thinking of her sons, and simultaneously of their own children (Beeman, personal communication, October 14, 2019).

20. For more details, see Iranian scholar Roja Fazaeli's presentation "Humiliated Men and Martyred Women: The War on Terror's Implication on Redefining Middle-Eastern Masculinities" at the panel "Cultural, Social and National Masculinities" at Emory Emory Law School, Emory University, September 27, 2009, http://www.youtube.com/watch?v=ES33sVoG_KM.

21. This uniqueness was made evident by the special placement of these two martyred soldiers on the hill in the town park and the elaborateness of their burial site. In contrast, Fars-Abad's other forty-four known martyrs were buried together in a small but well-kept martyrs' graveyard.

22. In Iran, a "carnation," or in Persian *mikhak*, is not just a flower. Carnations are called *mikhak* because they smell vaguely like cloves. The word for "cloves" is also *mikhak*, which means literally "little nail." Carnation thus evokes the symbolism of nails, of something hard, sharp, and resistant.

23. Contrary to conventional wisdom, Iran's pre-Islamic heritage was not always downplayed by Islamists in favor of a universal or anti-nationalist Islamism. Aghaie (2014), for instance, argues that scholars should accept the possibility that many Islamists were nationalists.

CHAPTER 4. CREATING AN ISLAMIC
NATION THROUGH FOOD

1. The Imam Khomeini Relief Foundation (IKRF) was established after the 1979 Revolution and was mandated to uproot poverty, support the deprived, and provide relief to the oppressed. Its ubiquitous blue boxes appear not only at the

mausoleum but at street corners across Iran (Farzanegan and Alaedini 2016, 4). Interestingly the IKRF has, to some extent, replaced self-organized kin networks of mutual support with state-organized networks of state welfare (Harris 2017, 105). The services provided through the fund include financial aid and health insurance to low-income families, interest-free loans for housing, scholarships for young Iranians, and stipends for the elderly poor in rural areas. The IKRF solicits donations from the public but relies on the Iranian government for most of its funds (Harris 2017, 106).

2. For instance, the complex (the dome and minaret) includes a *qibla* wall, indicating the direction of Mecca and orienting prayer. There are, however, key differences. The grill that encloses the tomb of Khomeini is made of metal strips rather than the silver- and gold-plated grills that enclose many tombs of Shi'i imams and Sufi saints. The four corners of the burial enclosure, which is covered by a green canopy, are embellished with bouquets of plastic flowers. This "cheap" decor is meant to convey an image of Khomeini as simple, unpretentious, and anti-elitist (Rizivi 2003).

3. The same sort of blessed food also appears in gatherings for Iranian presidents and their constituents. For instance, Basiji Islamic seminary women whom I met in Tehran said that they had attended a birthday party for former Iranian president Seyyed Mohammad Khatami, an event that was organized around the sharing of votive food.

4. See Najmieh Batmanglij's (1986) famous cookbook, *Food of Life: Ancient Persian and Modern Iranian Cooking and Ceremonies*, for an example of this cuisine as well as some tasty recipes.

5. See also how Sephardic Jews differentiate Jews from non-Jews through their use of kosher food practices (Sered 1988).

6. Here, citizenship is more than a legal status or set of rights. It is actively lived, embodied, and constituted. It is, moreover, a "political-ethical project" that is deeply entangled with power relations and structures of authority (Lazar 2012). And, as is the case for my Basiji hosts, it may be created, both from the top down and from the bottom up.

7. In some senses, these thinkers can be described as nativists who attempted to delegitimize and decenter Western modes of knowledge and thus counter Eurocentrism (Williams and Chrisman 1994, 14).

8. This is also the text in which he makes his public case for the "guardianship of the jurist" (*velāyat-e faqih*), the founding principle of the Islamic Republic. Also available at http://www.iranchamber.com/history/rkhomeini/books/velayat_faqeeh.pdf.

9. http://zamzamgroup.com.

10. Food imports to Iran have actually increased since the 1960s (Lahsaeizadeh 2001). Furthermore, scholars of nutrition in Iran have shown that dietary patterns—particularly those in Tehran and other urban centers—are shifting

from traditional diets to Western diets, which include greater consumption of red and processed meats, refined grains, and fried foods (Rezazadeh, Rashid-khani, and Omidvar 2010).

11. These kinds of venues have very basic seating, and the food isn't made to look fancy. Moreover, the coffee houses are men-only spaces where one can drink tea, smoke hookah, and eat simple foods. They are thought of by the elite urban youth as low-class hangouts.

12. Notably, the only other (prepared) food venues available in Fars-Abad during my research were traditional ice-cream shops, bakeries, pastry shops, small groceries, and sandwich venues.

13. See the newsstand magazine *Green Family Cooking* (آشپزی خانواده سبز) for this and similar articles (https://www.facebook.com/ash.ksabz.net/).

14. Moral rubrics are the different sets of ideals and values that are revealed as well as produced through discourses and actions in different moral registers (including the religious, the social, and the political-sectarian) (Deeb and Harb 2013).

15. Other illicit foods include the meat of animals not properly slaughtered, blood, and improperly used intoxicants (Regenstein, Chaudry, and Regenstein 2003; see also chapter 2).

16. The matter of interpretation of the Qur'an and hadiths is one of differences in center and periphery, class, hierarchy, religious authority, and claim to religious knowledge (Bowen 1993; Fischer and Abedi 1990; Lambek 1990, 23). Shi'i Islam allows for the possibility of "systematic original thinking" (*ijtehād*) and thus a diversity of rulings and opinions. However, while some believe that only clerics such as Ayatollah Khomeini, who have achieved the highest level of religious authority, that of a "source of emulation" (*marja'-e taqlid*), can offer interpretations, others debate who has the authority to interpret.

17. Amid these ongoing debates about what constitutes halal food, jurisprudents and state media highly recommend particular items for their purifying and/or health-promoting effects. These include, for instance, dates, honey, and pomegranates—which are mentioned in the Qur'an—as well as blessed or holy foods derived from the kitchens of the Imams; votive foods prepared at home or for distribution in shrines, graveyards, and streets; and food grown in the soil where Iranian martyrs died in the Iran-Iraq War.

18. For more see Schacht (1966, 121).

19. See also Shahshahani (2008) for gendered movement outside.

20. Maryam and Reza further linked the idea of ugliness (*zeshti*) to the immoral hosting practices of big-city dwellers, who, they explained, do not invite guests—"even their own uncles"—into their homes. In Fars-Abad, Reza said, as Maryam nodded, "We are 'warm/friendly' (*garm*) and love guests. People are purer/simpler in small towns [like Fars-Abad]. In Tehran, they are not warm at all." They both agreed: "They [Tehranis] have lost their humanity."

21. The ways in which class, family history, gender, urban/rural location, and generation shape contemporary Iranian foodways need further study.

22. Nushin, Fars-Abad, 8/7/2010.

23. My interlocutors said that the Night of Power occurs on one of the last ten days of Ramadan, specifically the nineteenth, twenty-first, or twenty-third, the latter being the most important. However, the nineteenth is also significant, as it is the night Imam 'Ali was attacked while worshiping in Kufa. He died on the twenty-first.

24. *Moshkel goshā* is a mixture of diverse nuts typically served and shared during the Iranian New Year but served on other occasions in Fars-Abad, such as picnics and commemorations, as a means of solving personal and family problems.

25. While women usually coordinate and cook for these occasions, men also participate, by buying ingredients, cooking, or spooning food into plastic containers for fellow pilgrims. The choice to make a *nazri* at a particular tomb may depend on logistics of proximity to that site, travel, and money, or it may reflect a feeling of shared intimacy with a particular saint (see also Betteridge 1985).

26. Members of my extended host family participated in the same votive offerings and local pilgrimage on a much smaller scale and almost on a weekly basis to the tombs of local *sayyed*s in the town graveyard.

27. Nasrin, Fars-Abad, 4/5/2010.

28. Nushin, Fars-Abad, 6/10/2010.

29. As with larger tombs of Shi'i saints, women cannot enter the inner enclave while they are menstruating, and all persons must perform ablutions before entering the sanctuary (*haram*) that houses the tomb.

30. Shrines are often the meeting place for teenage boyfriends and girlfriends, who meet in the courtyard or see each other from far away while texting.

31. In Persian, the concept of holy tomb or shrine (*haram*), too, is interchangeable with the word house (*khuneh*). Iranian pilgrims refer to the sacred mosque in Mecca (*al-masjid al-haram* in Arabic) as the "house of God." Likewise, shrines of the Twelve Imams and their descendants are similarly addressed: for example, the shrine of Imam Reza in Mashhad, Iran, is frequently referred to as "the house of the Imam" (*khuneh-ye Imam*).

32. In Arabic, the name Mashhad means "the place of martyrdom" and is the location of the martyrdom of Imam Reza.

33. This critique is particularly trenchant among Amal members and associates of Sayyed Fadlallah, who see themselves as leaders of Shi'i legitimacy and leadership.

34. These figures were given to me by my Islamic seminary student interlocutors and members of the Basij in 2010.

35. Shah Abdol Azim was a fifth-generation descendant of Imam Hassan, the Prophet's grandson and second Imam, after Imam 'Ali.

EPILOGUE

1. This ritual was first instituted at schools after the establishment of the Islamic Republic.

2. The women of Nistdar's generation often told me stories about this time before the Revolution: about how midwives knew how to turn a baby in the womb by rubbing the mother's stomach; how they pinched the joints of a child from the fingers to the elbows to relieve a fever; and about how, when a mother gave birth, she and the other women would stay in the garden all night. They would play the flute, talk, and eat dried nuts and fruits. They would ward off jinn or spirits by performing an "egg-breaking ritual." They told me about the purity rituals surrounding birth and the special foods that were given to the new mother. For forty days, they said, a mother couldn't eat food next to anyone else because it was impure. She must perform ablutions. She would eat *kāchi*, a special food to give strength and produce milk, and she would eat cumin.

3. Perhaps surprisingly, some of my Basiji hosts held similar views. "The veil should be a choice," chador-wearing Haleh confided. Clearly, the call for change is not limited to urban, secular youth.

4. Nader, Fars-Abad, 9/4/2010.

References

Abu-Lughod, Lila. 1989. "Zones of Theory in the Anthropology of the Arab World." *Annual Review of Anthropology* 18: 267–306.
Adelkhah, Fariba. 1999. *Being Modern in Iran*. London: Hurst, Centre d'Etudes et de Recherches Internationales.
Afary, Janet. 2009. *Sexual Politics in Modern Iran*. Cambridge, UK: Cambridge University Press.
Afary, Janet, Khosrow Mostofi, and Peter William Avery. 2020. "Iran." In *Encylopaedia Britannica*. www.britannica.com/place/Iran.
Afshar, Haleh. 1998. *Islam and Feminisms: An Iranian Case-Study*. New York: St. Martin's Press.
Aghaie, Kamran Scot. 2004. *The Martyrs of Karbala: Shi'i Symbols and Rituals in Modern Iran*. Seattle: University of Washington Press.
———. 2011. *The Martyrs of Karbala: Shi'i Symbols and Rituals in Modern Iran*. Seattle: University of Washington Press.
———. 2014. "Islamic-Iranian Nationalism and Its Implications for the Study of Political Islam and Religious Nationalism." In *Rethinking Iranian Nationalism and Modernity*, edited by Kamran Scot Aghaie and Afshin Marashi, 181–204. Austin: University of Texas Press. www.jstor.org/stable/10.7560/757493.12.
Akbarzadeh, Marzieh, and Nasrin Sharifi. 2010. *Morāqabat-hā-ye Hāmelagi va Zāimān az Didgāeh Eslām* [Pregnancy and childbirth from the perspective of Islam]. Shiraz: Takht-e Jamshid.

Alaedini, Pooya, and Hamid R. Ashrafzadeh. 2016. "Iran's Post-Revolutionary Social Justice Agenda and It Outcomes: Evolution and Determinants of Income Distribution and Middle-Class Size." In *Economic Welfare and Inequality in Iran: Developments since the Revolution*, edited by Mohammad Reza Farzanegan and Pooya Alaedini, 15–46. New York: Palgrave Macmillan.

Al-e Ahmad, Jalal. (1962) 1997. Gharbzadegi (Westernstruckness). Translated by John Green. Costa Mesa, CA: Mazda Publishers.

Allison, Anne. 1991. "Japanese Mothers and Obentas: The Lunch-Box as Ideological State Apparatus." *Anthropological Quarterly* 64 (4): 195–208.

Alonso, Ana Maria. 1994. "The Politics of Space, Time, and Substance: State Formation, Nationalism and Ethnicity." *Annual Review of Anthropology* 23: 379–405.

Amin-Esmaeili, Masoumeh, Afarin Rahimi-Movaghar, Maryam Gholamrezaei, and Emran Mohammad Razaghi. 2016. "Profile of People Who Inject Drugs in Tehran, Iran." *Acta Medica Iranica* 54 (12): 793–805.

Anderson, Benedict. 1983. *Imagined Communities*. London: Verso.

Ansari, Ali M. 2007. *Modern Iran: The Pahlavis and After*. 2nd ed. London: Pearson Education.

Appadurai, Arjun. 1981. "Gastro-Politics in Hindu South Asia." *American Ethnologist* 8 (3): 494–511.

———. 1988. "How to Make a National Cuisine: Cookbooks in Contemporary India." *Comparative Studies in Society and History* 30 (1): 3–24.

Aryan, Hossein. 2008. "Iran's Basij Force—the Mainstay of Domestic Security." Radio Free Europe/Radio Free Liberty, December 7. www.rferl.org/content/Irans_Basij_Force_Mainstay_Of_Domestic_Security/1357081.html.

Asad, Talal. 1993. *Genealogies of Religion: Discipline and Reasons of Power in Christianity and Islam*. Baltimore, MD: Johns Hopkins University Press.

Attar, Maryam, Khalil Lohi, and John Lever. 2016. "Remembering the Spirit of Halal: An Iranian Perspective." In *Halal Matters: Islam, Politics and Markets in Global Perspective*, edited by Florence Bergeaud-Blackler, Johan Fischer, and John Lever, 55–71. London and New York: Routledge. https://doi.org/10.4324/9781315746128-11.

Azkia, Mostafa. 2002. "Rural Society and Revolution in Iran." In *Twenty Years of Islamic Revolution: Political and Social Transition in Iran since 1979*, edited by Eric J Hooglund, 96–119. Syracuse, NY: Syracuse University Press.

Bahloul, Joëlle. 1996. *The Architecture of Memory: A Jewish-Muslim Household in Colonial Algeria, 1937–1962*. New York: Cambridge University Press.

Bahramitash, Roksana. 2003. "Revolution, Islamization, and Women's Employment in Iran." *Brown Journal of World Affairs* 9 (2): 229–41.

———. 2012. "Gender Transformation in Iran: Thirty Years and Thirty Revolutions." In *Navigating Contemporary Iran: Challenging Economic, Social and*

Political Perceptions, edited by Eric Hooglund and Leif Stenberg, 49–58. Routledge Advances in Middle East and Islamic Studies. London: Taylor & Francis Group.

Bajoghli, Narges. 2017. "The Politics of Counting: Pro-Regime Media Strategy in the Islamic Republic of Iran." Mossavar-Rahmani Center Seminar Series, Princeton University, April 4.

———. 2019. *Iran Reframed: Anxieties of Power in the Islamic Republic*. Stanford, CA: Stanford University Press.

Bakhash, Shaul. 1984. *The Reign of the Ayatollahs: Iran and the Islamic Revolution*. New York: Basic Books.

Bateson, M. C., J. W. Clinton, J. B. M. Kassarjian, H. Safavi, and M. Soraya. 1977. "Safa-Ye Batin: A Study of the Interrelationships of a Set of Iranian Ideal Character Types." In *Psychological Dimensions of Near Eastern Studies*, edited by Norman Itzkowitz. Princeton, NJ: Darwin Press.

Bateson, Mary Catherine. 1979. "'This Figure of Tinsel': A Study of Themes of Hypocrisy and Pessimism in Iranian Culture." *Daedalus* 108 (3): 125–34.

Batmanglij, Najmieh. 1986. *Food of Life: A Book of Ancient Persian and Modern Iranian Cooking and Ceremonies*. Washington, DC: Mage Publishers.

Bear, Laura. 2013. "'This Body Is Our Body': Vishwakarma Puja, the Social Debts of Kinship, and Theologies of Materiality in a Neoliberal Shipyard." In *Vital Relations: Modernity and the Persistent Life of Kinship*, edited by Susan McKinnon and Fenella Cann, 155–78. Santa Fe, NM: School for Advanced Research Press.

Beeman, William O. 1976. "Status, Style and Strategy in Iranian Interaction." *Anthropological Linguistics* 18 (7): 305–22.

———. 1986. *Language, Status, and Power in Iran*. Bloomington: Indiana University Press.

———. 2001. "Emotion and Sincerity in Persian Discourse: Accomplishing the Representation of Inner States." *International Journal of the Sociology of Language* 148: 31–57.

———. 2003. "Performative Symbols and Their Relative Non-Arbitrariness: Representing Women in Iranian Traditional Theater." *Semiotica* 145 (1/4): 1–19.

———. 2005. *The "Great Satan" vs. the "Mad Mullah."* Chicago: University of Chicago Press.

Behrouzan, Orkideh. 2016. *Prozak Diaries: Psychiatry and Generational Memory in Iran*. Stanford, CA: Stanford University Press.

Betteridge, Anne. 1985. "Gift Exchange in Iran: The Locus of Self Identity in Social Interaction." *Anthropology Quarterly* 58 (4): 190–202.

———. 1992. "Ziarat: Pilgrimage to the Shrines of Shiraz." PhD diss., University of Chicago.

Bloch, Maurice. 1999. "Commensality and Poisoning." *Social Research* 66 (1): 133–49.
Bolourchi, Neda. 2018. "The Sacred Defense: Sacrifice and Nationalism across Minority Communities in Post-Revolutionary Iran." *Journal of the American Academy of Religion* 86 (3): 724–58. https://doi.org/10.1093/jaarel/lfx089.
Boroujerdi, Mehrzad. 1996. *Iranian Intellectuals and the West : The Tormented Triumph of Nativism*. Syracuse, NY: Syracuse University Press.
Bourdieu, Pierre. 1984. *Distinction: A Social Critique of the Judgement of Taste*. Cambridge, MA: Harvard University Press.
Bowen, John R. 1993. *Muslims through Discourse: Religion and Ritual in Gayo Society*. Princeton, NJ: Princeton University Press.
Boylston, Tom. 2014. "Food, Life, and Material Religion in Ethiopian Orthodox Christianity." In *A Companion to the Anthropology of Religion*, edited by Janice Boddy and Michael Lambek, 255–73. New York: John Wiley & Sons. https://doi.org/10.1002/9781118605936.ch14.
Bryant, Rebecca. 2002. "The Purity of Spirit and the Power of Blood: A Comparative Perspective on Nation, Gender and Kinship in Cyprus." *Journal of the Royal Anthropological Institute* 8 (3): 509–30.
Bynum, Caroline Walker. 1997. "Fast, Feast, and Flesh." In *Food and Culture: A Reader*, edited by Penny Van Esterik and C. M. Counihan, 138–59. New York: Routledge.
Cannell, Fenella. 2007. "'Recognition': Mormon Adoption, American Kinship and Religion." Paper presented at the 106th Annual Meeting of the American Anthropological Association in Washington, DC, December 1.
———. 2013. "The Re-Enchantment of Kinship." In *Vital Relations: Modernity and the Persistent Life of Kinship*, edited by Susan McKinnon and Fenella Cannell, 217–40. Santa Fe, NM: School for Advanced Research Press.
———. 2017. "'Forever Families': Christian Individualism, Mormonism and Collective Salvation." In *New Directions in Spiritual Kinship: Sacred Ties across the Abrahamic Religions*, edited by Todne Thomas, Asiya Malik, and Rose Wellman, 151–69. Contemporary Anthropology of Religion. New York: Palgrave Macmillan. https://doi.org/10.1007/978-3-319-48423-5_7.
Carrington, Christopher. 2012. "Feeding Lesbigay Families." In *Food and Culture: A Reader*, edited by Penny Van Esterik and C. M. Counihan, 187–211. New York: Routledge.
Carsten, Janet. 1995. "The Substance of Kinship and the Heat of the Hearth: Feeding, Personhood and Relatedness among Malays of Pulau Langkawi." *American Ethnologist* 22 (2): 223–41.
———, ed. 2000. *Cultures of Relatedness: New Approaches to the Study of Kinship*. Cambridge, UK: Cambridge University Press.
———. 2004. *After Kinship: New Departures in Anthropology*. Cambridge, UK: Cambridge University Press.

———. 2013. "Introduction: Blood Will Out." *Journal of the Royal Anthropological Institute* 19 (S1): S1–23. https://doi.org/10.1111/1467-9655.12013.

Cave, Damien. 2010. "Pastor's Plan to Burn Korans Adds to Tensions." *New York Times*, August 25, sec. U.S. www.nytimes.com/2010/08/26/us/26gainesville.html.

Chatterjee, Partha. 1989. "Colonialism, Nationalism, and Colonialized Women: The Contest in India." *American Ethnologist* 16 (4): 622–33. https://doi.org/10.1525/ae.1989.16.4.02a00020.

Chehabi, H. E. 2003. "The Westernization of Iranian Culinary Culture." *Iranian Studies* 36 (1): 43–61.

———. 2007. "How Caviar Turned Out to Be Halal." *Gastronomica* 7 (2): 17–23.

Chelkowski, Peter. 1979. *Taʻziyeh: Ritual and Drama in Iran*. New York: New York University Press.

Chelkowski, Peter J., and Hamid Dabashi. 1999. *Staging a Revolution: The Art of Persuasion in the Islamic Republic of Iran*. New York: New York University Press.

Clarke, Morgan. 2007a. "The Modernity of Milk Kinship." *Social Anthropology* 15 (3): 287–304. https://doi.org/10.1111/j.0964-0282.2007.00022.x.

———. 2007b. "Closeness in the Age of Mechanical Reproduction: Debating Kinship and Biomedicine in Lebanon and the Middle East." *Anthropological Quarterly* 80 (2): 379–402. https://doi.org/10.1353/anq.2007.0022.

———. 2009. *Islam and New Kinship: Reproductive Technology and the Shariah in Lebanon*. New York: Berghahn Books.

Connerton, Paul. 1989. *How Societies Remember*. New York: Cambridge University Press.

Copeman, Jacob. 2013. "The Art of Bleeding: Memory, Martyrdom, and Portraits in Blood." *Journal of the Royal Anthropological Institute* 19 (S1): S149–71. https://doi.org/10.1111/1467-9655.12021.

Coulson, N. J. 1971. "Inheritance in Shīʻī Law." *Succession in the Muslim Family*. https://doi.org/10.1017/CBO9780511557965.009.

Deeb, Lara. 2009. "Emulating and/or Embodying the Ideal: The Gendering of Temporal Frameworks and Islamic Role Models in Shiʻi Lebanon." *American Ethnologist* 36 (2): 242–57. https://doi.org/10.1111/j.1548-1425.2009.01133.x.

Deeb, Lara, and Mona Harb. 2013. *Leisurely Islam: Negotiating Geography and Morality in Shiʻite South Beirut*. Princeton, NJ: Princeton University Press.

Delaney, Carol. 1986. "The Meaning of Paternity and the Virgin Birth Debate." *Man* 21: 494–513.

———. 1991. *The Seed and the Soil: Gender and Cosmology in Turkish Village Society*. Berkeley: University of California Press.

Dodson, Jualynne E., and Cheryl Townsend Gilkes. 1995. "'There's Nothing Like Church Food': Food and the U.S. Afro-Christian Tradition: Re-Membering

Community and Feeding the Embodied S/Spirit(s)." *Journal of the American Academy of Religion* 63 (3): 519–38.

Donovan, Jerome. 2011. *The Iran-Iraq War: Antecedents and Conflict Escalation*. New York: Routledge.

Doostdar, Alireza. 2018. *The Iranian Metaphysicals: Explorations in Science, Islam, and the Uncanny*. Princeton, NJ: Princeton University Press.

Dorraj, Manochehr. 1997. "Symbolic and Utilitarian Political Value of a Tradition: Martyrdom in the Iranian Political Culture." *Review of Politics* 59 (03): 489–522.

Douglas, Mary. 1972. "Deciphering a Meal." *Daedalus* 101 (1): 61–81.

Ehsani, Kaveh. 2017. "War and Resentment: Critical Reflections on the Legacies of the Iran-Iraq War." *Middle East Critique* 26 (1): 5–24. https://doi.org/10.1080/19436149.2016.1245530.

Eickelman, Dale F. 1998. *The Middle East and Central Asia: An Anthropological Approach*. 3rd ed. Upper Saddle River, NJ: Prentice Hall.

Eilers, W., E. Elāhī, and M. Boyce. (1987) 2011. "ĀŠ." In *Encyclopædia Iranica*, 7:692–94, sec. II. www.iranicaonline.org/articles/as-2.

Ellison, Susan Helen. 2018. *Domesticating Democracy: The Politics of Conflict Resolution in Bolivia*. Durham, NC: Duke University Press.

Euben, Roxanne L., and Muhammad Qasim Zaman. 2009. *Princeton Readings in Islamist Thought: Texts and Contexts from Al-Banna to Bin Laden*. Princeton, NJ: Princeton University Press.

Fajans, Jane. 1988. "The Transformative Value of Food: A Review Essay." *Food & Foodways* 3 (1–2): 143–66.

Farquhar, Judith. 2002. *Appetites: Food and Sex in Post-Socialist China*. Durham, NC: Duke University Press.

Farzanegan, Mohammad Reza, and Pooya Alaedini. 2016. Introduction to *Economic Welfare and Inequality in Iran: Developments since the Revolution*, edited by Mohammad Reza Farzanegan and Pooya Alaedini, 1–14. New York: Palgrave Macmillan.

Fathi, Nazila. 2009. "Neda Agha-Soltan Becomes a Symbol of Iran Protests through Video." *New York Times*, June 22, sec. Middle East. www.nytimes.com/2009/06/23/world/middleeast/23neda.html.

Faubion, James D. 2001. "Introduction: Toward an Anthropology of the Ethics of Kinship." In *The Ethics of Kinship: Ethnographic Inquiries*, edited by James D. Faubion, 1–29. Lanham, MD: Rowman & Littlefield.

Fazaeli, Roja. 2009. "Humiliated Men and Martyred Women: The War on Terror's Implication on Redefining Middle-Eastern Masculinities." Presented at a panel titled "Cultural, Social and National Masculinities," Emory Law School, Emory University, September 27. https://www.youtube.com/watch?v=ES33sVoG_KM.

Feeley-Harnik, Gillian. 1981. *The Lord's Table: Eucharist and Passover in Early Christianity*. Philadelphia: University of Pennsylvania Press.
———. 1995. "Religion and Food: An Anthropological Perspective." *Journal of the American Academy of Religion* 63 (3): 565–582.
———. 1999. "'Communities of Blood': The Natural History of Kinship in Nineteenth-Century America." *Comparative Studies in Society and History* 41 (2): 215–62. https://doi.org/10.1017/S0010417599002078.
Feldman-Savelsberg, Pamela. 1996. "Cooking Inside: Kinship and Gender in Bangangté Idioms of Marriage and Procreation." In *Gender, Kinship, Power: A Comparative and Interdisciplinary History*, edited by Mary Jo Maynes, Ann Waltner, Birgitte Soland, and Ulrike Strasser, 177–200. New York: Routledge.
Fischer, Michael M. J. (1980) 2003. *Iran: From Religious Dispute to Revolution*. Madison: University of Wisconsin Press.
———. 2010. "The Rhythmic Beat of the Revolution in Iran." *Cultural Anthropology* 25 (3): 497–543. https://doi.org/10.1111/j.1548-1360.2010.01068.x.
Fischer, Michael M. J., and Mehdi Abedi. 1990. *Debating Muslims: Cultural Dialogues in Postmodernity and Tradition*. Madison: University of Wisconsin Press.
Flaskerud, Ingvild. 2010. *Visualizing Belief and Piety in Iranian Shiism*. London: Continuum.
———. 2012. "Redemptive Memories: Portraiture in the Cult of Commemoration." *Visual Anthropology* 25 (1–2): 22–46. https://doi.org/10.1080/08949468.2012.627830.
Foucault, Michel. 2000. *Ethics: Subjectivity and Truth*. Vol. 1. London: Allen Lane.
Gheissari, Ali. 1998. *Iranian Intellectuals in the 20th Century*. Austin: University of Texas Press.
Goffman, Erving. 1956. *The Presentation of Self in Everyday Life*. Edinburgh: University of Edinburgh, Social Sciences Research Centre.
Golkar, Saeid. 2015. *Captive Society: The Basij Militia and Social Control in Iran*. New York: Columbia University Press.
Gruber, Christiane. 2012. "The Martyrs' Museum in Tehran: Visualizing Memory in Post-Revolutionary Iran." *Visual Anthropology* 25: 68–97.
Haeri, Shahla. 1989. *Law of Desire: Temporary Marriage in Shi'i Iran*. Syracuse, NY: Syracuse University Press.
Halbwachs, Maurice. 1992. *On Collective Memory*. Translated by Lewis A. Closer. Chicago: University of Chicago Press.
Harbottle, Lynn. 2000. *Food for Health, Food for Wealth: Ethnic and Gender Identities in British Iranian Communities*. New York: Berghahn Books.
Harding, Susan F. 1987. "Convicted by the Holy Spirit: The Rhetoric of Fundamental Baptist Conversion." *American Ethnologist* 14 (1): 167–81. https://doi.org/10.1525/ae.1987.14.1.02a00100.

———. 1991. "Representing Fundamentalism: The Problem of the Repugnant Cultural Other." *Social Research* 58 (2): 373–93.
Harris, Kevan. 2017. *A Social Revolution: Politics and the Welfare State in Iran*. Oakland: University of California Press.
Hegland, Mary Elaine. 1983a."Aliabad Women: Revolution as Religious Activity." In *Women and Revolution in Iran*, edited by Guity Nashat, 171–94. Boulder: Westview Press.
———. 1983b. "Ritual and Revolution in Iran." In *Political Anthropology*, volume II, *Culture and Political Change*, edited by Myron J. Aronoff, 75–100. New Brunswick, NJ: Transaction.
———. 1998. "Women and the Iranian Revolution: A Village Case Study." In *Women and Revolution: Global Expressions*, edited by M. J. Diamond, 211–25. Dordrecht: Springer Netherlands. https://doi.org/10.1007/978-94-015-9072-3_11.
———. 2013. *Days of Revolution: Political Unrest in an Iranian Village*. Stanford, CA: Stanford University Press.
Heng, Geraldine, and Janadas Devan. 1992. "State Fatherhood: The Politics of Nationalism, Sexuality and Race in Singapore." In *Nationalisms and Sexualities*, edited by Andres Parker, Mary Russon, Doris Sommer, and Patricia Yaeger, 343–64. New York: Routledge.
Ho, Engseng. 2006. *The Graves of Tarim: Genealogy and Mobility across the Indian Ocean*. Berkeley: University of California Press.
Hobsbawm, Eric. 1983. *The Invention of Tradition*. Cambridge, UK: Cambridge University Press.
Holtzman, Jon D. 2006. "Food and Memory." *Annual Review of Anthropology* 35 (1): 361–78.
Hoodfar, Homa. 2001. "The Veil in Their Minds and on Our Heads: Veiling Practices and Muslim Women." In *Women, Gender, Religion: A Reader*, edited by Elizabeth A. Castelli, 420–46. New York: Palgrave Macmillan US. https://doi.org/10.1007/978-1-137-04830-1_22.
Hooglund, Eric. 2009. "Thirty Years of the Islamic Revolution in Rural Iran." *Middle East Report* 250 (Spring). https://merip.org/2009/03/thirty-years-of-the-islamic-revolution-in-rural-iran/.
Howell, Signe. 2003. "Kinning: The Creation of Life Trajectories in Transnational Adoptive Families." *Journal of the Royal Anthropological Institute*, no. 9: 465–84.
Izberk-Bilgin, Elif, and Cheryl C. Nakata. 2016. "A New Look at Faith-Based Marketing: The Global Halal Market." *Business Horizons* 59 (3): 285–92. https://doi.org/10.1016/j.bushor.2016.01.005.
Jamzadeh, Laal, and Margaret Mills. 1986. "Iranian Sofreh: From Collective to Female Ritual." In *Gender and Religion: On the Complexity of Symbols*,

edited by Caroline Walker Bynum and Richman, Paula, 23–65. Boston: Beacon Press.

Janowski, Monica. 2007. "Introduction: Feeding the Right Food: The Flow of Life and the Construction of Kinship in Southeast Asia." In *Kinship and Food in South East Asia*, edited by Monica Janowski and Fiona Kerlogue, 1–23. Copenhagen: Nordic Institute of Asian Studies.

Johnson, Christopher H., Bernhard Jussen, David Warren Sabean, and Simon Teuscher. 2015. *Blood and Kinship: Matter for Metaphor from Ancient Rome to the Present*. New York: Berghahn Books.

Joseph, Suad. 1994. "Brother/Sister Relationships: Connectivity, Love, and Power in the Reproduction of Patriarchy in Lebanon." *American Ethnologist* 21 (1): 50–73.

———. 1999. "Descent of the Nation: Kinship and Citizenship in Lebanon." *Citizenship Studies* 3 (3): 295–318.

Kalinock, Sabine. 2003. "Between Party and Devotion: Mowludi of Tehran Women." *Critique: Critical Middle Eastern Studies* 12 (2): 173–87. https://doi.org/10.1080/1066992032000130620.

Kashani-Sabet, Firoozeh. 2005. "Who Is Fatima? Gender, Culture, and Representation in Islam." *Journal of Middle East Women's Studies* 1 (2): 1–24.

———. 2014. *Frontier Fictions: Shaping the Iranian Nation, 1804–1946*. Princeton, NJ: Princeton University Press.

Kaur, Ravinder. 2010. "Sacralising Bodies: On Martyrdom, Government and Accident in Iran." *JRAS* 3 (20): 441–60.

Keddie, Nikki R. 2006. *Modern Iran: Roots and Results of Revolution*. New Haven, CT: Yale University Press.

Khajeh, Zahra, and Imran Ho-Abdullah. 2012. "Persian Culinary Metaphors: A Cross-Cultural Conceptualization." *GEMA Online® Journal of Language Studies* 12 (1). http://ejournal.ukm.my/gema/article/view/22.

Khan, Arsalan, Rose Wellman, and Amina Tawasil. 2013. "Rethinking Ethics and Sentiment among Muslims in Iran and South Asia." Paper presented at the 112th Annual Meeting of the American Anthropological Association, Chicago.

Khomeini, Ruhollah. (1970) 2005. *Islamic Government: Governance of the Jurist*. 2nd ed. Translated and annotated by Hanmid Algar. Tehran: The Institution for Compilation and Publication of Imam Khomeini's Works (International Affairs Department).

———. (1979) 2001. *The Position of Women from the Viewpoint of Imam Khomeini (May Allah Grant Him Peace)*. Translated by Juliana Shaw and Behrooz Arezoo. Tehran: The Institute for Compilation and Publication of Imam Khomeini's Works (International Affairs Division).

———. 1999. *Sahifeh-Ye Imam*. Vol. 3. Tehran: The Institute for Compilation and Publication of Imam Khomeini's Works (International Affairs Division).

———. 2003. *The Greatest Jihad: Combat with the Self.* 2nd ed. Translated by Muhammad Legenhausen. Tehran: The Institution for Compilation and Publication of Imam Khomeini's Works (International Affairs Department).

Khosravi, Shahram. 2008. *Young and Defiant in Tehran.* Philadelphia: University of Pennsylvania Press.

Khosronejad, Pedram. 2012. "Introduction: Unburied Memories." *Visual Anthropology* 25 (1–2): 1–21.

———. 2013. "Shrines of Un-Known Martyrs of Iran-Iraq War as Vocal Public Spaces in Tehran Universities." Paper presented at the Annual Conference of the BSA, Sociology of Religion Study Group, Durham, UK, April 10.

Khuri, Fuad I. 2001. *The Body in Islamic Culture.* London: Saqi Books.

King, Ralph. 2007. *The Iran-Iraq War: The Political Implications.* New York: Routledge.

Labby, David. 1976. *The Demystification of Yap: Dialectics of Culture on a Micronesian Island.* Chicago: University of Chicago Press.

Lahsaeizadeh, Abdolali. 2001. "Sociological Analysis of Food and Nutrition in Iran." *Nutrition & Food Science* 31: 129–35.

Lambek, Michael. 1990. "Certain Knowledge, Contestable Authority: Power and Practice on the Islamic Periphery." *American Ethnologist* 17 (1): 23–40.

———. 2010. *Ordinary Ethics: Anthropology, Language, and Action.* New York: Fordham University Press.

Laqueur, Thomas. 1999. "Pint for Pint." *London Review of Books,* October 14.

Lazar, Sian. 2012. "Citizenship Quality: A New Agenda for Development?" *Journal of Civil Society* 8 (4): 333–50. https://doi.org/10.1080/17448689.2012.738898.

Lob, Eric. 2017. "Development, Mobilization and War: The Iranian Construction Jehad, Construction Mobilization and Trench Builders Association (1979–2013)." *Middle East Critique* 26 (1): 25–44. https://doi.org/10.1080/19436149.2017.1282738.

Lob, Eric Sander. 2013. "An Institutional History of the Iranian Construction Jihad: From Inception to Institutionalization (1979–2011)." PhD diss., Princeton University.

Loeffler, Agnes G. 2008. "The Indigenisation of Allopathic Medicine in Iran." *Anthropology of the Middle East* 3 (2): 75–92.

Ludwig, Paul. 1999. "'Iranian Nation' and Iranian-Islamic Revolutionary Ideology." *Die Welt des Islams* 39 (2): 183–217.

Madelung, W. 2012. "ALĪ AL-REŻĀ." In *Encyclopædia Iranica,* 1/8:877–80. www.iranicaonline.org/articles/ali-al-reza.

Mahdavi, Pardis. 2009. *Passionate Uprisings: Iran's Sexual Revolution.* Stanford, CA: Stanford University Press.

Mahmood, Saba. 2005. *Politics of Piety: The Islamic Revival and the Feminist Subject.* Princeton, NJ: Princeton University Press.

Maloney, Suzanne. 2000. "Agents or Obstacles? Parastatal Foundations and Challenges to Iranian Development." In *The Economy of Iran: The Dilemma of an Islamic State*, edited by Parvin Alizadeh, 145–76. London: I. B. Tauris.

Mamdani, Mahmood. 2002. "Good Muslim, Bad Muslim: A Political Perspective on Culture and Terrorism." *American Anthropologist* 104 (3): 766–75. https://doi.org/10.1525/aa.2002.104.3.766.

Manoukian, Setrag. 2012. *City of Knowledge in Twentieth Century Iran: Shiraz, History and Poetry*. New York: Routledge.

Massé, Henri, and Charles A. Messner. 1954. "Persian Beliefs and Customs." In *Behavior Science Translations*, 527. New Haven, CT: Human Relations Area Files. https://ehrafworldcultures.yale.edu/document?id=ma01-007.

Mattingly, Cheryl. 2014. *Moral Laboratories: Family Peril and the Struggle for a Good Life*. Oakland: University of California Press.

McClintock, Anne. 1993. "Family Feuds: Gender, Nationalism and the Family." *Feminist Review*, no. 44: 61–80. https://doi.org/10.2307/1395196.

McKinnon, Susan, and Fenella Cannell. 2013. "The Difference Kinship Makes." In *Vital Relations: Modernity and the Persistent Life of Kinship*, edited by Susan McKinnon and Fenella Cannell, 3–38. Santa Fe, NM: School for Advanced Research Press.

Meneley, Anne. (1996) 2016. *Tournaments of Value: Sociability and Hierarchy in a Yemeni Town*. Toronto: University of Toronto Press.

Mintz, Sidney W., and Christine M. Du Bois. 2002. "The Anthropology of Food and Eating." *Annual Review of Anthropology* 31 (1): 99–119. https://doi.org/10.1146/annurev.anthro.32.032702.131011.

Mir-Hosseini, Ziba. 1998. "Rethinking Gender: Discussions with Ulama in Iran." *Critique: Critical Middle Eastern Studies* 7 (13): 45–59. https://doi.org/10.1080/10669929808720130.

———. 2004. "Sexuality, Rights, and Islam: Competing Gender Discourses in Post-Revolutionary Iran." In *Women in Iran from 1800 to the Islamic Republic*, edited by Lois Beck and Guity Nashat, 204–17. Urbana: University of Illinois Press.

———. 2010. "Sharia and National Law in Iran." In *Sharia Incorporated: A Comparative Overview of the Legal Systems of Twelve Muslim Countries in Past and Present*, edited by Jan Michiel Otto, 319–72. Leiden: Leiden University Press.

Moallem, Minoo. 1992. "The Ethnicity of an Islamic Fundamentalism: The Case of Iran." *South Asia Bulletin* 12 (2): 25–34.

———. 2005. *Between Warrior Brother and Veiled Sister: Islamic Fundamentalism and the Politics of Patriarchy in Iran*. Berkeley: University of California Press.

Mutahhari, Murtaza. 2009. "The Human Status of Women in the Qur'an." In *Princeton Readings in Islamist Thought: Texts and Contexts from Al-Banna to Bin Laden*, edited by Roxanne L. Euben and Muhammad Qasim Zaman, 254–74. Princeton, NJ: Princeton University Press.

Naef, Shirin. 2017. *Kinship, Law and Religion: An Anthropological Study of Assisted Reproductive Technologies in Iran*. Tübingen: Narr Francke Attempto. https://public.ebookcentral.proquest.com/choice/publicfullrecord.aspx?p=5043741.

Najmabadi, Afsaneh. 1987. "Iran's Turn to Islam: From Modernism to a Moral Order." *Middle East Journal* 41 (2): 202–17.

———. 1997. "The Erotic Vatan [Homeland] as Beloved and Mother: To Love, to Possess, and To Protect." *Comparative Studies in Society and History* 39 (3): 442–67.

———. 2013. *Professing Selves: Transsexuality and Same-Sex Desire in Contemporary Iran*. Durham, NC: Duke University Press.

Nash, Catherine. 2008. *Of Irish Descent: Origin Stories, Genealogy, & the Politics of Belonging*. Syracuse, NY: Syracuse University Press.

Nashat, Guity. 1983. *Women and Revolution in Iran*. Boulder, CO: Westview Press.

———. 2004. Introduction to *Women in Iran from 1800 to the Islamic Republic*, edited by Lois Beck and Guity Nashat, 1–37. Urbana and Chicago: University of Illinois Press.

Nazemi, Nader. 1993. "War and State Making in Revolutionary Iran." PhD diss., University of Washington.

Nikfarjam, Ali, Mostafa Shokoohi, Armita Shahesmaeili, Ali Akbar Haghdoost, Mohammad Reza Baneshi, Saiedeh Haji-Maghsoudi, Azam Rastegari, Abbas Ali Nasehi, Nadereh Memaryan, and Termeh Tarjoman. 2016. "National Population Size Estimation of Illicit Drug Users through the Network Scale-up Method in 2013 in Iran." *International Journal of Drug Policy* 31 (May): 147–52. https://doi.org/10.1016/j.drugpo.2016.01.013.

Noori, Neema. 2013. "Rethinking the Legacies of the Iran–Iraq War: Veterans, the Basij, and Social Resistance in Iran." In *Political and Military Sociology: An Annual Review*, edited by Neovi M. Karakatsanis and Jonathan Swartz, 40: 119–40. New Brunswick, NJ: Transaction.

Ohnuki-Tierney, Emiko. 1994. *Rice as Self: Japanese Identities through Time*. Princeton, NJ: Princeton University Press.

Olszewska, Zuzanna. 2013. "Classy Kids and Down-at-Heel Intellectuals: Status Aspiration and Blind Spots in the Contemporary Ethnography of Iran." *Iranian Studies* 46 (6): 841–62. https://doi.org/10.1080/00210862.2013.810078.

———. 2015a. *The Pearl of Dari: Poetry and Personhood among Young Afghans in Iran*. Bloomington: Indiana University Press.

———. 2015b. "Class Reshuffling among Afghan Refugees in Iran." *Middle East Report* 277 (Winter): 3.

Osanloo, Arzoo. 2009. *The Politics of Women's Rights in Iran*. Princeton, NJ: Princeton University Press.

Ott, Sandra. 1979. "Aristotle among the Basques: The Cheese Analogy of Conception." *Man* 14: 699–711.

Paidar, Parvin. 1995. *Women and the Political Process in Twentieth-Century Iran*. Cambridge, UK: Cambridge University Press.

Parkes, Peter. 2005. "Milk Kinship in Islam. Substance, Structure, History." *Social Anthropology* 13 (3): 307–29.

Pilcher, Jeffrey M. 1998. *Que Vivan Los Tamales: Food and the Making of Mexican Identity*. Albuquerque: University of New Mexico Press.

Reeves, Minou. 1989. *Female Warriors of Allah: Women and the Islamic Revolution*. New York: E. P. Dutton.

Regenstein, J. M., M. M. Chaudry, and C. E. Regenstein. 2003. "The Kosher and Halal Food Laws." *Comprehensive Reviews in Food Science and Food Safety* 2 (3): 111–27. https://doi.org/10.1111/j.1541-4337.2003.tb00018.x.

Reuters. 2010. "Iran Koran Protesters Scuffle with Police." September 13. www.reuters.com/article/us-iran-koran-protest-idUSTRE68C48M20 100913.

Rezazadeh, Arezoo, Bahram Rashidkhani, and Nasrin Omidvar. 2010. "Association of Major Dietary Patterns with Socioeconomic and Lifestyle Factors of Adult Women Living in Tehran, Iran." *Nutrition (Burbank, Los Angeles County, Calif.)* 26 (3): 337–41. https://doi.org/10.1016/j.nut.2009.06.019.

Rizvi, Kishwar. 2003. "Religious Icon and National Symbol: The Tomb of Ayatollah Khomeini in Iran." *Muqarnas* 20: 209–24.

Robbins, Joel. 2013. "Beyond the Suffering Subject: Toward an Anthropology of the Good." *Journal of the Royal Anthropological Institute* 19 (3): 447–62. https://doi.org/10.1111/1467-9655.12044.

Sachedina, Abdulaziz. 2009. *Islamic Biomedical Ethics: Principles and Application*. New York: Oxford University Press.

Sadeghi, Fatemeh. 2009. "Foot Soldiers of the Islamic Republic's 'Culture of Modesty.'" *Middle East Report: The Islamic Revolution at 30* (250). https://merip.org/2009/03/foot-soldiers-of-the-islamic-republics-culture-of-modesty/.

Saeidi, Shirin. 2010. "Creating the Islamic Republic of Iran: Wives and Daughters of Martyrs, and Acts of Citizenship." *Citizenship Studies* 14 (2): 113–26. https://doi.org/10.1080/13621021003594734.

Said, Edward W. 1978. *Orientalism*. New York: Pantheon Books.

Salehi-Isfahani, Djavad. 2019. "Order from Chaos: Iran's Economy 40 Years after the Islamic Revolution." https://www.brookings.edu/blog/order-from-chaos/2019/03/14/irans-economy-40-years-after-the-islamic-revolution/.

Schacht, Joseph. 1966. *An Introduction to Islamic Law*. Oxford: Clarendon Press.

Schielke, Samuli. 2009. "Being Good in Ramadan: Ambivalence, Fragmentation, and the Moral Self in the Lives of Young Egyptians." *Journal of the Royal Anthropological Institute* 15 (supp. S1): 24–40.

Schielke, Samuli, and Zentrum Moderner Orient. 2010. "Second Thoughts about the Anthropology of Islam, or How to Make Sense of Grand Schemes in Everyday Life." *ZMO*, no. 2: 1–16.

Schirazi, Asghar. 1997. *The Constitution of Iran: Politics and the State in the Islamic Republic*. London: I. B. Tauris.

Schneider, David M. 1969. "Kinship, Nationality and Religion in American Culture: Toward a Definition of Kinship." In *Forms of Symbolic Action*, edited by Robert F. Spencer, 116–25. New Orleans, LA: University of Washington Press.

SCI (Statistical Center of Iran). 2015. Time series Excel tables. www.amar.org.ir.

Seeman, Don. 2017. "Kinship as Ethical Relation: A Critique of the Spiritual Kinship Paradigm." In *New Directions in Spiritual Kinship: Sacred Ties across the Abrahamic Religions*, edited by Todne Thomas, Asiya Malik, and Rose Wellman, 85–108, Contemporary Anthropology of Religion. New York: Palgrave Macmillan. https://doi.org/10.1007/978-3-319-48423-5_4.

Sered, Susan Starr. 1988. "Food and Holiness: Cooking as a Sacred Act among Middle-Eastern Jewish Women." *Anthropological Quarterly* 61 (3): 129–39.

Shaery-Eisenlohr, Roschanack. 2007. "Imagining Shi'ite Iran: Transnationalism and Religious Authenticity in the Muslim World." *Iranian Studies* 40 (1): 17–35. https://doi.org/10.1080/00210860601138608.

Shahshahani, Soheila. 1990. "Women in the Kinship Structure of Iran." In *Structures and Strategies: Women, Work, and Family*, edited by Leela Dube, Rajni Palriwala. Delhi: Sage.

———. 2008. "Body as a Means of Non-Verbal Communication in Iran." *International Journal of Modern Anthropology* 1: 65–81.

Shariati, Ali. 1981. *Ali Shariati's Fatima Is Fatima*. Translated by Laleh Bakhtiar. Shariati Foundation.

Shirazi, Faegheh. 2005. "The Sofreh: Comfort and Community among Women in Iran." *Iranian Studies* 38 (2): 293–309.

Sutton, David, Nefissa Naguib, Leonidas Vournelis, and Maggie Dickinson. 2013. "Food and Contemporary Protest Movements." *Food, Culture & Society* 16 (3): 345–66. https://doi.org/10.2752/175174413X13673466711642.

Taliqani, Mahmud, Murtaza Mutahhari, Ali Shari'ati, Mehdi Abedi, and Gary Legenhausen. 1986. *Jihād and Shahādat: Struggle and Martyrdom in Islam*. Houston, TX: Institute for Research and Islamic Studies.

Tawasil, Amina. 2015. "The Howzevi (Seminarian) Women in Iran: Constituting and Reconstituting Paths." *Journal of Middle East Women's Studies* 11 (2): 258–59. https://doi.org/10.1215/15525864-2889189.

Thomas, Todne, Asiya Malik, and Rose Wellman, eds. 2017. *New Directions in Spiritual Kinship: Sacred Ties across the Abrahamic Religions*. Contemporary Anthropology of Religion. New York: Palgrave Macmillan.

Tober, Diane M., Mohammad-Hossein Taghdisi, and Mohammad Jalali. 2006. "'Fewer Children, Better Life' or 'As Many as God Wants'? Family Planning among Low-Income Iranian and Afghan Refugee Families in Isfahan, Iran." *Medical Anthropology Quarterly* 20 (1): 50–71.

Torab, Azam. 1996. "Piety as Gendered Agency: A Study of Jalaseh Ritual Discourse in an Urban Neighbourhood in Iran." *Journal of the Royal Anthropological Institute* 2 (2): 235. https://doi.org/10.2307/3034094.

———. 2007. *Performing Islam: Gender and Ritual in Iran*. Volume 4, *Women and Gender: The Middle East and the Islamic World*. Leiden: Brill.

Turner, Edith L. B. 1993. "The Reality of Spirits: A Tabooed or Permitted Field of Study?" *Anthropology of Consciousness* 4 (1): 9–12. https://doi.org/10.1525/ac.1993.4.1.9.

Turner, Victor W. 1967. *The Forest of Symbols: Aspects of Ndembu Ritual*. Ithaca, NY: Cornell University Press.

Varzi, Roxanne. 2006. *Warring Souls: Youth, Media, and Martyrdom in Post-Revolution Iran*. Durham, NC: Duke University Press.

Vaziri, Mostafa. 1993. *Iran as Imagined Nation : The Construction of National Identity*. New York: Paragon House.

Verdery, Katherine. 1999. *The Political Lives of Dead Bodies: Reburial and Postsocialist Change*. New York: Columbia University Press.

Weismantel, M. 1995. "Making Kin: Kinship Theory and Sumbagua Adoptions." *American Ethnologist* 22 (4): 685–709.

Wellman, Rose. 2015. "Regenerating the Islamic Republic: Commemorating Martyrs in Provincial Iran1." *Muslim World* 105 (4): 561–81. https://doi.org/10.1111/muwo.12111.

———. 2017a. "Sacralizing Kinship, Naturalizing the Nation: Blood and Food in Postrevolutionary Iran." *American Ethnologist* 44 (3): 503–15. https://doi.org/10.1111/amet.12525.

———. 2017b. "Substance, Spirit, and Sociality Among Shi'i Muslims in Iran." In *New Directions in Spiritual Kinship: Sacred Ties across the Abrahamic Religions*, edited by Todne Thomas, Asiya Malik, and Rose Wellman, 171–94, Contemporary Anthropology of Religion. New York: Palgrave Macmillan. https://doi.org/10.1007/978-3-319-48423-5_8.

———. 2018. "'Almost Mahram': Moments of Trust and Kinship in Iran." *Anthropology of the Middle East* 13 (1): 117–20. https://doi.org/10.3167/ame.2018.130109.

———. 2020. "In a Basiji Kitchen: Halal Jello, Biomorality, and Blessing in the Islamic Republic of Iran." *Gastronomica* 20 (1): 23–33. https://doi.org/10.1525/gfc.2020.20.1.23.

Weston, Kath. 1991. *Families We Choose.* New York: Columbia University Press.
———. 2001. "Kinship, Controversy, and the Sharing of Substance: The Race/Class Politics of Blood Transfusion." In *Relative Values: Reconfiguring Kinship Studies*, edited by S. Franklin and S. McKinnon, 147–74. Durham, NC: Duke University Press.
Wilk, Richard. 2006. *Home Cooking in the Global Village: Caribbean Food from Buccaneers to Ecotourists.* Oxford: Berg.
Williams, P., and L. Chrisman. 1994. *Colonial Discourse and Post-Colonial Theory: A Reader.* New York: Columbia University Press.
Worth, Robert F. 2010. "Ayatollah Speaks of Plot to Abuse Koran." *New York Times*, September 13, sec. Middle East. www.nytimes.com/2010/09/14/world/middleeast/14iran.html.
Wright, Robin. 2018. "Hijab Protests Expose Iran's Core Divide." *New Yorker*, February 7. www.newyorker.com/news/news-desk/hijab-protests-expose-irans-core-divide.
Yanagisako, Sylvia, and Jane Collier, eds. 1987. *Toward a Unified Analysis of Gender and Kinship.* Gender and Kinship: Essays Toward a Unified Analysis. Stanford, CA: Stanford University Press.
Yanagisako, Sylvia Junko, and Carol Lowery Delaney. 1995. *Naturalizing Power: Essays in Feminist Cultural Analysis.* New York: Routledge.
Yuval-Davis, Nira, and Floya Anthias, eds. 1989. *Woman, Nation, State.* Hampshire, UK: Macmillan.
Zafarghandi, Saberi, Mohammad Bagher, Mohsen Jadidi, and Narjes Khalili. 2015. "Iran's Activities on Prevention, Treatment and Harm Reduction of Drug Abuse." *International Journal of High Risk Behaviors & Addiction* 4 (4). https://doi.org/10.5812/ijhrba.22863.
Zigon, Jarrett. 2008. *Morality: An Anthropological Perspective.* Oxford: Berg.
———. 2014. "Attunement and Fidelity: Two Ontological Conditions for Morally Being-in-the-World." *Ethos* 42 (1): 16–30. https://doi.org/10.1111/etho.12036.
Zubaida, Sami. 2004. "Islam and Nationalism: Continuities and Contradictions." *Nations and Nationalism* 10 (4): 407–20. https://doi.org/10.1111/j.1354-5078.2004.00174.x.

Index

Abbas (older brother of Kobra), 65
Achaemenid Empire, 25
Agha-Soltan, Neda, 149
Ahmad, 7, 8, 9, 10, 14–15, 16, 21–22, 38, 45–46, 86, 90, 91, 175; and on protecting the āberu of his family, 66, 69; buying of meat by, 93–94; cooking and sharing of blessed food by, 77; grief over the death of his father, 50; on the importance of doing good, 62; the making of pomegranate sauce, 97–98; on not celebrating the festival of Eid, 70; prayers of, 111–12; ancestry of his son-in-law, 59; self-description of, 88–89; service of in the Iran-Iraq War, 66, 129; support of for various Ayatollahs, 120–21; on visiting his family, 72–73
Ahmadinejad, Mahmoud, 12, 14, 18, 195, 202n10
Akbarzadeh, Marzieh, 209n4
Al-e Ahmad, Jalal, 159–60
Ali (son of Nushin and Ahmad), 66, 71–72, 76, 86, 121–22
alcohol, 93, 99, 129, 167, 168, 170
Allah. *See* God/Allah
almonds, 95, 100
alms, 110, 112

Anderson, Benedict, 148
animal husbandry, 94
Appadurai, Arjun, 79, 158
apricots, 95
"Aqiqeh Prayer," 119–20
Asghar, Ali, 57
āsh, 119, 156, 164, 181, 187, 193, 213n38; āsh-e mash, 213n38; āsh-e reshteh-ye posht-e pā, 213n38; āsh-e sholeh qalamkār, 213n38
'Ashura (day of mourning for the martyrdom of Imam Husayn at the Battle of Karbala), 23, 61, 130, 175. See also *ziarat-e 'āshura'*, why it "saved us"
Ataturk, nation-building of, 19
Atefeh (niece of Ahmad), 48, 49, 50, 54
Avicenna, 104
Avini, Seyyed Morteza ("Martyr of the Pen"), 134
Ayatollah Khamenei, 12, 13–14, 60, 134; *sayyed* status of, 58
Ayatollah Khomeini, 11–12, 16, 60, 102, 109, 121, 124, 129, 133, 134, 150, 155, 160–161, 167; distinguishing of the spiritual and moral virtue of the Iranian Revolution by, 60–61; tomb of, 153–155, 216n2; vision of Iran, 23–24, 160

INDEX

Ayatollah Mohammad Taghi (Taqi) Bahjat Foumani, 121
Ayatollah Montazeri, 19, 150; opinion of nationalism, 19
Ayatollah Morteza Mutahhari, 19, 44–45, 121, 130–131, 206n9, 206n12
Ayatollah Taleqani, 129
Azim, Shah Abdol, 186, 218n25
Azkia, Mostafa, 34

Bajoghli, Narges, 18, 25
Bangangté people of Cameroon, 79
barley, 30, 95
Basij(is) (Sāzmān-e Basij-e Mostaz'afin [Mobilization of the Oppressed]), 3, 6, 7, 13–15, 25, 44–45, 60, 90–91, 128, 151–52, 155, 157, 165–66, 170, 206n12; Basiji Islamic law students, 119; Basij membership cards, 15; and the experience of the Iran-Iraq War, 129; as a foil to modern youth, 17, 170; mass membership of 14; non-elite Basijis, 18–19; service of in the Iran-Iraq War, 208n34; scholarly accounts of, 18–19; "Sister's Basij" (Basij-e Khāharān), 24; "Special Basij" and other categories, 14, 203n14; strong reactions to the term "Basiji," 17; writing of Basiji lives, 15–18, 194
Basseri nomads, 49, 88, 116
Battle of Karbala, 24, 56, 57, 62, 126–27, 128, 129, 142, 149, 150, 151, 185, 204n24
Bibi Hur, 115
Bibi Khatun, 168
Bibi Nur, 115
Bibi Seshambe, 115
birun (outside, external), 79, 170, 209n1
Bloch, Maurice, 84
blood, 127–28, 150–51, 152, 197, 207n17; alternate discourses of, 149–50; female, 50, 145; male martyrs' blood, 140–143, 214n9; menstrual blood, 56, 109, 207n18, 214–15n17, 218n29; "physio-sacred" qualities of, 41, 205n4, 209n6; and prophetic genealogy, 52–60; visibility of in Iran's home life and politics, 5, 140–142. *See also* blood, beyond blood and family as an object of ethical and religious cultivation; blood of kinship
blood, beyond blood and family as an object of ethical and religious cultivation, 60–61; brothers, sisters, and secrets, 66–69; and degrees of kinship, 69–70; and family tensions, 64–65; inner purity, outer corruption, and forging the family household (pure family households), 61–62, 63–64; persons and households, 63–64; and saving family face, 66; and visiting extended family, 70–73
blood of kinship, 5; and the intersection with the blood of martyrs, 140–42; and female martyrs, 142–46; martyrs as national kin, 146–48
Book of Kings, 149
bread, 87–89; the "bread provider" (*nunāvar*), 113; buying of, 88–89, 210n16; connection of with good character, 87–88; "Fars-Abadi bread," 88; making of, 210n15
brothers and sisters of Islam, 23–25, 170, 171, 174, 185, 186, 189, 190, 197, 204n23

Cannell, Fenella, 42
Captive Society (Golkar), 12–14, 17, 203n13–15
carnation (*mikhak*), 215n22
caviar, 167
chador(s), 164, 165–66, 201n1, 212n32; black chadors, 143, 147, 153, 164, 201n2, 204n26; flowered chadors, 179
Chatterjee, Partha, 24–25
Christians, 22, 214n6
citizenship/citizens, 157, 216n6; food, kinship, and citizenship, 190–91; Iranian citizenship, 159; kindred citizens, 36, 145, 156, 161, 190, 209n5; virtuous (*bā-taqvā*) citizenry, 158
coldness/hotness (*sardi/garmi*), 103–4
Committee for Finding Missing Soldiers, 132–33
conception, 47–48
Connerton, Paul, 137
Constitutional Revolution (1905–11), 23
Construction Jehad (Jehād-e Sāzandegi), 33, 205n31
consumerism, postsocialist, 159
cucumbers, 30, 95
cultural invasion, 13, 36, 123, 126, 159, 169

darun (inside, internal), 101, 209n1
"Day of Sacrifice" (Eid-e Qorbān), 92
Delaney, Carol, 42
dietary laws, 93, 167
"divine grace"/"blessing" (*barakat*), 53, 85, 87
[Divine] Healing and Remedy with the Qur'an (Rezai), 65

Dorraj, Manochehr, 149
Douglas, Mary, 79
drug addiction, 62, 72, 139, 205n2; to opium, 63, 86

Ebrahami, Sara, 163–64
eggs, 47, 92, 111, 193, 210n13, 211n27
Egypt, Islamic Revival Movement in, 60–61
Ehsan, 38–39, 108, 143; burial of, 39–40, 73–75; death of, 39, 74, 76
Eid al-Fitr ("Festival of the Breaking of the Fast"), 70, 108
Elham (Tehrani seminary student), 187
Esfahan, 26
Esteem/reputation (*āberu*), concept of, 66; protection of, 67–68
ethics, 207m27; ethical work, 35, 41, 61, 73, 80
"evil eye," the, 72, 76, 209n1

Fahmideh, Hossein, 134
family of the Prophet (*ahl-e beyt*), 24, 38, 45, 53–54, 56, 62, 86, 140, 143, 195
Fariba (niece of Ahmad), 48–49, 50, 81
Farquhar, Judith, 159
Farrin (niece of Nushin), 48
Fars-Abad, 1, 2, 7, 15, 62, 172, 211n26; commemoration of martyrs in, 138–39, 146–47, 148, 188; "core" community of, 178; edge of town as a desert, 30; fasting in, 107–8; "foundations" of kinship in, 52; lack of opportunity in, 33–34; local class politics of, 32–34; localness of food in, 94–95, 98–99; oldest parts of, 29; orchards of, 30; parks in, 29; Ramadan and Islamic piety in, 212n35; *sofrehs* in, 85; state elites in, 25. *See also* Fars-Abad, kinship and Islam in; Fars-Abad, landscape and history of
Fars-Abad, kinship and Islam in, 43–45; and gendered substances, inheritance, and procreation, 48–52; and procreation as God's creation, 45–48
Fars-Abad, landscape and history of, 25–30, 27*fig.*, 28*fig.*; changes to as a result of the Iranian Revolution, 32–34; Rustam Relief of, 25–26; then and now, 30–32
Fars-Abadis, 15, 49, 51; on the purity of the *sayyeds*, 54
fasting, 212n34; and family, 111–13; and family protection, 107–8; fasting, Ramadan, and Islam, 108–10, 205n1

Fatemeh (Fati, daughter of Nushin), 38–39, 59, 69, 118, 145
Fatemeh Al-Zahra, 22–23, 155, 192, 215nn18–19; commemorating the martyrdom of, 142–46, 145*fig.*
Fatima Is Fatima (Shari'ati), 143–44
Fatemeh Ma'sumeh, shrine of, 155
Fazaeli, Roja, 215n20
Ferdowsi, 149
Festival of Fetr (*eid-e fetr*), 112
fetriyeh, giving of, 112–13
food: "blessed food" (*tabarrok*) 2, 4, 6, 77, 122, 156, 157, 174, 178–180, 184, 188–89, 190, 216n3; entanglements of food, religion, and kinship, 79–80; food, kinship, and citizenship, 190–91; foods that may harm a family, 78; and halal relations, 77; home-cooked food, 211–12n29; and the ideal proportions of daily meals, 210n12; illicit foods, 217n14; imports of to Iran, 216–17n10; for pious families in Iran, 80; and the potential to "change the soul," 78–79; regulation of, 23; as religiopolitical, 80; and the "right" kind of kindred Islamic spirit, 78; spiritual foods, 109; untrustworthy foods, 86; state-sponsored blessed food and the kitchen of the Imams, 184–89; various food practices, 118–21; Western food practices and moral decay, 159–60. *See also* food, sharing of; votive food; dietary laws
food, sharing of: food sharing in town by Hajji Hamed, 175–78, 176*fig.*; sharing of votive food (*nazri*), 77, 115, 144, 175, 178, 209n3, 218n25; sharing of blessed foods during Ramadan, 178–80; sharing of on a national scale, 174; sharing of the "right" food, 123
Foucault, Michel, 207n27
Foundation for the Preservation of Heritage and the Distribution of Sacred Defense, 2, 125, 134, 202n5, 214n14
Friday Imam(s), 2, 16, 58, 125–26, 136, 148

Galen, 104
gender, 47–48, 156, 167, 170, 175, 187, 198, 206n10, 206n12; gender segregation, 179, 183, 209–10n8; masculine, 141; mixed, 165
generational labels/differences, 49, 166–67, 208n30
"Girls of Revolution Street Protest," 195–96

God/Allah, 4, 12, 59, 70, 77, 86, 101, 129, 152, 156, 197; and creation/procreation, 45–48; design of for men and women, 206n8; "God's divine banquet," 109; as lacking a body (*jesm*), 47
Goli-Mehrebun (mother of Nushin), 8, 31, 80–81, 87–88, 101, 193
Golkar, Saeid, 17, 203n13
Goltab (sister of Nushin), 84
Green Family Cooking, 163, 217n13
Green Movement, 12, 18, 127, 133, 149, 195; post–Green Movement, 14, 19

hadiths, 140, 207n17; interpretation of, 217n16
Hagar (niece of Nushin), 66–68
halal ("lawful," "religiously permissible"), 208n29; halal relations, 77, 106–7; halalness and localness of food ingredients, 94, 99. *See also* halal appetites; halal, and the discernment of halal, local, and processed food; halal, and the forging of a halal nation-state; halal and the preparation of "right," balanced foods with "pure intention" (*kholus-e niyyat*)
halal appetites, 167–68; gendered appetites, 170–72
halal, and the discernment of halal, local, and processed food, 92–93, 217n17; factory processed food as "worthless," 95–100; halal foods, 93–94; local foods, 94–95
halal, and the forging of a halal nation-state, 158–61; and postrevolutionary foodscapes, 162–64
halal and the preparation of "right," balanced foods with pure intention (*kholus-e niyyat*), 100–103; and humoral balance (balance of hot and cold), 103–6
Halal World Institute (HWI), 167
Halbwachs, Maurice, 137
Haji Nazari (brother of Nushin), 21–22
Hajj Bibi (mother of Ahmad), 8, 88, 193
Haleh (niece of Ahmad), 6–7, 12–13, 68, 156, 164–66, 183, 186, 189, 207n18, 214–15n17
Hamideh (kin of Ahmad), 116, 117
harām (unlawful, opposite of halal), 167, 168, 169, 187
Harbottle, Lynn, 211–12n29
Hassan (older brother of Hagar), 67
hegemony, Western, 160
hermaphrodites, 44
hijab, 20, 164, 196, 206n10, 208n34

Ho, Enseng, 53
Hossein (younger brother of Hagar), 68

Idris, Vafa, 146
Imagined Communities (Anderson), 148
Imam 'Ali, 60, 65, 87, 143, 161, 168, 179, 185, 201n3; burial site of, 181
Imam Husayn, 4, 24, 30–31, 53, 114, 122, 142, 156, 170; martyrdom of, 61, 126, 129–31, 149, 175, 202n6; meeting house of, 11, 56–57, 71, 155, 179; shrine of, 155, 185
Imam Khomeini Relief Foundation (IKRF), 215–16n1
Imam Musa Al-Kazem, 168
Imam Reza, 168, 185, 186; descendants of, 170; shrine of, 187–88
Imam Sadeq, 65, 71, 121, 133
Imamzadeh Hamza, shrine of, 168, 169*fig.*, 170, 183
imperialism: cultural, 62; Western, 130
infant mortality, 33, 193
inner purity (*safā-ye bāten*), 36, 61, 62, 63, 76, 158, 161, 190, 197
Iran Civil Code, Article 976 of, 141
Iranian Constitution (1979), 24, 204n23
Iranian Islamic Broadcasting Network, 212–13n37
Iranian landscape, naturalizing and sacralizing of, 150–52
Iranian New Year (Nowruz), 209–10n8; celebrations of, 7, 82–84
Iranian regime, 17, 128–29, 130, 196; aspirations of, 203n16; "regime class," 34; regime consolidation, 150; supporters of, 13, 15, 18, 32, 40, 43, 139, 146, 155, 201n2
Iranian Revolution (1979), 3, 4, 20, 23, 32–33, 44, 64, 138, 151, 193, 202n9, 204n24; founding of, 204n28. *See also* Iranian regime; Islamic Republic of Iran, postrevolutionary
Iran-Iraq War, 4, 13, 18, 23, 63, 126–27, 138, 141, 147, 151, 208n30; casualty numbers of, 213n5; history of, 128–32; origins of, 201–2n4
Islam, 51; spirit of, 20; true Islam, 72, 126. *See also* brothers and sisters of Islam
Islamic Government (Ayatollah Khomeini), 65
Islamic open universities, 33
Islamic Republic of Iran, 2, 3, 15, 20, 62, 64, 120, 140, 148, 150, 151, 161, 195; defense of, 16–17, 23; and nationalism, 19–20; population of growth of, 204n29; as a

INDEX 241

Shi'i country, 177–78, 204n22; statecraft of, 128; support for, 10–13, 24, 40, 149. *See also* Islamic Republic of Iran, contours of
Islamic Republic of Iran, contours of, 19–20; Ahmad and Haji Nazari, 21–22; Mehdi, 20–21; Zahra, 22–23
Islamic Republic of Iran, Constitution of, 62
Islamic Republic of Iran, postrevolutionary, 53, 158–59, 172–3
Islamic Revolutionary Guard Corps (IRGC), 13–14, 15, 25, 33, 133, 143, 195, 202n12
Islamic State of Iraq and Syria (ISIS), 25

Jalal (kin of Nushin), 64
Jews, 22, 204n22
Jones, Terry, 11
Joseph, Suad, 68

kashk, 211n22
Kaur, Ravinder, 133
kebab, 209–10n8; "sultan kebab," 163
King Cyrus, 26
kinship, 41, 59–60, 205n4, 207n16; "acts of kinship," 41–42; blood of, 4, 5; degrees of, 69–70; entanglements of food, religion, and kinship, 79–80; food, kinship, and citizenship, 190–91; food and the purification of kin relations, 6; "foundations" of, 52; and gender difference, 43–44; Iranian kinship, 6; kindred citizens, 161; "kinning," 156; kin relations, 5–6, 51; "kinship maps," 51–52; milk kinship (*ridā*), 43, 51; and nation-making, 5, 152, 190; and the occupation of a "third space," 42–43; as physio-sacred, 152, 205n4; as a process, 43; sacralizing of, 4–6, 42–43; Shi'i Islamic kinship, 6, 43; trope of kindred religious nationhood, 23, 24. *See also* blood of kinship and the intersection with the blood of martyrs; kinship, and state politics; *sofreh*, kinship at
kinship, and state politics, 196–98; and conservative state politics, 198–99
kitchens of Imams, 184–188
Kobra (niece of Nushin), 64–65

lamb, 91–92, 95, 107, 111, 120, 177
Laqueur, Thomas, 128
Lazar, Sian, 196–97
Leila (kin of Ahmad), 48

Mahdavi, Pardis, 196
Mahmad (brother of Nushin), courtyard of, 80–81
Mahmood, Saba, 60–61
Mahmud (brother of Ahmad, husband of Parvin), 7, 8, 155, 165
mahram, 44
Malay people, 79
"male backbone" (*posht*), 49–50; as a gloss for male seed, 50
Marjan (niece of Nushin), 48
Martyrs' Expedition Brigade, 132
martyrs/martyrdom: commemoration of, 124–26, 157–58, 185, 189, 214n13; blood of, 214n9; families of, 58–59; and gender, 141; historical context of (the Iran-Iraq War), 128–32; mothers of, 136*fig.*; as not a matter of choice, 131; as selfless, 131; setting the stage for the commemoration of, 126–28; sign created for the commemoration of, 138*fig.*; traits of, 130–31; unknown martyrs (*shahid*), 1, 2, 124–25, 133–36, 138–39, 146, 148, 202n5, 214n14; welcoming of martyrs to their final resting place, 137*fig. See also* blood of kinship and the intersection with the blood of martyrs; martyrs/martyrdom, and the exhuming of martyrs' bodies
martyrs/martyrdom, and the exhuming of martyrs' bodies, 132–33; female martyrs, 142–46; and the sacralizing efficacy of martyrs' blood, 133–39
Maryam (daughter of Nushin and Ahmad), 7, 38, 45, 83, 107, 108, 119, 144–45, 168, 170–71, 179–80; on the idea of "ugliness" (*zeshti*), 217n20
Mashhad, 180, 185, 187–88, 218n31
Massé, Henri, 206–7n15
matrilateral/patrilateral relationships, 50–51, 52
Mausoleum of Ruhollah Khomeini, 153–55, 154*fig.*
McClintock, Anne, 198
Mehdi (son of Mahmud and Parvin), 20–21, 47
Middle East, US meddling in, 41
milk: hot milk, 157*fig.*, 157; "milk-suckling" (*shir-khor*), 56
Mirbagherzadeh, S. M., 132
Mir-Hossenni, Ziba 203n19
modernity: American, 42; hegemonic narratives of, 3

modernization, 159
modesty (*ru-dar-bāyesti*), conventions of, 171
Mohadeseh (kin of Nushin), 58
Mojahedin-e Khalq, 149
Mona (kin of Ahmad), 48
moral rubrics, 166, 217n14
moshkel goshā ("problem-solving candy"), 179, 218n24
Mousavi, Mir-Hossein, 12
Mr. Hosseini, 45–46; diagram of the course of human existence rendered by, 46*fig*.
Muharram, 126, 128, 140, 150, 175, 176; sixth day of, 56; tenth day of, 23. *See also* 'Ashura'
Muslims, 43, 188, 194, 201n3; linkage of Muslim society to God, 16; Shi'i Muslims, 15, 43, 87, 108–9, 126, 142, 150, 204n22; Shi'i Muslim law, 206n14; Sunni Muslims, 43, 177

Najaf, 146
Najambadi, Afsaneh, 161
Naraghi, Ehsan, 160
nature, 44, 45, 47, 110, 160, 206n8; Islamic law of, 206n6
Night of Power (Shab-e Qadr [Persian], Laylat Al-Qadr [Arabic]), 108, 112, 179, 205n1, 218n23
Nistdar, 56, 192–93, 219n2
nursing, of a Christian child by a Persian, 206–7n15
Nushin, 1–2, 3, 6, 7, 9, 16, 38, 40–41, 60, 83, 86, 90, 91, 104, 144, 147, 202n8; concerns of for her children, 169–70; on the consumption of breast milk, 51–52; cooking and sharing of blessed food by, 77; and fasting, 212n34; on the importance of doing good, 62; and the making of pomegranate sauce, 97–98; on not celebrating the festival of Eid, 70; positive assessment of local foods, 94; prayers of, 66; royal ancestry of her son-in-law, 59; on the sacrifice of Iman Husayn at the hands of Yazid, 61–62; spiritual food of her dreams, 182; on visiting both sides of her family, 72–73; visits of to a *sayyed* grave, 54–55, 55*fig*.

onions, 116, 117

Pahlavi, Mohammad Reza (Reza Shah), 160, 185, 202n9

Pahlavis, reign of, 159
panj tan ("five bodies"), 49, 140, 143, 202n8, 206n13
Parvin (wife of Mahmud), 7, 63, 104, 113, 155, 156; on blessed food, 184–85; on the importance of doing good, 62; on martyrdom, 131–32
Peak of Eloquence (*Nahj Al Balāgheh* [Imam 'Ali])
patriarchal authority, ideologies of, 5
peaches, 95
Persia/Persian Empire, 149
pilgrimage/pilgrims, 157, 170; Shi'i pilgrimage destinations, 185. *See also* pilgrimage/pilgrims, and votive food distribution
pilgrimage/pilgrims, and votive food distribution, 180–82; and local pilgrimage 54, 114, 125, 181–83; pilgrimage to Mecca and the use of Zamzam water, 66, 183–84; pilgrimage to the Mausoleum of Ruhollah Khomeini, 155
pizza, 100, 162, 165, 166; and halal ingredients, 173; as not a real food, 163–64; the "pizza eater" (*pitza khor*), 163, 164, 173
plums, 95, 158
pomegranates, 96–97, 158, 217n17; pomegranate sauce, 10, 95, 97–98; 97*fig*.; pomegranate statue, 96*fig*.
pork, 85, 93, 167
prayer, 66, 72, 75, 111–12, 209n2; "prayer taking," 72, 76–77. *See also* "Aqiqeh Prayer"; votive soup, as an act of prayer
pregnancy, 57, 79, 104, 115, 209n4
Pregnancy and Childbirth from the Perspective of Islam (Akbarzadeh and Sharifi), 209m4
Prophet Muhammad, the, 109, 127, 135, 143, 202n8; lineage/descendants of, 52–53, 56, 71, 140
"pure intention" (*kholus-e niyyat*), 65, 78, 91, 97, 100–103, 213n37; and martyrdom, 127, 131
purity (*pāki*), 6, 21, 40–42, 62, 74, 77; of descendants of the Prophet, 24, 53–54, 62, 87; 53–54, 58; as a quality of food, 78, 87–88, 93, 105, 109, 123; of (martyrs') blood, 133, 137. *See also* inner purity (*safā-ye bāten*)

Qajars dynasty, 32
Qassem (brother of Ahmad and Mahmud), 8
Qom, 121, 149, 153, 155, 180, 207n18, 214–15n17

qowm-o-khish (relatives, kinsmen), 48–49, 140
quinces, 158; quince lime syrup, 10, 95, 98
Qur'an, the, 10, 11, 44, 70, 110, 120, 140, 178, 207n17; first verse of (Surat al-Fātihah), 54, 119, 171; healing benefits of, 65; interpretation of, 217n16; Surah Al-Qadr verse of, 112

rahem (womb), 70–71; seleh-e rahem, 71
Ramadan, 7, 73, 171–72; in Fars-Abad, 212n35; fasting during, 107–8, 108–10, 205n1; first day of, 111–12; prayers during, 111–12; sharing of blessed foods during, 178–80; significance to Shi'i Muslims, 108–9
relatedness, 49, 139, 199
religion: entanglements of food, religion, and kinship, 79–80; true religion, 115, 121
Reza (son of Nushin and Ahmad), 2, 50, 86, 124–25, 171, 172, 192; and fasting, 212n34; on the idea of "ugliness" (zeshti), 217n20
rice, 2, 83, 88, 98, 103, 104, 158, 175, 186–87, 188; barberry rice, 163; fenugreek stew with rice, 163; lentil rice, 107, 163, 188; local rice, 98; rice pudding, 77, 85, 114, 174; saffron rice, 77, 85, 98, 105, 122, 163, 174, 179, 181; sweet rice, 114, 122; votive rice, 57
Rezai, Mojtabi, 65
Rouhani, Hassan, 195
Russian Orthodoxy/Russian Orthodox Church, 61

Saeidi, Shirin, 147
salt, 9, 87–88, 106–7, 212n33
Sami (brother of Nushin), 31, 89
Sami (younger brother of Kobra), 64–65
sandwiches, 160, 171; sandwich shops/venues, 172, 217n12
sayyeds ("descendants of the Prophet"), 51, 52–53, 147; association of with fertility, 56; donation of sacrificial meat to, 54–55; lineage of, 56; non-sayyeds, 56; "prophetic genealogy" of, 53–54; sayyed infants' proximity to God and purity of, 53, 54
sayyedah ("female descendant of the Prophet"), 51
scarves, 2, 134, 165, 214n15
Schacht, Joseph, 208n29

Schneider, David M., 42
Seed and the Soil, The: Gender and Cosmology in Turkish Village Society (Delaney), 42
sex/sexuality: as God given, 44; premarital sex, 62
Shaery-Eisenlohr, Roschanack, 185–86
Shah Cheragh, 182, 183
Shari'ati, Ali, 62, 143–44, 160, 215n18
Sharifi, Nasrin, 209n4
Shayegan, Daryush, 160
Shi'a Marja', 121, 217n16
Shiraz, 2, 62, 135, 139, 141, 171–72
shrines, 114, 181, 183, 185, 187, 202n5, 214n14, 217n17; food distribution at, 182; kitchens at, 184–188; of Imams, 174, 180, 181, 218n31
Siavash, 149
sofreh ("dining cloth"), 77–78, 102, 103, 156, 163, 175; arrangement of, 212n33; the breakfast sofreh, 86–89; incorporation of food into, 85–86; kinship at, 80–84; the lunch sofreh, 89–91, 94; as the mother's or wife's work, 105–6; and sacrifice for family protection, 91–92; spread of sofreh (sofreh ro pahn kon), 81, 83; three kinds of, 209n7; votive sofreh, 82fig., 115–16, 177–78; Zoroastrian sofrehs, 213n39
Soraya (Tehrani seminary student), 187
sovereignty, "inner"/"spiritual" domain of, 24–25
spirit (ruh), 47, 48, 52, 78, 89, 109, 123
state elites, 5, 6, 20; in Fars-Abad, 25. See also Friday Imam(s)
Supplication of Kumail, 2, 188
Sassanid Empire, 25

ta'arof, definition of, 210n10
Tabatabaei, Sayed Ali Qadhi, 121
Tawasil, Amina, 18
tea, 71–72, 76, 84, 91, 104, 111, 120, 144, 172, 179, 180, 210n11, 212n31; black tea, 84, 87; contaminated tea, 72; drinking of, 10, 22, 40, 72, 83, 121, 192, 217n11; golden tea, 61; and prayers, 84; sharing of, 84; tea brewers, 84; teacups, 84
Tehran, 2, 26, 62, 139, 141, 211n17; Ekbatan suburb of, 7, 12; Imam Khomeini Square in, 85–86; Restaurant 1 in Tajrish, 164–65, 166; and Restaurant 2 (the Sofreh House of the Garden of Ferdous), 165–67; upscale neighborhoods and restaurants in, 162–63

temperament (*tab'*), 41, 58, 104
Torab, Azam, 141–42
Twelfth and Hidden Imam (Imam Mahdi), 12, 16, 135, 147

United States, 63; cultural understanding of family in, 198–99; meddling of in the Middle East, 41

Varzi, Roxanne, 196
Vaziri, Mostafa, 20
velāyat-e faqih ("guardianship of the jurist"), 11–12, 203nn16–17, 216n8
Verdery, Katherine, 150
visiting, 35, 41, 64, 70–75, 91, 119, 195; *shab neshini* ("night visiting"), 71
votive food, 179–80; *See also* pilgrimage/pilgrims, and votive food distribution; votive offering
votive offering (*nazri*), 77, 144, 116*fig.*, 117*fig.*, 157, 176–77, 187, 209n3; as prayer and vow making, 113–15; and āsh, 213n38; and sharing of blessed/votive food, 81, 115, 144, 175–178, 209n3, 218n25; and food practices, 118–21; for teaching, 116–18; teething soup, 116*fig.*, 118. *See also* āsh, *sofreh*, votive *sofreh*

walnuts, 74, 77, 95, 100
Week of the Sacred Defense, 133–34, 147
Wellman, Rose, fieldwork of, 6–9; and becoming "almost Mahram/almost daughter," 9–10
Westernization, 159
"Westernstruckness," 3, 36, 62, 159, 163
Weston, Kath, 140
wheat, 30, 88, 95, 115, 160; sweet wheat porridge, 39, 114, 119, 156, 174; wheat noodles, 116
World Islamic Head Quarters for Remembering Martyrs, 145–46

Yazid, 61–62

Zahra's Paradise, 7, 132, 141, 155, 156
Zamzam cola, 162, 165
Zamzam water, 183–84
Zaynab bint Ali (granddaughter of the Prophet), 24, 38, 215n18
ziarat-e 'āshura' ("prayer for Imam Husayn"), 76; why it "saved us," 121–23, 209n2
Zigon, Jarrett, 61
Zoroastrians, 22, 138, 209–10n8, 214n6; Zoroastrian *sofrehs*, 213n39
Zumbagua people, 79

Founded in 1893,
UNIVERSITY OF CALIFORNIA PRESS
publishes bold, progressive books and journals
on topics in the arts, humanities, social sciences,
and natural sciences—with a focus on social
justice issues—that inspire thought and action
among readers worldwide.

The UC PRESS FOUNDATION
raises funds to uphold the press's vital role
as an independent, nonprofit publisher, and
receives philanthropic support from a wide
range of individuals and institutions—and from
committed readers like you. To learn more, visit
ucpress.edu/supportus.